WÎPLÎCHEZ WÎBES REHT

DUQUESNE STUDIES

PHILOLOGICAL SERIES
15

A MODERN HUMANITIES RESEARCH
ASSOCIATION MONOGRAPH

WÎPLÎCHEZ WÎBES REHT

*A Study of the Women Characters
in the Works of
Wolfram von Eschenbach*

BY
MARION E. GIBBS

DUQUESNE UNIVERSITY PRESS
Editions E. Nauwelaerts

For my Mother

Contents .

Preface

THE LITERATURE which treats Wolfram von Eschenbach and his works is immense, and the growth of such literature within the last 25 years is amply attested by the recent study of Wolfram research by Joachim Bumke.[1] A further contribution at this stage therefore seems to need a certain amount of justification, and, indeed, one is aware of the extent to which one must inevitably depend on earlier interpretations and take for granted factors which have long been commonplaces accepted by scholarship. To acknowledge at all points one's debt to previous research is impossible, and a select bibliography cannot really imply the range of scholarship in this subject.

D. M. Blamires writes in the preface to his study of the characters in *Parzival* of the lack of an investigation of Wolfram's character-portrayal, and his own work is a very full and detailed contribution to this strangely neglected aspect of Wolfram's work.[2] In some respects his approach anticipates my own, but his intention is not the same by any means. His is an investigation of Wolfram's technique of characterization with special reference to the notion of individuality as it emerges in his character depiction. My concern has been to show how this individualization is compatible with the concept of the ideal, in Wolfram's portrayal of his female characters.

The very presence of so many women characters, some of them dominant figures in the works, and even the minor ones often very significant, would seem to prompt investigation of Wolfram's attitude to woman in general and the use he makes of his individual heroines. The absence of a full-scale study of this kind means that the understanding of this fascinating and complex writer is strangely incomplete, even though the significance of individual heroines has sometimes been fully appreciated.[3] Almost any attempt to interpret *Parzival* leads to a discussion of such obviously important heroines as Herzeloyde, Sigune and Condwiramurs, and again the bibliography and references within the text can give only some idea of the extent to which one is indebted in general terms to past research.

An early discussion of some of the women characters in *Parzival* is that by Karl Kinzel,[4] who saw that the heroines deserved particular attention but draws no general conclusions from Wolfram's depiction of them. Ursula Heise, on the other hand, is fully aware that the women have a special significance, and her article is a perceptive and sensitive study of the rôle of the major heroines in relation to Parzival.[5] What has interested me is the way in which the qualities of the major heroines are repeated in the less obviously significant ones, so that each character has a right to a place in a consistent whole. Some of the lesser figures have received little attention from research which has been concerned with the major issues of the work in all their puzzling complexity. Often such figures—Belakane, Cunneware and Cundrie, for example—have been appreciated for their rôle in their particular context; but my aim has been to show how they, and the really minor heroines, too, have a part to play in a whole which in its turn reflects a very vital aspect of Wolfram's view of life.

The study by Marlis Schumacher of Wolfram's concept of marriage comes close in intention to the present study, though the focus of attention is clearly different.[6] A thorough examination of Wolfram's view of marriage was needed, to draw together much of what was well known to earlier scholarship and to show how, in this respect too, Wolfram is wonderfully consistent and most firm in his views. Human relationships, of which marriage is among the great-

est, were a matter of intense interest to Wolfram, but his concept of
the nature of the bond between man and woman rests on something
more fundamental, his sense of the intrinsic nature of the two individuals, and of this he has much to say. *Parzival* establishes beyond doubt his view of woman and the rôle she has to play in the life
of man, and in *Willehalm* this view receives its fullest expression
in the perfection of the union of Gyburc and Willehalm. Again, in
some respects, one is aware that one is treading paths which are
familiar and that, perhaps above all, the study of *Willehalm* by
Joachim Bumke points the way to a very close understanding of
this great work.[7] Yet, again, I hope to have indicated the relationship between the two works in this single but very important aspect
and so to have shown that Wolfram's view of woman remains consistent through the developing thought which binds them together.

With a great artist like Wolfram something new emerges at
every reading, and the works speak differently to every reader. It
is this conviction which prompts yet another contribution in an already well-worn field, as well as the conviction that Wolfram speaks
as clearly to the later years of the twentieth century as he has ever
done, and that in his view of the nature of human life we may today
find food for thought, and for hope.

I should like to express my gratitude to the Modern Humanities
Research Association for its support of the publication of this study,
and in particular I wish to thank Professor R. A. Wisbey for his
close scrutiny of the manuscript: I am indebted to him for so gen-
erously allowing me to benefit from his scholarship, and for his
tactful understanding of my intention.

NOTES

1. Joachim Bumke: *Die Wolfram von Eschenbach Forschung
   seit 1945. Bericht und Bibliographie*, Munich, 1970.
2. D. M. Blamires: *Characterization and Individuality in Wolfram's 'Parzival,'* Cambridge, 1966.

3. For example Herzeloyde, Sigune, Condwiramurs and Gyburc. The following are just some of the outstanding works which treat individual heroines:

W. J. Schröder: *Die Soltane-Erzählung in Wolframs 'Parzival,'* Heidelberg, 1963.

Ingeborg Giese: 'Sigune. Untersuchungen zur Minneauffassung Wolframs von Eschenbach,' Diss. Rostock, 1952.

B. Rahn: *Wolframs Sigunendichtung. Eine Interpretation der Titurelfragmente,* Zürich, 1958.

G. Meissburger: 'Gyburg,' *ZfdPh.* 83, 1964, 64-99.

W. Schröder: 'Armuot,' *DVjs.* 34, 1960, 501-526.

W. Schröder: 'Süeziu Gyburc,' *Euphorion* 54, 1960, 39-69.

4. K. Kinzel: 'Die Frauen in Wolframs *Parzival,' ZfdPh.* 21, 1889, 48-73.

5. Ursula Heise: 'Frauengestalten im *Parzival* Wolframs von Eschenbach,' *Deutschunterricht* 9, 1957, 37-62.

6. Marlis Schumacher: *Die Auffassung der Ehe in den Dichtungen Wolframs von Eschenbach,* Heidelberg, 1967.

7. Joachim Bumke: *Wolframs 'Willehalm.' Studien zur Epenstruktur und zum Heiligkeitsbegriff der ausgehenden Blütezeit,* Heidelberg, 1959.

Introduction

EARLY IN *Parzival* Wolfram says that he is about to tell a story

> daz seit von grôzen triuwen,
> wîplîchez wîbes reht,
> und mannes manheit alsô sleht,
> diu sich gein herte nie gebouc.   (4,10-13)[1]

Clearly, then, the women characters are to be important in the work, and their virtues as essential to it as the knightly virtues displayed by the men. The nature of the particular virtue of woman is referred to by Wolfram on other occasions. At one point he exclaims:

> wîpheit, dîn ordenlîcher site,
> dem vert und fuor ie triwe mite.   (116,13-14)

and again he says:

> wîpheit vert mit triuwen.   (167,29)

Side-by-side with this great virtue of loving loyalty is the virtue of purity which he will praise in women when he finds it:

> swelhem wîbe volget kiusche mite,
> der lobes kemphe wil ich sîn.   (115,2-3)

Kiusche, as Wolfram uses it, goes far beyond the basic meaning of womanly purity, for it is an aspect of humility itself, an aspect of that *scham* which Wolfram sees as an essential virtue:

> scham ist ein slôz ob allen siten. (3,5)

These are, for Wolfram, the vital virtues of true womanhood, the *essential nature of womanly woman* which, as he claims, will be the matter of his tale. It is these virtues which inspire Trevrizent to tell Parzival to honour women and priests alike, with the implication that women, too, have some mysterious link with God, and it is such virtue which Parzival has in mind when, having rejected God, he commends Gawan to woman:

> friunt, an dînes kampfes zît
> dâ nem ein wîp für dich den strît:
> diu müeze ziehen dîne hant;
> an der du kiusche hâst bekant
> unt wîplîche güete:
> ir minn dich dâ behüete. (332,9-14)

These words are uttered by Parzival in great sorrow, and they appear to come close to blasphemy; yet in the light of Wolfram's view of woman they may be seen as completely acceptable. Parzival stresses that the woman who can guide the hand of man must be pure and virtuous, and in a work which extols the power of perfect love and sees it as a means to God, this commendation of man to pure womanhood may be seen, not as a rejection of God, but as an indication of the way to Him.

The courtly love lyric had tended to give a special place to woman, raising her up as the object of devotion and yearning praise. Very often, however, the awe in which she was held was due to her inaccessibility rather than to any real virtue, and in fact she is often shown as a cold, ruthless woman, indifferent to her lover and the suffering she is causing him. For Wolfram, a relationship of this kind was uncongenial, and the consistency with which, in his narrative works, he presents love, both in marriage and, outside it, between two people who are free to love one another, is in accordance with his relatively small contribution in the field of the *Minnesang*. He could not happily lend himself to this genre which displayed, and often extolled, a relationship which was essentially amoral, if taken seriously, and insincere, if regarded merely as a convention of literature. It is true that two of Wolfram's poems[2] adopt the conventional pose of the lover towards his lady, but it is for a different kind of love lyric that he is remembered, and his fame for the dawn-song bears witness in itself to his attitude towards the whole genre. The love which he shows in these poems is not the conventional love of the *Minnesang*, for it is a mutual love, between people he sees as equals.[3] Yet, though it is a deep and sincere love, Wolfram sees it as far from perfect, standing as it does in constant danger of discovery. He shows this illicit love as an uneasy one, threatened by the light of day which is heralded by the watchman. His last word is contained in the poem which begins 'Der helden minne ir klage,'[4] where the lovers have no fear of the light of day, since their love is protected by the supreme bond of marriage. Now there is no need for the watchman, and the couple can await the day together.

For Wolfram, then, the only perfect love is the one between two people who have a right to it, and so the word *minne* has a special significance for him in describing the love between a man and his wife. The basic idea of the *Minnesang* had been the enslavement of the lover to the woman, but this is not Wolfram's notion of *minne*. For him it is a relationship between equals, and one to which each contributes equally. Though he does show relationships in which the woman seeks to wield her power over the man, these are not the lasting ones. The most perfect love which Wolfram shows is the one which finds supreme expression in marriage, and the marriages of Parzival and Condwiramurs, Willehalm and Gyburc, are central to the two works. Wolfram could not have expressed himself more clearly on this subject than in these two affirmations of the state of marriage. For Wolfram 'reht minne ist wâriu triuwe' (*Parzival* 532, 10), so the studied displays of love of the *Minnesänger* were not *minne* in his sense of the term. Moreover, *minne* has a distinct spiritual significance, since God Himself is the true *minnære* (*Parzival* 466,1). Love is not an emotion to be played with, then, but a great gift, shared by the Creator with His creatures. Thus Wolfram sees love as something which stems from God and leads back to Him, and so the situation of Gyburc is possible, in whom love of Willehalm and love of God are united and allow her to radiate love to those about her.

The loyalty which Wolfram exalts is far from the devotion of the love-lorn *Minnesänger* to his remote lady. Each partner in the relationship of true *minne* owes loyalty to the other, and it is in the perfect marriages which he presents that Wolfram allows the loving devotion of the man to be matched by that of the woman. Though the contribution which each makes to the marriage is of a different kind, it is essential to Wolfram's concept of ideal marriage that each partner *does* contribute equally with the other, and this view of marriage is best expressed by Gurnemanz when he tells Parzival:

> man und wîp diu sint al ein;
> als diu sunn diu hiute schein,
> und ouch der name der heizet tac.
> der enwederz sich gescheiden mac:
> si blüent ûz eime kerne gar. (173,1-5)

Man and woman are manifestations of the same basic reality, as inseparable from one another as day and sunlight.

Though there still exist in Wolfram's works some examples of the relationship which is based on the courtly idea of service and reward, there is in general a changed view of the relationship between a knight and his lady. Where the woman places conditions upon her love, that love is often doomed, so that Belakane and Sigune lose their lovers, while Obie and Orgeluse bring their lovers and themselves to the brink of tragedy. Condwiramurs does not place any conditions on her love, but Parzival knows that he must prove his love for her, and she remains at home to prove the constancy of her love for him. In the earlier work, this mutual contribution towards a higher goal is explicit, for together they prove that their marriage fits them for the rule of the Graal. Later, in *Willehalm*, Wolfram was to depict another perfect marriage, sustained equally by husband and wife, but the achievement of the marriage of Gyburc and Willehalm is not a unique and tangible goal, but something wider and hardly to be limited by expression, the unity of mankind through love which is the theme of the whole work.

In Wolfram's works, then, marriage is the supreme expression of love, and love itself stems from God. Thus it is clear why Sigune can hope that the marriage which she believes to exist between herself and Schionatulander will lead her to God, and why the King of the Graal, with the highest honour of Christendom, must be married to a pure woman. For Feirefiz, marriage and Christian baptism are inextricable, as they are for Gyburc, for the love which each experiences for a Christian leads directly to God, the true Lover. In this changed view of the relationship between men and women, the nature of woman changes accordingly, for the sincerity and spirituality which are essential to Wolfram's concept of love demanded a very different type of heroine from the exalted and barely human lady of the courtly love lyric. Whereas her acclaim had rested on her lofty dignity and usually on her total inaccessibility to her enslaved lover, the praise which Wolfram offers to his heroines is prompted by actual qualities. Yet, though he has removed woman from the false pedestal on which *Minnesang* had placed her, he has adopted a new and equally exalted view, which sees in woman the embodiment of great virtue.

Wolfram has made a deliberate choice in his depiction of his women characters, consistently electing to display them in their conformity to his ideal, and even, if need be, overlooking clear deviations from this ideal and explaining such deviations in a positive way.[5] That Wolfram was himself aware that he was establishing an ideal is certainly to be assumed. He is in other respects realistic in his view of human nature, though compassionate in his attitude towards human failings. More potent evidence of a deliberate choice on his part is, however, given by Wolfram himself, when he speaks, briefly but emphatically, of those women who are false and who will not receive his praise (3, 7-24). Yet here, in the Prologue to *Parzival*, he deliberately turns his back on such women and expresses his firm intention of telling rather of virtuous women. If he later speaks of the woman who has earned his lasting hatred (114, 7-18), it is so that he can bring into relationship with this one false woman the many of whom he has uttered only praise. This rejection of the negative which he knows to exist is an essential factor in Wolfram's view of woman, and the exalted picture which he gives gains in significance with the knowledge that this is the ideal of a man who was fully aware of the real, yet chose not to depict it.

This exalted view of the nature of woman is borne out by the array of Wolfram's heroines. Together they form a vast spectrum, to which each contributes according to her stature. The whole has indeed the careful gradation of a spectrum, for, while not all the women can achieve the greatness of Herzeloyde, Sigune, Condwiramurs or Gyburc, even the smallest of them possesses some element by which she partakes of the ideal.

It is to the examination of Wolfram's women characters, and the way in which they demonstrate his lofty concept, that the following study is devoted. Any attempt at a rigid classification of the women characters fails, and this fact in itself bears witness to the close relationship among them which makes it impossible to separate absolutely one from the other. The only division which exists is that produced by the individuality of each woman, and the remarkable thing is that Wolfram succeeds in endowing each with her individual nature, which yet does not detract from her contribution towards the whole.

NOTES

1. All quotations are from the edition of Wolfram's works by K. Lachmann, 6th complete edition by E. Hartl, Berlin 1926, reprint Berlin 1960. Unless otherwise stated, quotations are from *Parzival*.
2. ed. cit. *Lieder* 5, 16: 'Ein wîp mac wol erlouben mir. . . .' and 7,11: 'Ursprinc bluomen, loup ûz dringen. . . .'
3. See 3,1: 'Den morgenblic bî wahters sange erkôs. . . .'; 4,8: 'Sîne klâwen durh die wolken sint geslagen. . . .'; 6,10: 'Von der zinnen wil ich gên. . . .'; 7,41: 'Ez ist nu tac, daz ich wol mac mit wârheit jehen. . .'.
4. ed. cit. *Lieder* 5,34.
5. See, for example, his treatment of Obie, Antikonie and Orgeluse.

PART I

CHAPTER ONE

Herzeloyde

THE MOST POWERFUL EXPRESSIONS of Wolfram's view of woman are clearly to be found in the three great heroines of *Parzival* and in the single heroine of *Willehalm*. Herzeloyde, Sigune, Condwiramurs and Gyburc are without doubt his foremost personifications of the ideal of woman and her rôle: yet this in no way means that they can be treated as a single lifeless concept, for herein lies the skill of Wolfram. These are four vivid and superbly differentiated figures, and even the ideal itself is presented differently in each. The achievement of Wolfram in this respect immediately anticipates the greatness of his art throughout, for close study of all the women reveals as many manifestations of a single ideal as there are women.

The character of Herzeloyde is decided for Wolfram by the fact that she is Parzival's mother, for the notion of heredity is a powerful one with him, and that his most noble hero should be the son of any but a truly noble woman is inconceivable. Thus her fitness to be the mother of Parzival is the clearest possible indication of her perfection, and to this is added Wolfram's assessment of her as

> ein wurzel der güete
> und ein stam der diemüete.   (128,27-28)

In view of the importance which Wolfram attaches to humility, showing it to be one of the essential virtues of the Graal King, he could offer no higher praise of Herzeloyde than that she is a stem

3

of humility, while his description of her as a root of goodness suggests absolute perfection.[1] Moreover, although he admires and extols other heroines, it is to Herzeloyde that he gives the most direct praise, when he says that she will be spared the pains of hell, suggesting, it seems clear, that the intermediate state of Purgatory is unnecessary for this woman who has suffered so much in life and proved herself so complete in human virtue. It is of the utmost importance that this statement occurs in juxtaposition to the one expressing her blessedness in being a mother:

> ir vil getriulîcher tôt
> der frouwen wert die hellenôt.
> ôwol si daz se ie muoter wart!   (128,23-25)[2]

Through her death as a devoted mother, Herzeloyde finds the way to eternal bliss, in the same way as Sigune's loving constancy to Schionatulander forges a link with God, and Arabel's love for Willehalm leads to her conversion to Christianity.

Herzeloyde's death marks the coincidence of the peak of her motherhood and the end of it. It is the end because, although her influence endures beyond Parzival's physical departure from her, she has done all she can do for him, and her responsibility as a mother is over; and it is the peak because, in at last allowing her son to ride away from her and accepting that her efforts to retain him will, in fact, be in vain, she is making the supreme sacrifice of the devoted mother. Like Sigune, who is able to die at last, when her duty towards Parzival is over, once he has come to the Kingship of the Graal and when she has herself achieved perfect harmony between earthly love and divine love, Herzeloyde dies at the moment of fulfilment.[3] This moment comes, however, only at the end of a long line of development, for of all Wolfram's heroines Herzeloyde is the one who develops most. It is true that Parzival's meetings with Sigune, combined with the picture given in *Titurel*, show the changes which take place in her, but she is rather the passive object of time, and in her are apparent the changes which must come with its passing. In the case of Herzeloyde, experience—not

merely the passage of time, but all that it brings with it—produces
the changes in her, and she develops from an immature girl, who is
still untouched by the hardship of life, into a mature woman who is
not only fit to bear the future Graal King, but wise enough to let
him ride away from her, knowing that she will never see him again.
Titurel offers additional light on her character, for she is known
first as the bride of the ill-fated Kastis, as the wife of Gahmuret,
and then as his widow.

It is *Titurel* which introduces Herzeloyde as a young girl, and
significantly it is as a member of the Graal Family that she is mentioned first, so that from the beginning her destiny is linked with
the destiny of the Graal, until at last her own son achieves the Kingship of the Graal 'als im daz gordent was' (827,7). She is named as
one of the children of Frimutel, together with Schoysiane, Repanse
de Schoye, Anfortas and Trevrizent (*Titurel* 9-10). To the reader
acquainted with *Parzival* the names thus juxtaposed are a striking
reminder of Parzival's involvement with the Graal Family, the
more so since each one—Schoysiane through her daughter Sigune—
makes a particular contribution to the story of Parzival. The story
contained in *Titurel*, though, is primarily that of Sigune and Schionatulander, and Herzeloyde is of minor importance in the work, although in taking Sigune into her care she is responsible for her
introduction to Schionatulander. What is stressed, however, even
here, where Herzeloyde is not the central figure, is her purity and
absolute goodness. She is mentioned for the first time by Titurel
himself, who is praising his son for his noble children:

> Dîn tohter Schoysîâne   in ir herze besliuzet
> sô vil der guoten dinge,   dês diu werlt an sælden geniuzet:
> Herzelöude hât den selben willen:
> Urrepanse de schoyen   lop mac ander lop niht gestillen.
> (Titurel 10,1-4)

Thus Herzeloyde, whose devoted love is later to permit her to sacrifice wealth and place in the world, is named with the two women
whose purity and devotion make them fit to bear the Graal. There

is no further mention of her until the death of Kastis, when she decides to take her young niece into her care. Nor does Wolfram dwell on her for long at this point, and he gives no indication that the early death of her husband left any particular mark on her. Like his stress on her virginity, the brevity of his treatment is certainly deliberate, to show that her love for Gahmuret was the only real love of her life (*Titurel* 27,1-29,2).

It is this love which brings about the great change in Herzeloyde and causes her to develop more than any of the other women. When Gahmuret first meets her, Herzeloyde is very much a lady of the court, and the manner of her wooing suggests her complete adherence at this point to the conventions of the court which she is later to reject. The sorrow of the Graal Family has not yet come to her, and her short-lived marriage to Kastis was clearly an insufficiently profound experience to have left her with any lasting grief. Grief comes only with Gahmuret, who brings with him both her first experience of real love, and the sorrow which Wolfram sees as its inevitable companion.

Gahmuret meets Herzeloyde in a situation which is essentially a product of the courtly life. Moreover, it is one which she has herself created, for she has arranged the tournament and offered her hand in marriage to the victor. Thus she gains in a tournament the man whom she is later to lose in battle, and she prizes him not least for his excellence in the practice of the chivalric code which she is later to strive so hard to keep from his son. Such contrasts are striking and point to the changes which take place within her during this brief period of her life. Striking, too, is the contrast between the manners in which Gahmuret wins Herzeloyde and Belakane. Belakane is in dire distress, faced with physical danger, and from this Gahmuret frees her. He rides into battle with the thought of her in his mind. Theirs is a relationship of mutual love and spontaneous attraction, and one which can surmount the problems of race and religion.[4] Herzeloyde is in no such danger: the tournament is the result of a mere whim and the product of a mind preoccupied with the courtly life. Gahmuret attracts her at first for his valour and handsome appearance, and he is no less impressed by her exceptional beauty. The memory of Belakane is with him still, however, and will remain with him for a long time to come, marring his happiness in this new acquaintance. In the mind of the reader is a further memory, which Gahmuret does not possess: of the grief of Belakane, left to mourn with her new-born son. This memory tends to prejudice the view of Herzeloyde at this stage, as she proceeds with such ruthless determination to usurp the place of Belakane in Gahmuret's heart. Her manner ignores the claims of the wife and the obvious reluctance of Gahmuret himself, and it betrays her own frankly sensual desire. She behaves with immature indiscretion, singling him out for her kiss, until, with his delicate social sense, he is forced to remind her of the rules of etiquette, that there are other kings and princes present who are also entitled to it (83,17-20). As she draws Gahmuret close to her, Wolfram remarks with some hint of criticism:

> si was ein magt und niht ein wîp,
> diu in sô nâhen sitzen liez.   (84,6-7)

At this stage she gives the impression of a young girl untouched by the seriousness of life, and this impression is strengthened when she is compared—and comparison is inevitable—with Belakane, who, although she can hardly have been much older in years, attains a certain maturity by her very situation when Gahmuret meets her. She is seen as a woman in extreme danger against the background of the battlefield, while Herzeloyde stands in the splendour of the court, secure and supremely confident.

Yet Wolfram is careful to tell of Gahmuret's own feelings for Herzeloyde, for Parzival must be the product of a perfect, mutual love. The first sight of Herzeloyde produces an involuntary response in Gahmuret:

> von dem liehten schîne,
> der von der künegîn erschein,
> derzuct im neben sich sîn bein.   (64,4-6)[5]

7

In this single touch, Wolfram betrays the spontaneous interest of Gahmuret for Herzeloyde, and on several occasions he says that it is the memory of Belakane which prevents his falling in love with Herzeloyde (84,16-18; 90,17-91,8).[6] Possibly Herzeloyde senses his feelings towards her and is thus encouraged in her efforts to persuade him. Strangely, she uses the same argument to him as he had used in his parting letter to Belakane, that he cannot feel bound by marriage to a heathen, but the reason does not convince him any more now than when he used it himself. Ironically, it is not this argument of Herzeloyde's which persuades him, but a more obscure one, for it is only when Gahmuret accepts that it is his duty as a knight to marry Herzeloyde, since he has been pronounced the victor in the *vesperîe*, that he agrees to do so, prompted by his loyalty, not to Herzeloyde, but to Ampflise, the woman who gave him his knowledge of knighthood. To this irony is added another, for it must be remembered that it was not Herzeloyde who spurred Gahmuret in the combat itself, but Ampflise, whose messengers had just arrived with letters reminding him of this woman who is truly his liege-lady (76,23-77,28). Thus it is not Herzeloyde for whom Gahmuret fights but Ampflise: it is Ampflise who brings him victory, and the memory of Ampflise and the code she taught him combines with his 'art von der feien' (96,20) to persuade him to marry Herzeloyde. The irony is both for Herzeloyde and for Ampflise herself. For the first time, though she is not yet aware of it, the happiness of Herzeloyde is threatened: the shadow of irony is cast over her splendid confidence, and it may well be recalled that for a brief moment in *Titurel* Herzeloyde betrays the fear she feels for the woman she recognizes as her rival, when she seizes on the strange notion that it is Ampflise who has inflicted love on Sigune and Schionatulander, as an obscure means of revenge on Herzeloyde herself (*Titurel* 122).

Almost immediately a further threat comes into Herzeloyde's life, when Gahmuret insists that she should free him each month to practise the art of chivalry. Gahmuret is still too fresh from the

grief which he inflicted on himself and Belakane to desire a repetition of the experience, and he admits now that it was the longing
for adventure and combat which drove him in secret from his first
wife (96,29-97,4). Thus, in insisting that Gahmuret should marry
her, Herzeloyde brings upon herself this condition and is thus
doomed to lose him at some point. Perfectly content herself in her
love for him, she must nevertheless share him with the life of chivalry which eventually takes him from her. The perfection of their
union is symbolized in the ritual by which Gahmuret goes into battle wearing the garment of Herzeloyde, who puts it on again when
he returns, regardless of its stained and torn state. The action suggests that Herzeloyde accompanies Gahmuret in battle as much as
Condwiramurs does Parzival, or Gyburc Willehalm. It suggests, too,
Herzeloyde's acceptance of this other half of her husband's life,
for the ceremony takes place eighteen times during their time together, until the occasion when Gahmuret does not return. Yet even
then the garment, stained this time with his blood, is returned to
her for burial, an additional symbolic touch which suggests that
Gahmuret returns to her even in death (111,25-112,4). Moreover,
Herzeloyde desires, as before, to put it on her own body, in token
of her love for him and her complete acknowledgement of his chivalry. It is important that the mission which brings Gahmuret's death
is no mere venture after knightly honour, but the fulfilment of a
duty towards a friend who calls upon him in time of need, the
Baruch of Baldac whom he has served for so long. So Herzeloyde
does not lose her husband in a foolish errand, but for the sake of an
allegiance which is even greater than the one he bears her, because
it is bound too with knightly activity.

Like Condwiramurs who has 'den wunsch ûf der erde' in her love
for Parzival, Herzeloyde exists for her husband, and his return becomes an essential ingredient of her happiness:

> do er ûze beleip ein halbez jâr,
> sîns komens warte si für wâr:
> daz was ir lîpgedinge.   (103,15-17)

Like Belakane before her, she is cast into grief when she is left alone, and, like Belakane, she is left to bear her son alone. Yet she finds hope in her unborn son, whom she regards almost as the reincarnation of her husband:

> ich trage alhie doch sînen lîp
> und sînes verhes sâmen. (109,26-27)

Belakane had kissed Feirefiz especially on those white patches which were all that remained to her of Gahmuret, but Herzeloyde expresses the same idea more positively, and it is significant that Gahmuret's death is followed so closely by the birth of Parzival. Parzival is the re-formation of Gahmuret, with the vital addition of all the feminine virtues of Herzeloyde.[7]

It is at the birth of Parzival that Herzeloyde comes to perfect womanhood, as Wolfram sees it, for he allows her to compare herself with the Virgin Mary:

> [frou] Herzeloyde sprach mit sinne
> 'diu hœhste küneginne
> Jêsus ir brüste bôt,
> der sît durch uns vil scharpfen tôt
> ame kriuze mennischlîche enphienc
> und sîne triwe an uns begienc. (113,17-22)

Significantly, this is the only time that Wolfram ever makes an actual comparison with the Virgin, and significantly it is a comparison of motherhood, which is the reflection of perfect womanhood in both the Virgin Mary and Herzeloyde. The picture of this woman whom he regards as supremely good, with the child who is to gain the highest reward of Christian knighthood, echoes the familiar picture of the Virgin and Child, but the comparison is even more precise, for it is one of purity and humility, born of love. Moreover, the grief of Herzeloyde may well be seen in its relation to the Sorrows of Mary,[8] although Wolfram shows that grief is a part of the experience of all women and in no way peculiar to Herzeloyde.[9]

10

The humility which allows Queen Herzeloyde to suckle her child, against the custom of royal ladies, is the beginning of the humility which is to allow her, in her grief for Gahmuret and her fear to lose her child, to sacrifice worldly possessions and rank, in order to withdraw into the forest. The *armuot* which Wolfram speaks of in reference to Herzeloyde's sacrifice (116,15) is not only physical poverty, the absence of riches, but a positive quality, reminiscent of the biblical 'poor in spirit,' where poverty in spirit is the state of being unattached to material things, a part, therefore, of the positive virtue of humility. Herzeloyde thus becomes the forerunner of Gyburc, for whom *armuot* represents a positive quality, beginning, it is true, as it does with Herzeloyde, with the sacrifice of worldly goods, but widening into an attitude of mind, a way of life, which has its source in love.[10] In both these women, *armuot* and *diemuot* become one, and when Wolfram talks of Herzeloyde as 'ein stam der diemüete,' he is referring not only to her ability to give up her wealth and rank and live in poverty, but also to the humility which allows her to do so, and which allows her now to nurse her child. Moreover, of the milk which waits for her child she says:

> 'du bist von triwen komn.
> het ich des toufes niht genomn,
> du waerest wol mîns toufes zil.
> ich sol mich begiezen vil
> mit dir und mit den ougen,
> offenlîch und tougen:
> wande ich wil Gahmureten klagn.'   (111,7-13)

Both the milk and the tears which she sheds are the product of her love for Gahmuret, and she sees them both as the possible substitute for baptismal water. She regards love itself, then, as a means to Christian baptism, and that this is Wolfram's own view is clear from the earlier occasion, when he said of Belakane:

> ir kiusche was ein reiner touf,
> und ouch der regen der sie begôz.   (28,14-15)

11

Belakane's love for Isenhart, reflected in her tears now that he is
dead, serves to make her a Christian in spirit. This notion may then
be taken further, for it is love for Willehalm which actually leads
to Gyburc's baptism, love for Repanse de Schoye which makes Feirefiz agree to be baptised, and Sigune, a Christian already, comes to a
closer love of God through her love for Schionatulander. These
other examples emphasize the value which Wolfram places on the
triuwe of Herzeloyde and which allows him to compare her with
the Virgin Mary. Even without them his meaning is unambiguous,
but their presence adds support to what is a basic ingredient in his
conception of her character.

Herzeloyde withdraws from the life of the court which has been
marred for her by the death of Gahmuret and lives in the forest,
determined that her son shall not come to know of this life.[11] Although Wolfram does say

> der knappe alsus verborgen wart
> zer waste in Soltâne erzogn,
> an küneclîcher fuore betrogn;   (117,30-118,2)

he does not appear to blame Herzeloyde, since she does this from
the best of motives, love for her son, even if this can be interpreted
as selfish love, a possessive desire to cling to her child.[12] The pre-
cautions which she takes to protect Parzival from the world outside
are implied by the reaction of the servants who fear to lose their
lives when they realize that he may have been in contact with the
strange knights. It is a shock, therefore, to Herzeloyde, when she
learns of Parzival's acquaintance with the life of the court, an acquaintance which must be accompanied in the child of Gahmuret
by the desire to become a part of it. Herzeloyde, of course, is too
deeply versed in the courtly life and too conscious of the claims of
knighthood not to understand her son's wish to go to Arthur's Court.
She may hitherto have hoped to keep him from the knowledge of
its existence, but she knows that she cannot now prevent his desire
to go there. Nor, in fact, would she really wish to, for in Gahmuret

she loved a man of valour and nobility, and a man who did not possess these qualities would not long satisfy this woman whose values and view of life are deeply rooted in the courtly life. Yet her immediate and natural desire as a mother is to keep her son with her, and, although she does not prevent his departure, her reluctance to see him leave leads her to dress him in the clothes of a fool, in the hope that the mockery of the world will prove too much for him and send him back to her (126,22-127,10). On first consideration, this would seem to be the action of a foolish, even a cruel mother, for she is exposing him to the ridicule of a world of which he has no knowledge, but again Wolfram does not seem to blame her, for she is prompted by real love for Parzival, and she never doubts that in keeping him from the courtly life she is keeping him from suffering, perhaps even from death. Moreover, though she gives expression to her love in one way, by dressing him in the clothes of a fool, she does so in another way, too, by insisting that he should stay one more night, so that she may give him some final words of advice. This procrastination may be construed as a part of her desire to put off the moment of departure which she knows to be inevitable, but this is not her only motive: clearly, if he must go from her into the unknown world, she wishes him to have at least some basic rules of conduct.[13]

It is not Herzeloyde's fault that the instructions she gives to her son are limited and misleading. Despite her love for him—or perhaps precisely because of it—it is not in her power to offer him better advice, nor is he ready to receive it; knowledge will come to him later, when experience has already taught him a certain amount. He is not ready for complex instructions regarding religion: such instruction will come very much later from Trevrizent, but until then he can exist in the knowledge of a God who is 'liehter denne der tac' and to whom he may turn in time of need (119,17-24). The bald and misleading teaching of Herzeloyde about his behaviour towards women will be enlarged upon and made clear by Gurnemanz, but only after Jeschute has suffered through his over-literal adherence to his mother's words. Her instructions that he should avoid dark waters and give his greeting to everyone he meets on his way have less serious consequences when he follows them too closely, and her advice that he should listen attentively to the teaching of a wise, grey-haired man has positive effect, echoing as it does both in his meeting with Gurnemanz and, much later, with the Pilgrim and then with Trevrizent. Such brief and ambiguous instructions are all that Herzeloyde is capable of giving to her son, and perhaps all that he is capable of absorbing at this stage, but she sets him on the path towards the knowledge which she cannot give him.[14] Her work of teaching is taken up by others, Gurnemanz, Sigune, the Pilgrim and Trevrizent, and it is significant that Sigune and Trevrizent are both closely related to her and so most fitted to succeed her in the task of educating her son.[15]

When Gurnemanz tells Parzival to refrain from constant reference to his mother, Wolfram comments that Parzival did indeed keep silent but did not forget her in his heart.[16] The memory of Herzeloyde remains, however, not only to her son, but in the mind of the reader, for, just as Feirefiz shows in his physical appearance the two distinct races which gave him life, so does Parzival possess in his nature a duality which bears witness to his parentage. When Herzeloyde seemed to see her son as the re-incarnation of his father, she was perhaps partly right, for he is truly the son of a noble and valiant father, skilled in combat and eventually versed in the ways of the court. He is more than this, however, for as the son of Herzeloyde he is endowed with other qualities of mind and heart which did not belong to his father. It is these qualities which make Parzival different from Gahmuret, and which also make him a more complex character and his life fraught with conflict, until he learns, as he can learn only by faith supported by experience and instruction, to reconcile the two distinct parts of his nature. On many occasions he is mentioned as the child of one or other of his parents, and although this may be regarded as a common practice of mediæval authors, Wolfram seems to use it on some occasions with more specific intention. When he refers to Parzival as the son of Gahmuret he usually wishes to stress his perfection in the courtly arts.[17] It is to be expected that Parzival is more often mentioned as the son of Gahmuret, for manly virtue was the foremost attribute of the mediæval knight, so that the occasions on which Wolfram refers to him as the son of Herzeloyde stand out with an even greater significance. Sometimes the relationship is mentioned with no apparent intention of stressing a particular quality in Parzival (434,3-5; 781, 3-5), but there are some outstanding connections in which Parzival is mentioned deliberately as the son of Herzeloyde. When Cundrie comes to reproach Parzival for his failure at the Graal Castle, she laments that he should have behaved in a manner so unworthy of the son of Gahmuret but then exclaims with greater force:

> ôwê daz ie wart vernomn
> von mir, daz Herzeloyden barn
> an prîse hât sus missevarn!   (318,2-4)

Contributing to her horror are two considerations: first, that Herzeloyde, the daughter of the Graal Family, should have a son who apparently ignored the plight of the whole kingdom and failed to use the opportunity he was given to relieve both Anfortas and all his people, and secondly that the child of the gentle, compassionate Herzeloyde should seem to be so lacking in human compassion. Moreover, in Wolfram's closing words, he refers to Kyot, who told

> wie Herzeloyden kint den grâl
> erwarp, als im daz gordent was,
> dô in verworhte Anfortas.   (827,6-8)

Thus it is as Herzeloyde's child that Parzival achieves the Graal Kingship, as he is destined to do, since, as her child, he is both related to the Graal Family and fitted for its kingship by those qualities of mind which he has inherited from her. From his father he inherited perfect manhood and knightly supremacy, essential virtues in one who was to receive the highest honour of chivalry, but his mother contributed those virtues without which no-one could come near to the Graal.

Thus it is at the turning-point of Parzival's journey towards his destiny that Wolfram again, and with the utmost significance, refers to him as Herzeloyde's son:

> hin rîtet Herzeloyde fruht.
> dem riet sîn manlîchiu zuht
> kiusch unt erbarmunge:
> sît Herzeloyd diu junge
> in het ûf gerbet triuwe,
> sich huop sîns herzen riuwe. (451,3-8)

Parzival has passed through grief and despair, indignation and rebellion, and now, at his lowest ebb, he has met the Pilgrim who, inspired by his daughters to charity and pity, has directed him to Trevrizent's hermitage, where he will find a renewal of faith. The compassion thus shown to him inspires him, too, to compassion, and this virtue, combined with purity and manly breeding, makes him truly the son of Herzeloyde. With the side of his nature which was his mother's legacy to the fore, he becomes once more a man in whom knightly perfection combines with feminine sensitivity, so that, prompted by the human kindness of the pilgrims, he feels again the need to love and to turn to God. He feels this need, says Wolfram, because he is the son of a woman who loved and endowed him, too, with the power to love and to need love, hence with the power to repent before God. Only by repentance can Parzival come to the Graal once more, and only with a simple expression of pity can he achieve its Kingship. Repentance is an aspect of humility, the virtue demanded of those who would serve the Graal and of the Graal King above all. Anfortas lost sight of this virtue and suffered terribly in consequence, while Trevrizent withdrew from the world in order not to become a victim of arrogance. Only Herzeloyde possesses natural humility, and as her son Parzival, too,

16

possesses latent humility. As Gurnemanz tells him, however, this is a virtue which must be nurtured (170,28-30), and it is only when he allows that part of him which is Herzeloyde's legacy to come forward that he truly possesses the humility which can lead him back to God through repentance, and hence to the Graal. Thus as Herzeloyde's son he possesses the key to his destiny, in the form of the two great virtues of love and humility, and in his vital comment on the encounter with the pilgrims Wolfram shows them to be manifested in him, with most potent effect.

It is apt that Herzeloyde should bequeath to Parzival the virtues which will make him fit for the Graal Kingship, for as the daughter of Frimutel she is deeply involved in its destiny.[18] As a child of the ill-fated Graal Family she must partake too of its sorrow, and bequeath this also to her son. Nor is this only the sorrow which overtakes them all by virtue of their birth into a stricken family, but also the personal sorrow which comes to all its members. Kyot must suffer the death of his young wife, and his child is Sigune, destined to a life of mourning for her dead lover. For Herzeloyde, personal grief comes with the death of Gahmuret and the departure of Parzival, yet both sorrows are the result of love, for, in Wolfram's mind, love and grief are inseparable companions. When Herzeloyde is grieving for the absent Gahmuret, Wolfram exclaims:

> ôwê unde heiâ hei,
> daz güete alsölhen kumber tregt
> und immer triwe jâmer regt!　　　　(103,20-22)

and Sigune says to Parzival, when he has shown pity for her slain lover:

> du bist geborn von triuwen,
> daz er dich sus kan riuwen.　　　　(140, 1-2)

Clearly she sees in him the power of his mother to love with an intensity which must bring grief, even though at this point she has no idea who this mother is. Thus Parzival, too, as part of his destiny, must know very great love, together with the grief which comes with its loss, and the greater sorrow of his loss of trust in God. He must experience the grief which results from his failure in his appointed task, the grief of loneliness and despair: all this is part of his heritage, but it is the lesser part. Above all his mother bequeathed him the power of love, and, in its finest manifestations, Wolfram shows that love is no destructive force, bringing only grief to those who know it, but a great gift, which can raise its bearers above the trials of the world and bring them into relationship with the Divine. Thus Sigune and Gyburc, the foremost bearers of this message, can hope for ultimate peace through love, and Parzival, blessed with the gift of love from his parents, may demonstrate it in his relationship with Condwiramurs and in his faith in God, and so come to the Graal.

It is indeed as the son of Herzeloyde that Parzival comes to the Graal, fails there and comes again to succeed, after years of despair and suffering. It is because he is her son that he encounters problems which would not have troubled the less complex Gahmuret, and it is precisely the complexity which distinguishes him from his father which fits him to be King of the Graal. Without the struggle for inner harmony, Parzival might indeed have been a very great knight, like his father, but he needed this struggle to emerge at last as a deeper, more integrated being, complex still, but with the conflicts in his nature resolved by suffering and experience. In his early boyhood, the complexity of Parzival's nature is revealed in his ambiguous reaction to the birds' song, and the incident stresses too the connection between the nature of the mother and the nature of the son. The sweetness of the song makes Parzival weep, and Wolfram observes

des twang in art und sîn gelust   (118,28)

for from Herzeloyde—and indeed from Gahmuret too—he has inherited both the sensitive delight in beauty and an indefinable mel-

18

ancholy which senses sorrow lurking close to joy at all times. With the same kind of intuition which made Herzeloyde grieve that Sigune should have come to know love so early (*Titurel* 109), she now recognizes the fatal susceptibility of her husband in her son and senses that such sensitivity will bring him into conflict and danger in the world: without knowing why, she turns her anger on the birds which have aroused this emotion in Parzival and orders them to be killed. Yet she is equally quick to respond to his appeal that the birds should be spared, for such brutal disregard for life is not in the nature of this gentle woman, save in the attempt to keep her son from the anguish which she knows must come to him.

This incident, which comes very early in the story of Parzival, goes beyond the simple and the idyllic and serves to prepare the way for Wolfram's treatment of the character of his hero. It shows the extent to which the rational and the intuitive are bound together in the mother as in the son, and the close relationship between the two people. Herzeloyde is an outstanding example of the depth of Wolfram's conception of his characters, based as she is on the barely defined widow of Chrétien's version. Although she dies early in the work, her influence remains throughout, until the memory of her is given new life in the awareness, through the words of Wolfram at the end of the work, that it is the child of Herzeloyde who achieves the Graal.

NOTES

1. W. J. Schröder (*Die Soltane-Erzählung in Wolframs 'Parzival*,' p. 61), has drawn attention to the similarity here with the symbolism used of the Virgin Mary.
2. The notion of Herzeloyde's passing straight into heaven recalls the idea of the Assumption of the Virgin Mary. Although this did not take the form of a doctrine until very recently, it was a part of Catholic belief already in the 8th century.
3. A very different view of the death of Herzeloyde is taken by

D. M. Blamires (pp. 80-81). He sees her death as a sign of weakness, the revelation of her inability to live without the support of Gahmuret and Parzival.

4. See below, p. 87-89.

5. For a discussion of Gahmuret's first sight of Herzeloyde, see also M. F. Richey: *Gahmuret Anschevin*, Oxford, 1923, p. 30. Wolfram frequently describes the beauty of his women characters as a radiant light, and again it is interesting that this was the way in which other writers saw the beauty of the Virgin Mary. See, for example, the *Marienleben* of Priester Wernher (*Maria*, ed. C. Wesle, Halle 1927: Altdeutsche Textbibliothek 26):

> dâ lac diu maget reine
> in einem grôzen liehte   (ll. 4150-4151)

and (line 22) 'ir chûsche liuhtet uberal.'

6. See below, p. 91.

7. W. J. Schröder (*Die Soltane-Erzählung in Wolframs 'Parzival,'* p. 12) puts it even more strongly: "In Herzeloydes Sinn sind also Vater und Sohn in gewisser Weise identisch."

8. cf. *The Oxford Dictionary of the Christian Church*, ed. F. Cross, Oxford, 1957, p. 1273.

9. On the relationship between Herzeloyde and the Virgin Mary, see D. M. Blamires (p. 93ff).

10. See the discussion of Gyburc, below.

11. It is important to note that at this point Wolfram is independent of Chrétien, whose narrative begins with the widow in the forest with her son. The motivation of the woman in living thus isolated is not mentioned, and the character of Herzeloyde represents an outstanding development of the source.

12. D. M. Blamires (p. 86) seems also to take the more positive view of her behaviour, though accepting that it could be viewed negatively.

13. It may be argued that all that Herzeloyde does at this stage is

selfish, but this is not how Wolfram himself sees her behaviour and one must be guided by him in judging a character whom he prizes so highly. cf. D. M. Blamires (p.96).

14. See W. J. Schröder (*Die Soltane-Erzählung in Wolframs 'Parzival,'* p. 21) "Herzeloydes Rat an den Sohn ist also bloßer Antrieb zum Tun, weiter nichts. Sie hat ihm nicht gesagt, *wie* er kämpfen und minnen soll, sondern nur, *daß* er es soll. . . . Was Herzeloyde 'lehrt' und Parzival 'lernt' kann im eigentlichen Sinne nicht gelehrt und gelernt werden. Wirklich Lernbares erfährt Parzival erst durch Gurnemanz."

15. On Herzeloyde's education of Parzival see in particular D. M. Blamires (pp. 85-92). This is, however, a key episode, which is discussed in most interpretations of the work as a whole.

16. An interesting echo is noted by S. Singer (*Wolfram und der Gral. Neue Parzival-Studien,* Bern 1939, p. 39): He quotes the *Kreuziger* of Johannes von Frankenstein, 9697ff:'Doch sand Bernhard des vergicht: Ob Christus mit dem munde nicht Habe bedûhtet mûter nam, Doch ûz dem sinne im nicht kam Der spruch, alleine in der munt Nicht bî namen machte kunt.' This is certainly an interesting comparison with *Parzival* 173,8-10.

17. For example, when Parzival is just beginning to learn the art of knightly combat (174,24-25); in the battle with Clamide (212,2-3); when Parzival rides away from the castle of Gurnemanz, grieving for Liaze (179,24-26); when Gawan wishes to present Parzival to the four great ladies, it is the son of Gahmuret who expresses his qualms (695,25-27).

18. This is not, however, the view of D. M. Blamires who says of Herzeloyde (p.67) that her relationship with the Graal Family is 'a purely external one' and that the Graal has 'no significance whatsoever' in her life. It is difficult to see how he can uphold this view, which seems contrary to Wolfram's intention. cf. S. M. Johnson: 'Herzeloyde and the Grail,' *Neophilologus* 52, 1968, pp. 148-156.

CHAPTER TWO

Condwiramurs

THE END OF Book IV links Herzeloyde and Condwiramurs as the mother and the wife of Parzival must be linked. In Condwiramurs Parzival has chosen a wife who comes close to his mother in purity and love, and that the likeness is evident to him is made clear when, at the height of his happiness with Condwiramurs, he begs leave to go and seek his mother. This idea is already present in *Le Conte del Graal*,[1] but there little stress is placed on the link between the two women: it is not apparent that Perceval feels a real need to share his new-found joy with his mother, nor does Blancheflor sense the compliment which is being paid to her, for she protests and so forces Perceval to go without her leave. Not so Condwiramurs: her love for Parzival is so great, says Wolfram, that she will deny him nothing, even though she must suffer the grief of separation (223, 27-30), and Condwiramurs proves during the years of Parzival's absence that she is capable of the same constancy which bound Herzeloyde to Gahmuret even beyond death.

Unlike Herzeloyde, though, Condwiramurs is not seen to develop during the course of the work. She does not grow towards perfection: rather is she perfect from the start. It is true that external circumstances touch her, but they do not change her, as they do Herzeloyde. The effect of such external circumstances—marriage to Parzival, separation from him, the call to the Graal Kingdom—is rather to prove again the worth already established at their first meeting. It is very interesting that, of all Wolfram's major heroines, Condwiramurs is the least deliberately characterized.[2] Much is left unsaid about her nobility and virtue, because there is no need to extol individual virtue in a woman who loves, and is loved by, the future Graal King. Certainly, the ultimate evidence of her great worth comes in her call to the Graal Kingdom: all other praise is superfluous, in view of the honour which is to be hers, and Wolfram makes it clear that this honour is due not to the consort of Parzival, but to a woman in her own right.

When Parzival left Gurnemanz, he gave as his reason that he was not ready to accept the love of Liaze: he must first prove himself worthy of her. Whatever his unconscious yearnings at this point, this was certainly a genuine consideration with him, for Liaze had to be won, in accordance with the code of chivalry given to him by her father. He rides away, then, leaving the sorrowing Gurnemanz with the hope that he may one day return to claim his bride. Almost immediately he involves himself in an act of valour which would certainly prove him worthy of Liaze, but it is not Liaze whom he wins by the defence of Pelrapeire, but her cousin, Condwiramurs, who exceeds her in beauty and whose love for him will contain all the devotion of true *minne* in Wolfram's sense of the term. Although this vital element had been absent in his relationship with Liaze, without her Parzival would have been ill-prepared for Condwiramurs, in whom he recognizes immediately the qualities which he came so near to loving in Liaze:

> Lîâze ist dort, Lîâze ist hie.
> mir wil got sorge mâzen:
> nu sihe ich Lîâzen,
> des werden Gurnemanzes kint.   (188,2-5)

What he sees in Condwiramurs is that womanhood which he met for the first time in Liaze, but Liaze's physical beauty is enhanced in Condwiramurs, as Wolfram suggests:

> Lîâzen schœne was ein wint
> gein der meide diu hie saz.   (188,6-7)[3]

23

Since physical beauty is so often the reflection of spiritual beauty for Wolfram, the implication is that Condwiramurs is more perfect too in virtue, but, despite the difference, Parzival connects the two in his mind. Nor does Wolfram himself wish to undermine this natural reaction in his young hero, so he, too, stresses the connection between the two women, while making it clear that, for Parzival, Condwiramurs is the only possible wife.[4]

When Parzival meets Condwiramurs and seems to find Liaze again, Wolfram is surely suggesting that he has fallen in love with her already, since in Condwiramurs he sees a renewed version of the girl he has loved, though without intensity, and whom he has remembered since leaving her with pain and some regret. Already there is a note of inevitability, and as Parzival and Condwiramurs sit together, Wolfram draws attention to the splendid match, echoing the previous occasion when Parzival had sat at table with Liaze, and they, too, had seemed such a well-matched couple.[5] Both women kiss Parzival in greeting, and although this is a conventional greeting, it is significant that Wolfram sees fit to mention it: in both cases he draws attention to the redness of the women's lips, but only when Parzival kisses Condwiramurs does he point out how his lips match hers in redness, hinting perhaps at the love which is to be mutual between them (187,2-3). A further hint is contained in the slight touch which Wolfram adds, of their sharing the last crumbs which remain to the starving household. (191,5-6). The distress in which Parzival finds Condwiramurs is similar to that suffered by Gyburc, and by Belakane. All three women must endure imminent danger from a powerful enemy, and all three must suffer, too, the knowledge that they are the cause of hardship, even death, to those who serve them. The relationship between Condwiramurs and Belakane is strangely close: both are in immediate danger and urgently need the aid of a brave knight. Moreover, just as Gahmuret was prepared to fight for the queen of the besieged city even before he had met her, so is his son now ready to help Condwiramurs, with no thought for the reward which may be his as a result. When Condwiramurs comes to Parzival at night, Wolfram is at pains to stress the purity of her intention: she comes only to plead for help in her desperate need, and even the garment which she is wearing Wolfram describes as the attire of war:

> dô gienc diu küneginne,
> niht nâch sölher minne
> diu sölhen namen reizet
> der meide wîp heizet,
> si suochte helfe unt friundes rât.
> an ir was werlîchiu wât,
> ein hemde wîz sîdîn:
> waz möhte kampflîcher sîn,
> dan gein dem man sus komende ein wîp? (192,9-17)

Not for him is the nocturnal adventure of his source, nor the wholly distasteful behaviour of Chrétien's Blancheflor.[6] Parzival promises his aid to her, and she leaves him with an expression of her thanks, so that their relationship begins with the promise of aid on the one hand, and gratitude on the other.

Yet for Wolfram, though he had chosen to solve the immediate problems posed by his source in this way, such a relationship was not to be the basis for the perfect and most potent love of Parzival and Condwiramurs. Already he has hinted very gently at the perfection of their match, and it is significant that it is when Condwiramurs mentions Liaze that Parzival agrees to fight for her. Wolfram comments that he does this for love of Liaze (195,11), but the way from love of Liaze to love of her cousin is a straight one: although at the time all conscious thought of a new love may be absent from his mind, its seed is already planted in the memory of the old one. On the following day, moreover, Condwiramurs is preoccupied with the thought of him during Mass, and already there is the hint of the spirituality of their love, which does not intrude, such is its purity, even on the religious service. Without doubt, it is with the picture of her in his mind that he goes out to fight with Kingrun,[7] and subsequently he thinks to send his defeated opponent to her, as a first act of service towards the woman whom he is to serve for ever. When he returns, Condwiramurs greets him with the declaration that no other man will be her husband, and this is no unbecoming act on her part, but the expression of a consciousness of the pre-ordained and the unchallengeable. There is no question of the fitness of the marriage of this perfectly matched couple: Wolfram omits the details of the preliminaries of the marriage, and that evening Parzival rules over the house and the kingdom as its lord, and the husband of its queen. Parzival and Condwiramurs are already married before his victory over Clamide frees her from danger, because for Wolfram this further act of valour alone was insufficient basis for a marriage.

When Parzival rides out to meet Clamide, Wolfram comments that this combat will show whether God wishes him to keep Condwiramurs or not. Their marriage is conceived as an act of divine will, and more than anywhere else it is in the case of Parzival and Condwiramurs that Wolfram extols the state of marriage, showing it to be a sacred union. Gurnemanz had told Parzival of the relationship between a man and his wife:

> man und wîp diu sint al ein;
> als diu sunn diu hiute schein,
> und ouch der name der heizet tac.
> der enwederz sich gescheiden mac:
> si blüent ûz eime kerne gar. (173,1-5)

Parzival himself recalls this when he finds joy in physical union with Condwiramurs:

> von im dicke wart gedâht
> umbevâhens, daz sîn muoter riet:
> Gurnemanz im ouch underschiet,
> man und wîp wærn al ein. (203,2-5)

The oneness of man and wife goes deeper than physical union, and Condwiramurs becomes an essential part of Parzival, the reason behind his striving and his constant support in grief and loneliness, united with the Graal as his inspiration and his goal. When Parzival leaves Arthur's Court and embarks on his long quest, Wolfram states explicitly that the thought of her will spur him in many undertakings:

> Condwier âmûrs,
> dîn minneclîcher bêâ curs,
> an den wirt dicke nu gedâht.
> waz dir wirt âventiure brâht!   (333,23-26)

Already, though, the Graal and Condwiramurs have been linked by Wolfram, when, on the plain of Plimizoel, he speaks of the double anguish of Parzival:

> sîne gedanke umben grâl
> unt der küngîn glîchiu mâl,
> iewederz was ein strengiu nôt.   (296,5-7)

At this stage, however, it is the separation from his wife which is causing him the greatest suffering:

> an im wac für der minnen lôt   (296,8)

for as yet the full impact of his failure at the Graal has not been brought home to him: the acute realization of his failure and dishonour will come only with the speech of Cundrie at Arthur's Court. At this point his love overwhelms all other desires, when he becomes transfixed by the sight of the blood in the snow. Knightly honour itself has no meaning for him in this state, and his actions, even the wounding of Kei which fulfils his very dear ambition of avenging Cunneware, depend upon his position in relation to the drops of blood. Condwiramurs is the powerful central force in his life, and so it is possible for the sight of the blood in the snow to prompt him to an outburst of praise of God, Who has created the beauty of Condwiramurs: nor is there anything unfit-

27

ting in this, for Condwiramurs is all-virtuous and may well be seen as a supreme manifestation of the power of the Creator (282,24-283,3).

— Soon, however, Parzival is to renounce the God he now extols and to turn from his wife, the source of all his joy; yet his turning from Condwiramurs in no way represents a rejection of her, for it is the inevitable consequence of his having fallen into dishonour. That he has no thought of rejecting her is clear from his great speech to Gawan, in which he commends his friend to the hands of a virtuous woman who will guide him in time of need (332,1-14). Having just rejected the power of God, he turns to woman as a substitute, and there is no doubt that he looks to the memory of his wife to sustain him, nor that she does so. What he does not realize at this early stage is what Wolfram makes clear during the course of the rest of the work: that woman is not a substitute for God, but a means to Him, that only through the love of his wife will he return to trust in God, and that, on the other hand, reunion with his wife can come only through renewal of his love for God. Moreover, the Graal itself, which he is later to seek so avidly, demands of him both trust in God and abiding love for his wife. He believes that only by coming to the Graal and succeeding where he failed before can he again claim the love of his wife, but Wolfram makes it clear that the reverse is also true, that only through the sustaining love of Condwiramurs for Parzival, and his for her, can they achieve the rule of the Graal. It is essential to Wolfram's concept of their marriage, as to his concept of the nature of the Graal, that they achieve it together; and this he expresses unambiguously when he tells that their names appear side-by-side in the inscription on the stone (781,17-19). Moreover, she is already on her way to meet him when he hears of their call, so that they can journey together towards their kingdom. Each has contributed equally to the achievement of the Graal, though in a different way.[8] Without the support afforded by the constancy of Condwiramurs during their long separation, all the striving of Parzival would have been in vain, for it is without doubt the awareness of her love, coupled with the hope of coming again to the Graal, which sustains him through the years of lonely wandering. The power of this love is made more apparent by the fact that during all this time Condwiramurs does not appear in the work, save in the thoughts of Parzival. Thus Wolfram emphasizes their separation even more, and Condwiramurs appears in the final book as the physical proof of the love which has been their single bond during the five years of separation.

When Parzival leaves Condwiramurs, he is going in search of the fame which will make him worthy of her. Although he says that he is anxious to see his mother again, this is not the only reason, and, unlike Gahmuret with Belakane, he is prepared to admit to his wife that the desire for adventure and fame urges him to leave her. In this Parzival shows the maturity which his father did not possess, and Condwiramurs is spared the fate of Belakane. At Pelrapeire, Parzival has achieved maturity as a knight and as a man: in his defeat first of Kingrun and then of Clamide, and in his mercy to them once he has defeated them, he has shown himself master of the art of noble combat, and in winning Condwiramurs and loving her as a true husband he has become master of the other aspect of knighthood. As yet, though, his is a superficial maturity, which conforms to the values of society but goes no deeper. His maturity must be tried, by suffering and loss, grief and degradation, before he can emerge finally as a truly mature man. The part played by Condwiramurs in the growth towards maturity is a considerable one, and the recognition of it comes when she is named with him on the Graal. Before that moment of joy, Condwiramurs must share in the grief of Parzival, and it is apt that this marriage which is to know almost five years of grief and separation should begin, not in the splendour of the court, but in a town in very real distress, in a state of siege and threatened by an apparently invincible army. It is indeed Belakane who is the forerunner of Condwiramurs, rather than Herzeloyde, close though the resemblance may be in some ways between Parzival's mother and the woman he chooses as his wife.

Once Cundrie has drawn attention to his failure at Munsal-væsche, Parzival cannot return to Condwiramurs, since, thus dishonoured, he is not worthy of her love. Moreover, he states explicitly that he will abstain from all joy until he has seen the Graal again (329,25-30), and Condwiramurs is the centre of all his joy. Later he tells Sigune how he paid for his reticence at the Graal with the companionship of his wife:

> dâ hân ich freude vil verlorn.
> der grâl mir sorgen gît genuoc.
> ich liez ein lant da ich krône truoc,
> dar zuo dez minneclîchste wîp.   (441,4-7)

At Trevrizent's hermitage he says:

> mîn hôhstiu nôt ist umben grâl;
> dâ nâch umb mîn selbes wîp:
> ûf erde nie schœner lîp
> gesouc an keiner muoter brust.
> nâch den beiden sent sich mîn gelust.   (467,26-30)

On both occasions, Parzival places his yearning for the Graal higher than his yearning for his wife: as a spiritual goal, the Graal must clearly take precedence over a human being. Moreover, it is essential that the desire for the Graal does not detract from his love for Condwiramurs, and, in any case, in coming to the Graal a second time he will atone for his former failure, thus re-establishing his honour and proving himself worthy of her. Although the Graal is the foremost object of his striving, the desire for his wife is intense and constant.[9]

When, at Arthur's Court, amid the joy which ends Gawan's adventures, Parzival feels himself alone and very sad, he himself expresses the link between his search for the Graal and his love for his wife:

> sol ich nâch dem grâle ringen,
> sô muoz mich immer twingen
> ir kiuschlîcher umbevanc.   (732,19-21)

It is at this point, when he rejects all love save that for his wife, that he sets off on the final stage of his quest. He deliberately turns his back on the joy which is so prevalent about him but which is barren since it lacks the single essential ingredient of his joy; in doing so he turns towards the realization of the only true joy for him, anticipated at the close of Book XIV in the oncoming dawn. The way ahead leads through the fight with Feirefiz, and it is above all in this fight that the saving power of the love of Condwiramurs reveals itself. She is the force which turns the action, when Parzival is almost succumbing to the might of his half-brother. Wolfram describes the way in which strength comes to Feirefiz each time he calls the name of Sekundille's city, and he desperately urges Parzival to think of his own wife, who can save him from death now:

> ern welle an minne denken,
> sone mager niht entwenken,
> dirre strît müez im erwerben
> vors heidens hant ein sterben.
> daz wende, tugenthafter grâl:
> Condwîr âmûrs diu lieht gemâl:
> hie stêt iur beider dienstman
> in der grœsten nôt dier ie gewan.   (740,15-22)

Once more, the Graal is named before Condwiramurs, but her power is no less than its power. Wolfram grows exasperated when Parzival is slow to think of his wife (742,27-30), but at last relief comes to Parzival with the thought of his wife and of her noble love:

> der getoufte nam an kreften zuo.
> er dâht (des was im niht ze fruo)
> an sîn wîp die küneginne
> unt an ir werden minne.   (743,23-26)

31

The effect is immediate, and with the thought of her and the shout of *Pelrapeire!*, strength returns to him. Thus the intolerable consequence, the death of Parzival at the hand of his half-brother, is averted, when with renewed vigour he aims a blow at Feirefiz which breaks his own sword and so, thanks to his opponent's generosity and courtliness, terminates the fight. Nowhere is the power of the love of Condwiramurs more apparent than here, where Wolfram describes it as coming to Parzival across four kingdoms and unmarred by the years of separation. At this fateful moment, it is the inspiration of Condwiramurs which saves him, not directly that of the Graal, but by now the two things are so closely related that they are synonymous in his mind.

It is not at Pelrapeire, which belongs to their past and the early days of their love, that Parzival and Condwiramurs meet once more, nor at Munsalvæsche itself, where their future together lies. Wolfram chooses rather a place which has been endowed with a special significance in the story of their love: the meadow by the Plimizoel. Here, as he twice reminds us, Parzival was once held entranced by the sight of the blood in the snow (797,8-10; 802,1-5) and here he now finds his wife in person. Moreover, between the two occasions lies another, vital in the progress of Parzival, for it was here too that Cundrie appeared before Parzival to accuse him and so cast him into despair. Here he lost his wife, when he determined to abandon all joy, and here he now finds her again. A further echo is present, for Wolfram tells how many of the army which once fought against Clamide now gather to sing Mass (802,23-26). The presence of these men, the vassals presumably of Condwiramurs, is not in itself surprising, but Wolfram reminds us of their earlier function and so himself supplies the link.[10] Thus their marriage, which began with Parzival's rescue of Condwiramurs from Clamide and which was conceived as an act of divine Will, now receives additional blessing and affirmation. The ultimate affirmation remains, however, the call of Parzival and Condwiramurs to the Graal, and the naming of their son as the future successor to Parzival.

Although Condwiramurs is given this supreme reward, and although Wolfram clearly means to imply her supremacy among women by making her equal to Parzival in the rule of the Graal, he is unusually reticent in his description of her. The reason is not hard to find: what need is there to elaborate on the virtue of one who is selected for such reward? He does, however, state that her beauty exceeds that of Liaze, Jeschute, Enite, Cunneware and the two Isoldes (187,12-19), raising her at once above other women who are acclaimed by himself and his contemporaries for their beauty. Later he says that only in Repanse de Schoye did Condwiramurs ever encounter a serious rival (811,1-3), yet even the lovely and virtuous Graal Bearer does not outshine Parzival's wife, nor does Orgeluse, although Wolfram admits that she comes very close to her in beauty (508,22-23).[11] In beauty, as in all else, Condwiramurs must remain supreme, and it is significant that her beauty is described at the first meeting as 'ir liehter glast' (186,5). Even though at this time she is suffering great distress and an actual lack of food, her beauty shines from her, and this radiance suggests a giving-out of all that lies beneath it, a great manifestation of virtue. Repeatedly, Wolfram takes up the same idea, using the adjective *lieht* to describe her (732,2; 740,20; 801,3; 811,1). Apart from this radiance, the beauty of Condwiramurs is epitomized in the image of the rose-bud:

> . . . als von dem süezen touwe
> diu rôse ûz ir bälgelîn
> blecket niwen werden schîn,
> der beidiu wîz ist unde rôt.   (188,10-13)

Wolfram thus prepares the way for Parzival's later response to the blood in the snow, and red and white become symbolic of Condwiramurs and of his love for her, with a hint even of the sorrow which is the traditional association of red and white.

What Wolfram does not say in detail of the virtue of Condwiramurs may justly be deduced. When he says that her beauty is supreme, the implication is that her virtue is also. That she inspires in Parzival the desire to see his mother suggests a close resemblance to Herzeloyde. When the all-virtuous Repanse de Schoye withdraws from the Graal, it is Condwiramurs who takes her place; and the Graal itself acknowledges her virtue when her name appears in the inscription. Moreover, she is the wife of one future Graal King, and the mother of another. Indirectly Parzival is speaking of her when he commends man to the hand of a woman in his speech to Gawan, for the woman who can come to the aid of man in his time of need must be one who possesses *kiusche* and *wîplîche güete*, and Trevrizent, too, makes an indirect reference to her when he tells Parzival that the Graal King must have a pure wife (495,9-10). There is no need, then, to extol her individual virtues, but Wolfram makes it clear that the devotion of Condwiramurs is her greatest possession, and the virtue in her which contributes most potently to Parzival's success:

> uns tuot diu âventiure kunt,
> wie von Pelrapeir diu künegin
> ir kiuschen wîplîchen sin
> behielt unz an ir lônes stat,
> dâ si in hôhe sælde trat. (734,10-14)

Her constancy to Parzival is rewarded when she herself comes to the Graal, but it is also the vital force which helps to bring him there. It is, above all, the virtue of *triuwe* which Wolfram shows in her, and this is intimately linked with her *kiusche*, the purity which keeps her true to him during their years of separation. This purity Wolfram had stressed in Condwiramurs very early, at the time of her visit to Parzival's bedside, and, later, in marriage, it joins with *triuwe* to form the abiding loyalty of which Parzival can be sure during their separation and which serves to keep him from total despair. Trust is the basis of their relationship, beginning when she goes to him, a stranger, at night and hopes to gain his help, and continuing when, as his wife, she releases him from her without the protests of Chrétien's Blancheflor or the conditions of Laudine. It is the knowledge that his wife has remained true to him which prevents Parzival's giving way to temptation himself, when he seems so far from her and so alone: inconstancy has no part in their relationship:

> stüend unser minne, mîn unt ir,
> daz scheiden dar zuo hôrte
> sô daz uns zwîvel stôrte,
> ich möht wol zanderr minne komn.   (733,10-13)

Knowing that this is so, Parzival gains the courage to continue in his search, and in the oncoming dawn he entrusts himself and his horse to fate. Significantly, it is at daybreak that he at last finds Condwiramurs:

> do ez tagt, dô vant er lieben funt.   (799,16)

The love which has not faltered during almost five years of separation and which, during that time, has prevented the total darkness of despair, comes at last to a reunion in the greyness of a new dawn.

NOTES

1. Chrétien de Troyes: *Le Roman de Perceval ou Le Conte du Graal*, ed. W. W. Roach, Geneva and Paris, 1959, 2993ff. All references are to this edition.
2. See D. M. Blamires (p. 233): 'The descriptions applied to Condwiramurs are unmistakably idealistic in intention and remarkably unspecific in their content. Wolfram's aim was to create an ideal beyond which nothing was possible, and by refusing to limit the beauty of Condwiramurs by describing her in particular terms he was able to realize this ideal. Individualization is impossible in this context and only occurs in the comparisons and in the extension of symbols: it would be foolish to expect anything further.'

3. H. Sacker (*An Introduction to Wolfram's 'Parzival,'* Cambridge 1963) says of these lines 'We are assured that there is no real comparison' (p. 38) but this does not seem to be Wolfram's meaning: rather is he at pains to point to the likeness, while making it clear that, in any such comparison, Condwiramurs must be superior to Liaze.

4. The relationship between the Liaze-episode and Parzival's marriage with Condwiramurs is examined in the article by G. Bauer ('Parzival und die Minne,' *Euphorion* 57, 1963, 67-96).

5. Compare 187, 24-29 and 176,26.

6. cf. B. Q. Morgan ('Some Women in Parzival,' *Journal of English and Germanic Philology*, 12, 1913, 175-198): '(Wolfram) has ennobled to a very remarkable degree a very ordinary romantic adventure' (p. 184). It is, of course, significant that Wolfram saw fit to change the name of the heroine. The relationship of Perceval and Blancheflor is on a much more superficial level than that of Parzival and Condwiramurs. Blancheflor is the 'bele amie' of Perceval (2417 and 2912), whereas it is essential to Wolfram's conception of the love of his couple that it culminates in a marriage in which man and woman are one. The memory of Blancheflor could not remain, even in the name. Moreover, the name Blancheflur exists also in Gottfried's *Tristan*, and again Wolfram may have wished to avoid the comparison.

7. This seems clear from Wolfram's juxtaposition in the lines 196,18-20.

8. J. Bumke (*Wolframs 'Willehalm,'* p. 144, note 3) comments: 'Condwiramurs wird zwar Gralkönigin, aber ihr fehlt jede innere Affinität dazu.' This seems to ignore Wolfram's own meaning in allowing them to be named together on the Graal, as well as his exalted view of Condwiramurs.

9. The desire for the Graal may not detract from Parzival's love for Condwiramurs: the achievement of the first implies the

achievement of the second. For this reason, the view expressed by C. F. Bayerschmidt ('Wolfram von Eschenbach's Christian Faith,' *Germanic Review*, 29, 1954, pp. 214-223) does not seem quite just: '. . . . although he is drawn to his wife with all the bonds of love, he is drawn even more to the Graal and everything which its possession implies' (p. 222). The view of W. J. Schröder (*Der Ritter zwischen Welt und Gott*, Weimar, 1952) is more satisfactory: 'Der Sinn ist: obwohl der Schmerz um die verlassene Gattin den Helden mit starker Gewalt zur Rückkehr treibt, bleibt er doch dem Streben nach dem Grale treu' (p. 153). Schröder is thus able to express the situation in the following way: 'Je mehr die Kraft der Liebe zur Gattin betont wurde, um so mehr muβte auch der Drang zum Gral hervortreten.'

10. A further link between the two episodes is present in Wolfram's mention, at the time of Cundrie's attack on Parzival at the Plimizoel, that Parzival is sitting beside Clamide: 311,7. Clamide, the rejected suitor of Condwiramurs, had witnessed the disgrace of Parzival which led to his separation from Condwiramurs, and now those who once defeated Clamide rejoice at the reunion of Parzival and Condwiramurs and the re-establishment of Parzival's honour.

11. D. M. Blamires (p. 229) observes the relative lack of description of Condwiramurs and sees that a vital part of Wolfram's conception of her beauty rests in the comparison with Jeschute, whom he has described at unusual length (130,3-25): 'he would have found it well-nigh impossible to make another detailed portrait surpassing it, and so he is content to leave this in his audience's memory and state, with obvious effect, that Condwiramurs' beauty excels even this.'

CHAPTER THREE

Sigune

A SINGLE SCENE in Chrétien's *Conte del Graal*[1] appears to have been Wolfram's only source for the mysterious and intriguing figure whom he calls Sigune and who appears four times in *Parzival*. In the sight of the girl grieving over the dead knight he found the essence of a human tragedy which he could extend and deepen, until it took on a new significance, both in its own right and in the context of the whole work. The implications of Chrétien's isolated sketch seem to have occupied Wolfram so much that he needed another work to recount the history of Sigune, for this could not be contained in *Parzival*, where nothing might detract for long from the development of the hero himself.

Of all the central women characters in *Parzival*, only Sigune is given a story of her own, not directly connected with the main theme. The past of Belakane and Herzeloyde is faintly sketched, and the crucial period of their lives is their marriage to Gahmuret, culminating for each in the birth of his son. For Herzeloyde, the principal task of her life ends when Parzival leaves her, and of Belakane we hear no more, except to note her great worth, reflected in the only man who is a match for Parzival, and to learn from Feirefiz of her death. It is in marriage to Parzival that Condwiramurs comes to the fore, and her existence is inextricable from his. Sigune, on the other hand, comes closer in this respect to Gyburc, who led a full life before she knew Willehalm. Sigune's personal history is barely suggested, however, until *Titurel* provides a fuller explanation. In *Parzival*, she fulfils a rôle of the utmost importance to Par-

38

zival himself, and her ability to do so is increased for the reader by
the awareness that, hidden somewhere in her past, is the story of
love and bereavement which is the key to her present suffering.
Parzival is not the place for a full explanation of Sigune's state, and
the figure of the lamenting maiden is enhanced by the mystery which
surrounds it. The absence of explanation, and, even more, the tantalizing hints at an explanation, serve to raise Sigune above the
ordinary, so that her appearances are endowed with an almost
mystical significance, capable of numerous interpretations on different levels and from different angles, until, as a character of many
dimensions, she becomes one of Wolfram's most complex creations.[2]

In *Le Conte del Graal*, the unnamed maiden appeared, to instruct the boy, to tell him of his misfortune in failing to speak at
the Graal, to prompt him to guess his name, to tell him of their own
kinship and to inform him of the death of his mother.[3] This purely
functional rôle seems hardly to justify the picture of her with the
dead knight, but possibly in Chrétien there were already the seeds
of that conflict between love and death in combat which Wolfram
was to develop as the basic tragedy of the life of chivalry. Whether
the idea was in fact present in Chrétien or not, the inspiration certainly was. The picture which occurs three times in *Parzival*, of the
girl mourning her dead knight, is an impressive one, the more vivid
because it remains unexplained. In this single, masterly stroke, Wolfram epitomizes the situation which he conveys at greater length
on other occasions. We are moved by the grief of Belakane, both at
the death of Isenhart and later when Gahmuret leaves her virtually
a widow; and we have witnessed Herzeloyde's passionate suffering
when she hears of the death of Gahmuret. Gurnemanz, the lonely
father, is left to mourn his three sons, more resigned perhaps than
the women to accepting the reward of knighthood, but nonetheless
pitiful in his grief. Yet none of these more protracted expressions
of the tragic dichotomy of the life of chivalry has the sharp impact
of the picture of Sigune and Schionatulander, with the unambigu-

ous juxtaposition of mourning love and knightly death.[4] It is characteristic of the women in Wolfram's works that they respect absolutely the code of knighthood which deprives them of their menfolk. In Sigune's grief there is no bitter attack on the claims of chivalry: the emotion which consumes her is the intense distress of bereavement, coupled with remorse that she was the cause of Schionatulander's death. Although she misdirects Parzival at their first meeting, fearing that he may otherwise suffer a premature death at the hands of an experienced opponent, she does so, not to keep him from the first act of chivalry which he so desires, but out of pity for his youthful innocence and in order not to bring upon herself the responsibility for another death while the present one is so burdensome to her. When, at the second meeting, she learns of his reticence at the Graal Castle, she accuses him of having lost knightly honour there, yet this is her interpretation in his terms of his failure to express pity for Anfortas: knighthood is no mere abstraction for her, but the manifestation of the qualities she prizes most highly—love, pity and sensitivity towards others.

The realization of the precious nature of human life, which should not fall a prey to a mere whim and the misguided concept of valour, comes only with experience, however, in this age when knightly prowess is prized so highly. Parzival kills Ither because he desires his red armour, and even without the additional factors which make this a crime according to the code of chivalry,[5] he has committed a very wrongful act, for there was no valid reason for this taking of human life. Sigune, too, the events of whose life run in many ways close to Parzival's, was guilty of succumbing to a mere whim, as *Titurel* relates, when she insisted that her lover should win her by deeds of valour. With the growing wisdom of experience, she becomes fully conscious of her responsibility, and with this consciousness comes too a deep sense of remorse.[6] Thus when Parzival first encounters her she is in the first frenzy of grief, which finds expression in passionate cries and wild gestures. She reproaches herself for not giving Schionatulander her love without conditions:

> ich hete kranke sinne,
> daz ich im niht minne gap   (141,20-21)

and her reaction at this early stage of bereavement is to embrace
him physically now, giving him the love she denied him in life:

> nu minne i'n alsô tôten.   (141,24)

This is her spontaneous response to her loss: the knight is recently
slain,[7] and the whole scene rings with the uncontrolled anguish of
physical bereavement.

The strongest grief must become tempered with time, however,
and when Parzival next meets Sigune, she is more controlled, lamenting still, but with a less violent show of anguish. Whereas her
grief was more physical before, finding expression in cries and tearing of hair, Parzival is led to her this time by 'einer frouwen stimme
jæmerlîch' (249,12), suggesting a mournful lament. The scene
which greets him at the linden-tree is much softer than the earlier
one: time has passed, and the knight is now embalmed, the horror
of recent death removed from him. With the passing of time, Sigune's anguish has become an inward grief which reveals itself in
her appearance. Parzival does not recognize her, for he is not yet
sufficiently advanced in grief himself to look beneath the superficial: this will come at the third meeting, but meanwhile it is left
for Sigune to reveal her identity.[8]

Her life at this point is one of utter devotion to her knight, and
it is this devotion which Wolfram stresses above all in her, until
she becomes a great personification of this, to him, greatest feminine
virtue. He says now that

> al irdisch triwe was ein wint,
> wan die man an ir lîbe sach   (249,24-25)

and so he anticipates what is to come, for already her devotion has
raised her above the earthly, although she has yet to find its ultimate object. The scene offers a link between the purely physical,

earth-bound anguish of the first meeting, when Sigune's concern was with her loss, and the spirituality of the third, when she is looking heaven-wards, in the firm hope of a joyous reunion before God. Of all the meetings with Sigune, this is the most passive, presenting total resignation and single-minded devotion. The piercing cries of the first encounter[9] have given way to a melancholy lament, softened but perhaps even more pitiful, for youth and beauty have paid dearly for their folly, and at present there seems no hope, no sign that the sacrifice has been worthwhile. Of all the scenes with Sigune, this surely represents her at her lowest ebb, and it is hardly surprising that it is now that she upbraids Parzival so violently for his failure at Munsalvæsche.[10] Only the prospect of such a joyful event as the release of Anfortas from suffering and the whole of the Graal Kingdom from sorrow could provoke such lively enthusiasm in her now, and only the bitter disappointment of these hopes could rouse her to such a passionate invective against the unwitting culprit. In her own present state of hopelessness, she can offer no hope to Parzival, rejecting in bitter terms his suggestion that he could make amends:

> 'ir sult wandels sîn erlân,'
> sprach diu maget. 'mirst wol bekant,
> ze Munsalvæsche an iu verswant
> êre und rîterlîcher prîs.
> iren vindet nu decheinen wîs
> decheine geinrede an mir.' (255,24-29)

These are harsh words indeed, but they reflect her intense disappointment, which has its source in the belief that Parzival will have displayed again the compassion which she herself has experienced from him on both occasions. Time will prove that what now seems a brutal rebuff of the young man has a wholly salutary effect, for Sigune sends Parzival off on the path which will lead through the even more violent reproaches of Cundrie to humiliation, despair and the ability to atone. It has justly been pointed out that this very

42

harshness is one aspect of the great *triuwe* of Sigune, for she does not shrink from the harshness which belongs to her duty towards Parzival.[11] Moreover, it is now, when she is herself displaying the perfection of her own devotion to her dead lover that she reproaches Parzival with a lack of precisely that quality:

> ir truogt den eiterwolves zan,
> dâ diu galle in der triuwe
> an iu bekleip sô niuwe. (255,14-16)

She is the first to accuse him of this lack, but Cundrie and Trevrizent both base their accusations on the absence of this quality (316,2; 488,28-30). For all three, *triuwe* includes the sensitive concern for others which is part of a man's responsibility towards his fellow-man. This virtue Wolfram himself prizes so highly that he makes it essential to the achievement of the Graal Kingship, and he endows it with further tremendous value by making it the supreme feminine virtue.

When Parzival meets Sigune alive for the last time, her single-minded devotion is finding wider, more positive expression in the service of God. Now at last she has found her means to atone, for it is atonement which she is seeking in her lonely cell. Now at last, love for a human being has led her to love for God, and the two, seldom far apart in Wolfram's mind, have become one. Once more, Sigune anticipates Gyburc, whose love for Willehalm is to bring her to that love for God which will take on a wider significance as an all-embracing love for her fellow-men, for Sigune, too, is able to look with pity now on Parzival, the lonely man who has forsaken God. The hair-shirt which she wears is one of the conventional outward signs of the penitent, and she is offering penance to God for her guilt towards her human loved-one. The ring she wears on her finger is the symbol of the union which she believes to exist between herself and Schionatulander, and she firmly believes that this ring, the symbol of their marriage in the sight of God, will lead her before Him:

der rehten ê diz vingerlîn
für got sol mîn geleite sîn.   (440,13-14)

This symbol of true and abiding love which she continues to wear as a religious recluse lights up the whole of her cell, surely a sign that true love is the basic ingredient of the religious life.[12] It is because Parzival is still inexperienced that he appears insensitive and questions her right to wear the ring of marriage,since he has always heard that recluses should not allow themselves love relationships. Only later will he know that true love is the direct way to God (439, 9-15).[13]

Now that she has this new-found confidence in an eventual reunion with Schionatulander, Sigune no longer needs to contemplate his body as she knew it in life, so he now lies at peace in a coffin, which represents no barrier to these two who are united by the love of God. Thus, in these three meetings, Wolfram passes from the early state of bereavement, when Sigune refuses to be parted from the body of her lover, jealously guarding all that remains to her of him, to her final state, when she allows his physical remains to be obscured in a coffin, in the firm belief that they will meet again in eternal joy, so that present separation is merely a passing phase. The coffin remains in her cell, a permanent reminder of the death which will come to her. It is also a constant link with death while she lives, and, in this cell of pious devotion, a sign that she has come to know God through perfect human love. The way is prepared both for the death of Sigune in the attitude of prayer, and the reunion of the two lovers in the coffin, when Schionatulander is shown to be untouched by the decay of time.[14] Schionatulander, then, who never appears alive in *Parzival*, yet joins with Sigune in forming a kind of leitmotiv for the whole work, a symbol of perfect love which is eternal love.

The recurrence of the picture of Sigune and her dead lover points both to her individual significance and her relevance to the story of Parzival. Within the framework of *Parzival*, the story of Sigune must remain veiled in mystery, but this very mystery serves to arouse the curiosity in her which will be satisfied, to some extent, in *Titurel*. Thus, by what seems the negative means of concealment, Wolfram achieves, as he so often does, the positive effect of heightened interest. His own interest in the intriguing figure he has created is surely the beginning of his wish to expand her story. *Titurel*, then, serves as an appendix to *Parzival*, to explain something left unexplained in the earlier work, and to enlarge on the character of Sigune. It serves, moreover, to suggest the particular appropriateness of Sigune for the important rôle she plays in *Parzival*.

If *Parzival* shows the end of earthly love and its passage into eternity, *Titurel* shows its beginning, when the thought of death is far from the minds of the two young lovers. Yet the two works are inextricably linked, and the reader cannot escape from the awareness of what the end of this love will be. The youth and joy of *Titurel* are overshadowed by the picture of the mourning Sigune with the dead Schionatulander in her lap. Taken together, the two works cover the whole life of Sigune, from the birth which cost her mother her life, to the reunion in death with Schionatulander. Even this beginning, with the coincidence of life and death, is significant, for Sigune's life is to be one in which life and death are in constant juxtaposition: she is to witness the life in death of Anfortas and Titurel, to live on after the death of her lover, and ultimately to find a new life which comes to her through death. The history of the love of Sigune and Schionatulander has its source, too, in love and death. It is the death of Schoysiane and Kyot's consequent withdrawal in grief from the world, later the death of King Tampunteire, which bring Sigune to the care of Herzeloyde, widowed by the death of Kastis. The orphan Schionatulander is adopted by Ampflise who, in her love for Gahmuret, gives the boy to him as a squire. Thus the two come together through the union of Gahmuret and Herzeloyde: love has brought them together, and their own love will last beyond the grave.

Sigune is the daughter of a noble mother—'diu clâre und diu

stæte' (*Titurel* 19,1)—who is the predecessor of Repanse de
Schoye. She is, moreover, the daughter of a man whose love is so
great that he is prepared to forsake all that he has hitherto prized
most highly when his wife dies (*Titurel* 22,3-4). If this, her direct
heritage of service and devoted love, were not enough to ensure
Sigune's life of steadfast devotion, she is the niece and protegée
of Herzeloyde, whom Wolfram esteems so highly for her *triuwe*.
In talking of the young Sigune, Wolfram lays stress on the nobility which is hers as a member of the Graal Family,[15] but side-by-
side with this she inherits the sorrow which all its members must
know. Such sorrow is anticipated in the opening lines of *Titurel*,
with the mood of heavy sadness which is so much in contrast to the
rest of the work, for during the greater part of *Titurel* this sorrow
is obscured by the prevalent joy of youthful love and zest for life.
What gives to *Titurel* its melancholy is the memory of *Parzival*
and the fate of Sigune and Schionatulander: apart from that, although the poem moves with sonorous dignity, its content is not
dominantly sad. Only Herzeloyde, more deeply aware now of the
earnest nature of human life and of the dangers which loom beyond
the present, grieves that Sigune should have come to know love so
early. Sigune, in the innocence of her youth, is unaware of the sorrow which her love will bring to her, and she rejoices that her secret has been brought into the open (*Titurel* 131,1-4). The first
part of *Titurel* ends with this climax of Sigune's joy, when all seems
to point towards future happiness, and only the shadow of *Parzival* can mar this joy.

Sigune, perhaps more than any other of Wolfram's creations, is
the victim of the basic uncertainty of human existence. In view of
Wolfram's preoccupation with the recurrent elements in human
life, it is significant that he expresses this uncertainty in his words
on the doomed love of her father and mother:

sus nimet diu werlt ein ende: unser aller süeze am orte ie
                          muoz sûren. (*Titurel* 17,4)

46

What Sigune achieves at last is the harmony between the two sides
of human existence, but, as with Parzival, harmony comes only
with faith and love of God. These two, whose fates are so closely
linked, experience the peak of joy and the lowest depths of grief,
but they emerge, Parzival into a fuller earthly life and Sigune into
perfect fulfilment in death, when they have discovered the means
of reconciling conflicting elements. Herzeloyde also knows the
fluctuations of earthly fortunes, but, in her, the state of resignation
which in Sigune grows into perfect harmony is never established,
for she dies of grief when the claims of life prove too strong for her
love. While Wolfram in no way blames Herzeloyde for surrender-
ing to her nature and dying of grief, he presents in Sigune the ability of a woman to live on, though consumed with grief, sustained
always by what is a scarcely conscious awareness of a task still to be
fulfilled. During the years she lives after Schionatulander, Sigune
shows in her bearing the growth of that *triuwe* which Wolfram
prizes so highly in her; yet before she can come to this life of devotion, she must endure the despair and sorrow through which alone
she is able to reach the peak of happiness.

The agony which Sigune is later to suffer and which is to make
her story, seen as a whole, the more poignant, springs from her
sense of guilt, for it is her refusal to give Schionatulander the love
he desires until he has earned it which leads eventually to his death.
Yet this in itself was an innocent stipulation, the consequence of a
girlish delight in a new-found power, and made at a time when
the future stretched out into endlessness and no sense of impending disaster obscured her view. Schionatulander submitted, too, to
this stipulation, which was not an unusual one: it is a pact which
they make at the end of *Titurel*, and each is responsible for the
consequences. That Schionatulander agreed to her conditions is,
however, no consolation to the bereaved Sigune, for she is left to
bear the burden of loss, coupled with the sense of guilt, and it is
this sense of responsibility as much as actual grief at his death
which leads to the passionate outburst of her first meeting with

Parzival, when she reproaches herself with withholding her love. That the source of all her years of lonely sorrow is a moment of caprice in the innocence of youth, not only makes her story more heart-rending, but it binds her all the more closely with Parzival, who brought upon himself years of despair and remorse by a moment of ill-judged silence, when he firmly believed that he was conforming to the rules of knighthood. Thus it is that *Titurel* supplies the key to Sigune's rôle in *Parzival* and reveals her appropriateness to fulfil this rôle. Because this link is present, by implication in *Parzival* and extended in *Titurel*, Wolfram raises his Sigune far above the weeping maiden of his source, whose rôle was the functional one of instructing Perceval. Although Sigune does act as instructor and guide to Parzival on all three occasions, her significance extends far beyond this.

The fact that Sigune is already dead when Parzival, at the peak of fame and joy, and reunited with Condwiramurs, seeks her in her anchoress's cell, suggests the extent to which their destinies are linked. Her task is over, now that he has come to the Kingship of the Graal, and in some mysterious way the burden of responsibility drops from her and she is able to join Schionatulander at last, just as Herzeloyde may die when Parzival leaves her. Added to this is the fact that Parzival feels the need to visit her, sensing the way in which she is linked with him and desiring to share his joy with her, to appear before her in the perfection of his manhood, which she has seen at significant stages in his development. Perhaps there is an echo here of that earlier occasion, when he desired to see his mother again, to share with her his new-found joy with Condwiramurs. On neither occasion is he able to find alive the woman who has contributed so greatly to his present state, yet, particularly with Sigune, one feels that it is appropriate that death has set its seal on a task completed.

It has frequently been observed that the encounters with Sigune occur at evenly-spaced intervals throughout the work and at significant stages in Parzival's development.[16] He comes upon her by accident on the three occasions when he meets her alive, and he does so each time when he is in need of some kind of guidance. For the young Parzival, Sigune is able to continue the task which his mother began, in many ways filling the gaps left in his knowledge by Herzeloyde, telling him his name and his lineage. He is in urgent need of instruction, for in following his mother's advice too closely he has already brought upon himself the responsibility for Jeschute's distress. It remains for Gurnemanz to instruct him in the art of chivalry, and for Liaze to introduce him to the notion of love. Sigune contributes little in either sphere, save inasmuch as she and her dead knight present together a picture of devotion and of the sorrow which comes with the chivalric life. Parzival is too inexperienced as yet to see the implications of the scene he encounters. What is important is the fact that it prompts him to express his natural pity, to enquire about the knight and to desire, with the zest of youth for the unknown, to avenge her. Sigune, then, is the first person to receive his pity, and ironically it is she who will reproach him so bitterly for failing to show his pity for Anfortas. Now, in her grief, she is able to recognize his capacity for compassion as the product of a parentage of love:

> du bist geborn von triuwen,
> daz er dich sus kan riuwen.   (140,1-2)

Unlike Chrétien, Wolfram does not allow Sigune to tell Parzival of his mother's death on his departure: presumably she does not know of it, for this would have clouded her admiration for his natural sensitivity and so spoilt their relationship which rests at their first meeting on her belief in his innate goodness.

She sends him on his way with a knowledge now of his lineage but with no idea of the code of knighthood. Before they meet again, he is to commit the grievous sin of killing a kinsman, to learn of knighthood from Gurnemanz, and to know perfect joy in his love for Condwiramurs. Most important, he is to come to the Graal Castle and to ride away, oblivious of his failure there. So the Parzival who next meets Sigune is one experienced in some measure and stained by an offence of which he is not yet aware, standing between the peak of happiness which he knew in his victory on behalf of Condwiramurs and his love for her, and the destruction of all happiness which Cundrie's speech is to bring to him. Sigune, too, is in a state of transition, for she has lost the innocent, cloudless joy of her youth, and she has not yet achieved the harmony which she is to find in devotion to God and confidence in perfect love after death. In this state of hopeless gloom, she gives herself over to a violent invective against Parzival and thus helps to draw him to the same level of despair.

The years of despair which follow, when Parzival has forsaken God as a support and a means to happiness, correspond closely to Sigune's period of grief unrelieved by hope, so that when Parzival next meets her and finds her at peace with herself and leading a life of devotion to God, his own release is at hand. She is able to play a part in the impending turning-point in his life, for her whole being is an example of the faith through which alone he can return to the Graal:

$$\text{ir leben was doch ein venje gar.} \qquad (435,25)$$

Her clothing, too, the hair-shirt of the penitent, suggests that the way to God lies through humility, and that Parzival will find happiness only when he chooses to turn to God and abandon his arrogant belief that he can dispense with His aid. Not only does she point to God in her own being, but she actually commends Parzival to the hand of God 'dem aller kumber ist bekant' (442,10), taking up the theme of Herzeloyde, who had urged her child to turn to God in time of need (119,23). Sigune thus anticipates the Pilgrim and Trevrizent, who point the way more directly to God. She herself directs him in Cundrie's path, in the hope that he will thus come to the Graal. She doubts, in fact, that a second chance will come to him, but her manner is in sharp contrast to her earlier one, and she now feels so much pity for the lonely man that she cannot deny him this one slight chance. Although she directs him in all good faith towards the Graal Castle, Parzival cannot yet find it, for he is still unfit to come there and assume his destined rôle: first he must meet Trevrizent and so find God again, and it is noteworthy that Wolfram has already implied that God has guided Parzival to Sigune (435,12), for she now, in turn, commends him to God and, in this indirect way, guides him back to God. Thus Sigune's directions are important, as they are on each occasion, even though, on each occasion, the effect is not the one she intended. On the first occasion, she directed him purposely away from the slayer of her lover, and so he came to Arthur's Court: though in her effort to keep him from harm she unwittingly sent him to commit irreparable damage in his killing of Ither, Wolfram makes it clear that even this negative action has its place in Parzival's career. The second time, when her reproaches send him away in stunned silence, he meets Jeschute, and in righting the wrong he did her he sets himself on the path of atonement. Now, though he loses the track of Cundrie's mule, the way leads him to the encounter with the Graal Knight, so that, though he may not yet come to the Graal despite his physical proximity to it, he nevertheless approaches the great turning-point of his search riding on the horse of the Graal: it is this horse which he commends to the guidance of God and which brings him to the Graal.[17]

The amazement and horror which Parzival feels when Sigune tells him of his failure at Munsalvæsche and his loss thereby of knightly honour are increased by Cundrie, who upbraids him publicly and accuses the Round Table of having been disgraced by one of its members. Yet Wolfram makes an observation after Cundrie's speech which is very significant, both for Parzival's own development and for Wolfram's concept of the two women, who in this respect are so closely linked. He speaks of the *scham* which Parzival now experiences and which will keep him from real sin (319,8).[18] Only through the sorrow which shame brings with it can he come into the light of perfect happiness, for *scham* is an aspect of that all-important quality, humility, without which Parzival cannot become King of the Graal. Shame, or a sense of guilt, brings with it the desire to atone, and in atonement at Trevrizent's hermitage Parzival prepares himself for his great office. So, in this too, Sigune produces a salutary effect by what seems to be a destructive act. When she misdirects Parzival, he finds a right direction, and when she casts him into the despair of guilt, it is so that he can emerge purged of guilt. And even in her own life, Sigune is a model of the path which Parzival is to follow, for she passes from violent self-reproach to a state of passive acceptance of her burden, until she finds the way to God which leads through the desire to atone and the act of atonement.

It is fitting that it should be Parzival who performs the last service for Sigune, for this sets the seal on the bond which has existed between them throughout. United now with Condwiramurs in perfect love, he is able to see that Sigune and Schionatulander are united physically in the coffin, as she believed they would be spiritually in heaven, the undecayed state of the body of Schionatulander a testimony to the perfect and constant love between them (804,28-805,2).[19] Parzival's gesture is the completion of the series of their meetings, and it shows how far he has come since he made the facetious and unfeeling reference to her wedding-ring: now he knows that true love is eternally binding and God-given.

As on the other occasions, the scene is relevant, for Parzival comes to the cell which has been hallowed by love and faith, and he himself is filled with love and faith. It is evening, signifying the end of a day and the end of a phase for Parzival and Sigune, with Sigune at peace at last, and Parzival reigning as the wise and great ruler of the Graal.[20] The settings of the other three meetings are carefully described, too, for in each case the setting corresponds to Sigune's state. The stark outline of the rock prepares for the harsh, passionate grief of Sigune, when she sits with her knight so recently dead, while her later position, in the linden-tree, presents a gentler picture, with her grief hopeless as yet but softened, and her whole life devoted in love for Schionatulander.[21] It is this latter picture which Wolfram remembers in *Titurel* (78,1-4), for the Sigune whom *Titurel* anticipates is the one who leads a life of devotion to her earthly lover, rather than the devoted anchoress of the third meeting. The setting is the same at the third and fourth meetings, suggesting the easy transition of Sigune from a life of religious devotion to union with God in death. She dies in the attitude of prayer, with the unambiguous suggestion that prayer, the traditional manifestation of faith, is the direct link between life and death.[22] Already, at the third meeting, Sigune has told Parzival of her firm belief that her love, symbolized in the ring on her finger, would lead her to God (440,12-14). The two, then, love and faith, are inextricable from one another, and inextricable too from the cell where Sigune lived and died, where the ring which indicated love and marriage could be worn by one who also wore the hair-shirt of the penitent, and where the coffin of the dead lover did not detract from the sincerity of the religious recluse.

While she lives in her cell, Sigune is sustained by food brought from the Graal by Cundrie. The Graal, however one may interpret it, demands purity, love, faith and humility of those who serve it, so this miraculous sustenance in itself points to the perfect life which Sigune leads. It links her in another way with Parzival, who is destined to come to the Graal as its King. From the beginning there existed the ties of blood which bound them to one another and to the Graal, for each is the child of a daughter of the Graal. With these ties goes the heritage of grief which each must share, as part of the price of a noble lineage. Yet each, with the innate capacity for *triuwe* which belonged to Herzeloyde and Schoysiane, endures that grief with steadfast devotion and through love comes to conquer it. Their personal grief is different, and so is the object of their devotion, but the formula is the same. When he releases Anfortas with the simple question, Parzival lifts the grief from the whole of the Graal Family, so Sigune too is relieved of the life which con-

53

sisted of years of sorrowing for Schionatulander. Her death marks not only the completion of her task towards Parzival, but also the end of the personal grief which was her share of the sorrow of the whole family.[23]

In Sigune, Wolfram has created a figure who is complex and mysterious, highly individualized, yet also perfectly in accord with his other women. Although he offers no direct suggestion of a connection with the Virgin Mary, there are certain echoes which point to a connection in his mind. He describes her as 'rehter güete ein arke' (804,16) and the symbol of Mary as the Ark of the Covenant was a current mediæval one.[24] Yet Wolfram himself does not go further than this in offering the connection, as he does with Herzeloyde, and the reason is apparent: Mary achieved the height of her perfection in motherhood, and this is not given to Sigune. It has been suggested that Wolfram was inspired by the scene depicted by the Pietà,[25] and it is true that there is some immediate visual echo in the picture of Sigune bearing the body of Schionatulander; yet the situation is different, for Sigune is not the mother of the man in her lap, nor is she to be seen as the Bride of Christ.[26] She wears the ring of human marriage and hopes through it to come to God. Nevertheless Sigune does share some of the qualities of the most perfect of women. Above all, her devotion to her lover is extolled by Wolfram, together with the humility which allows her to withdraw into the forest and lead a life of dedicated seclusion. Although Wolfram never compares her with the Virgin, as he does Herzeloyde, and never calls her a saint, as he does Gyburc, she nevertheless leads the life of a saintly recluse. She has found a personal way to God, not guided by the formalities of the Church.

Clearly the life of Sigune becomes one of great spirituality, and an interesting point is that of her being fed once a week by food brought from the Graal: it may well be that Wolfram was remembering the idea that the Virgin Mary was brought food from heaven by the Angel Gabriel.[27] It seems clear that, despite the essential differences, Wolfram was drawing on much which was current in the mediæval concept of the Virgin Mary to create his Sigune. Like Mary, the Mother of Sorrows, Sigune loves with an intensity which brings great grief, yet both accept this suffering with humility increased by love itself. Repanse de Schoye is the pure virgin, dedicated to the Graal which she bears, while Herzeloyde is the devoted mother, nursing her child who is to be the greatest of all Christian knights. In both cases, the resemblance to the Virgin Mary is a closer one, but to Sigune, as indeed to Condwiramurs where the similarity is again not voiced, Wolfram nevertheless gives the virtues of Mary. With the other great heroines of his creation, she is a clear manifestation of his ideal of womanhood, with its capacity for humility and purity, and above all else for the love which brings forth suffering and yet can conquer it.

NOTES

1. ed. cit. 3428-3690.
2. G. Weber (*Parzival. Ringen und Vollendung*, Oberursel, 1948) describes her as 'die tiefsinnigste Gestalt unter allen seinen Schöpfungen.' In this study of all the women characters in Wolfram's works, it is clearly not possible to examine Sigune in all her complexity, but it is hoped to show her in her place among the other heroines. The Bibliography contains a number of works which discuss her in some detail, and particular attention should be given to the works by D. M. Blamires, I. Giese, U. Heise, D. Labusch, B. Rahn and M. F. Richey.
3. ed. cit. 3581-3606.
4. cf. M. F. Richey (*Schionatulander and Sigune*, London 1927, reprinted 1960): 'The picture of Sigune's life-in-death is sharply differentiated from that glowing pageant of worldly prowess and honour which Wolfram interprets with so keen and certain a sense of its heroic worth; yet is the one the corollary of the other. For so it must be in an age dominated

by adventure and hazard, where too often the award of valour is sudden death, and the heritage of true love, grief without healing. From time immemorial the glory of life in action has been linked in thought with its antithesis, the blankness of despair and the ineffable mystery of sorrow' (p. 24).

5. i.e. that Ither was a kinsman, that Parzival was not a knight, that he killed Ither without provocation and with an un-knightly weapon.

6. cf. B. Rahn (p. 76) for a discussion of Sigune's 'guilt.'

7. See the words of Orilus 135,20-24.

8. cf. D. M. Blamires (p. 187).

9. B. Q. Morgan (p. 186) speaks of the grief of Chrétien's maid-en as 'too shrill' and contrasts Wolfram's treatment, yet in fact Wolfram shows Sigune at the first meeting to be in a state of wild grief, stressing her cries (138,13) and tearing of hair (138,17-19). It is true that Wolfram tempers the grief later, but this first scene shows grief as violent as that shown by Chrétien (see, for example, ed. cit. 3432ff).

10. Chrétien had placed the encounter rather later, and so the *germaine cousine* had reproached Perceval at their first and only meeting. By describing three meetings with Sigune alive, Wolfram points out the passage of time and relates Parzival's development to the grief of Sigune. Thus Ursula Heise (p. 49) can say with some justice: 'So ist Sigune für Parzival ein Spiegel dessen, was er erlebt hat.'

11. cf. Dietlinde Labusch (pp. 76-77): '. . . denn Sigune beweist gerade durch den Fluch ihre echte *triuwe*, die sich in Härte und Strenge äußern muß, wenn es im Interesse des Andern ist.'

12. The ring seems to have a double significance and Wolfram allows it to remain ambiguous. It is both the symbol of the marriage which she believes to exist between herself and Schionatulander (cf. Marlis Schumacher pp. 55-57) and the symbol of her relationship with God, echoing as it does the ring donned by nuns. The two are compatible, of course,

which is precisely why Wolfram gives no explicit statement, despite the importance which Sigune attaches to the ring. D. M. Blamires comments (p. 186): 'The important aspect of their relationship is the way in which Sigune has transformed it into a spiritual marriage analogous to that of the nun with Christ.'

13. D. M. Blamires (pp. 186-187) discusses the third meeting with Sigune and draws a parallel between the relationship of Sigune and Schionatulander and the early relationship of Parzival and Condwiramurs: 'The latter relationship is a genuine marriage on all levels, and Sigune's constancy is a powerful example to Parzival to keep his faith to Condwiramurs, which as yet has not been seriously questioned. It is the transcendental nature of both relationships that is important, and the unity between each couple is essentially undisturbed despite the fact that Sigune is externally separated from Schionatulander in time and Parzival from Condwiramurs in space. The essence of the relationship continues in face of this.'

14. Wolfram deliberately makes this point (804,28-29) although he twice mentions that, in any case, Schionatulander's body is embalmed (249,16 and 804, 29). It is interesting to note that popular belief insisted that Héloïse had asked to be buried in the same coffin as Abelard, and legend told how Abelard held out his arms to greet her. (See C. Charrier: *Héloïse dans l'histoire et dans la légende*, Paris, 1933, p. 300ff.) Wolfram may well have had this pair of lovers in mind.

15. He tells how her birth gives her the right to be mentioned before Schionatulander: *Titurel* 43,1-4.

16. See U. Heise; D. M. Blamires pp. 174-189. This is, however, a matter of discussion in most of the commentaries on the work.

17. See my article 'Wrong paths in *Parzival*,' *Modern Language Review*, Vol. 63,4, 1968, pp. 872-876.

18. The question of *scham* is treated more closely in relation to Cundrie (p. 131 below).

19. But see note 14 above.

20. Dietlinde Labusch (p. 22) sees the evening as symbolic of fulfilment, and this is also true: 'Wie sich im Abend der Tag erfüllt, so hat auch Sigunes Leben die irdische Vollendung erreicht'.

21. The position of Sigune in the linden tree in its relationship to legends of mediæval tree saints is well known (cf. J. Schwietering: 'Sigune auf der Linde,' *ZfdA*, 57, 1920, 140-143) but Arthur Groos ('Sigune auf der Linde,' *Journal of English and Germanic Philology*, 67, 1968, pp. 631-646) makes another, very interesting point, when he observes that Wolfram has deliberately changed the oak tree of Chrétien to the linden: 'The linden tree in this context draws attention to the fact that Sigune's present suffering, like that of Trevrizent and Amfortas, stems from her past involvement with the forbidden cult of courtly love' (p. 638).

22. The link is further suggested by Wolfram in what seems to be a distinct verbal echo:

Sigûnen an ir venje tôt   (804,23)

of   ir leben was doch ein venje gar   (435,25).

23. For this reason it is perhaps not correct to speak of the story of Sigune as 'eine tragisch endende Liebesnovelle' (H. de Boor and R. Newald: *Geschichte der deutschen Literatur von den Anfängen bis zur Gegenwart*, Munich, 1949, Vol. II, p. 123). The end is not tragic for Sigune: cf. B. Rahn (p. 89) who concludes: 'Weil sie sich nun in der *triuwe* bewährt und sich durch ihre Leidensfrömmigkeit Gott nähert, kann er, der sie längst erwählt hat, sie am Schluβ erlösen. Am Ende von Sigunes Geschichte steht somit nicht der Zusammenbruch eines Weltbildes, sondern die Erlösung und damit die Verwirklichung eines Ersehnten, Erhofften und Erstrebten. Die *Sigune* kann folglich nicht tragisch sein.'

24. cf. A. Salzer: *Die Sinnbilder und Beiworte Mariens in der*

deutschen Literatur und lateinischen Hymnenpoesie des Mittelalters, Darmstadt, 1967, p. 5ff.

Wolfram uses the same image to describe Schoysiane (477, 12).

25. cf. J. Schwietering (op. cit.); B. Rahn (p. 84); D. Labusch (pp. 34-36).

26. Only if one extends the symbolism of the ring and relates it to that worn by a nun as the Bride of Christ can one interpret the figure of Sigune in these terms, but this is not stated by Wolfram as her motive, and she herself tells Parzival that she wears the ring out of love for Schionatulander (see 439,22-30 and note 12 above). That this love leads to a deepening of her love of God does not justify a changed view of her motive: the analogy is there, but it must remain an analogy only.

27. cf. Priester Wernher's *Maria* (ed. cit. 1389ff; 1436-7).

CHAPTER FOUR

Gyburc

THE WORLD of *Willehalm* is very different from that of *Parzival*, for Wolfram's mood and purpose had changed by the time he came to write the later work. *Parzival* is a work of optimism, displaying the victory of faith over despair, of good over evil, and its principal blackcloth is the sparkling world of the court, where beauty and valour, joy and love dominate. In *Willehalm*, the court serves only as an ironic contrast to the main scene of the action, the battlefield. In a world such as this, there is little place for joy, and the radiant beauty and happiness of Condwiramurs would be incongruous. Instead, the figure of Gyburc represents a new aspect of ideal womanhood, which embraces the beauty and virtues of her predecessors in *Parzival*, yet goes further. For Gyburc can endure the trials of siege and war, sorrow and hatred, to an extent which was never required of the other heroines. This does not imply that she is actually superior to Condwiramurs, with whom, as the wife of the other great hero, she is inevitably compared. Condwiramurs is, after all, never called upon to show physical courage: the two works represent two aspects of mediæval chivalry and so demand two different heroines. There is a similar difference between Willehalm and Parzival, yet it would be impossible to say which is the greater man. Greatness has many manifestations, and different circumstances will produce different aspects of greatness. Wolfram's concept of ideal womanhood involves its potentialities, the extent to which it will reach if the need is there. Thus, in *Parzival*, he had shown one ideal woman who could sustain her husband through despair and suffering, and so help to bring him to the highest honour of Christian knighthood, with herself as his apt consort. Gyburc's task, too, is to sustain her husband, but in a different way. Despite his moments of grief and profound discouragement, Willehalm does not experience the despair and spiritual suffering of Parzival: any past doubts have been overcome and he has learnt to know and love God and is prepared to fight for his love. As his wife, Gyburc is prepared, too, to fight for the sake of the God she has come to acknowledge: circumstances demand of her a demonstration of what remained in Condwiramurs an implied potentiality.

The rôle of Gyburc is decided, to a very considerable extent, by the theme of *Willehalm*. Basically this theme is the conflict between two great forces, and Gyburc's rôle is a particular one, because she stands between these forces, belonging completely to neither, yet deeply concerned with the fate of each. Nor is this concern a mere passive distress at the sorrow about her, for it is coupled with the awareness that she is the direct cause of it, as she tells her father-in-law:

> ich schûr sîner hantgetât,
> der bêde machet unde hât
> den kristen und den heiden!
> ich was flust in beiden.
> an mir wuohs leide in unt uns.　　(253,9-13)[1]

From the beginning, Gyburc is deeply involved, and it is precisely this involvement which governs her whole character and makes her so different from Wolfram's other heroines, despite the many features they have in common.

Willehalm is essentially a didactic work, pointing to the futility of war and the injustice of killing the heathens simply because they are heathen. Wolfram chose not only to allow the action itself to convey his message, but also to express it most powerfully through a major character. Thus Gyburc comes forward, transcending the rôle of Guibourc in the *Aliscans*, to bear this great message.[2] Who,

61

after all, has more right to bear it? Gyburc is bound by blood and
loyalty to the heathens and this she cannot forget, in spite of the
new bond of love which binds her to Willehalm and so to the Christian God and the whole of Christendom. Her appearances are few,
yet they are vital to the work and leave a profound impression on it.
The spirit with which she defends the city and the memorable words
in which she urges reconciliation pervade the work and exalt Gyburc
herself as a woman in whom courage and the readiness to fight for
a great cause mingle with love and compassion.

Gyburc is called upon to defend Orange, in order to defend her
husband and this she shows herself able to do. Her uplifted sword
is no idle gesture but a symbol of her readiness to fight, if the need
arises (227,12-17). It is indeed 'ein aktives und ihre frauliche
Schwäche überwindendes Eintreten für ihren Glauben':[3] the situation is a desperate one and calls forth this supreme effort. Yet, although she is capable of the courage and strength of a man, Wolfram does not wish to show this side of her more than necessary.
He prizes femininity highly, and, as soon as Willehalm returns,
Gyburc changes her masculine, warlike attire, to resume her true
place as Willehalm's consort. Wolfram is not sparing in his description of her now, giving a picture of beauty and elegance which is
in sharp contrast to the earlier one she gave of herself.[4] He stresses
that this is a conscious gesture on her part, an indication of her own
sense of her nature as a woman, when he allows her to order all her
ladies to put on their most beautiful clothes with her, to replace
their unattractive, grimy attire with the outward show of their femininity and so make light of their trials (247,1-10). That Gyburc
is able to transcend her true nature when the need arises, is admir-
able, but no-one—Willehalm, Wolfram or Gyburc herself—desires a woman to do this, save in exceptional circumstances.

This capacity to act with a courage resembling closely the courage of a soldier is called forth in Gyburc purely as a result of her
environment, and the demands made upon her. When she is required once more to be a lady of the court, she appears very like

Condwiramurs, who may also have possessed qualities of physical strength and courage which she was never called upon to exert. There is altogether in Gyburc a duality, of which this ability to act with manly courage is one aspect. She is, after all,

> Arabele Gyburc, ein wîp
> zwir genant. . . . . (30,21-22)

Clearly, Wolfram intended to show in Gyburc a woman torn between two loyalties and with two very different backgrounds contributing to her make-up.[5] Her baptism as Gyburc cannot erase her heathen name, any more than her new-found Christianity can obliterate from her mind the memory of her birth and the years she spent in her heathen kingdom. Her introduction to Christianity appears to her as a great gift, with which she has had the fortune to be endowed, and from which there is now no turning away for her. Yet the sense of her own fortune serves to make her the more eager to urge mercy towards those who have not known the joy of this gift.

The personal dilemma of Gyburc is very great: the ties of blood are strong and she cannot ignore them, nor can she escape her sense of the immorality of slaying the heathens. To demand of Willehalm, however, that he should withdraw from the battle is impossible, for, even if he could do so in the face of the enemy, it would suggest that she herself had no faith in the cause. Moreover, she would be forced to surrender herself once more to the heathens, forsaking God, her baptism and Willehalm. This she cannot do, for she shows herself at all times loyal to the religion she has adopted as her own. Her only course is the one she does, in fact, take, when she pleads for mercy towards the Saracens if they are defeated (306,28; 309,1-6). It is significant that she advocates mercy rather than tolerance, for mercy implies an attitude of the strong towards the weak. She does not demand that the Christians should accept the gods of the heathens, but that they should look with compassion upon those who have not become acquainted with the Christian God. Before she begins to urge mercy, she adds strength to her argument by stressing that the Christians have it in their power to increase their 'kristenlîch êre' (306,19) in their impending victory: her meaning is clear, for what irony there would be in the brutal slaughter of the spiritually weaker by the disciples of the Christian God!

Already, in *Parzival*, the virtue of *erbarmung* has been extolled, for only by asking a simple question which arises from natural compassion can Parzival come to the Kingship of the Graal. As Herzeloyde's son, he possesses the innate capacity for pity, and it is the compassion of the Pilgrim's daughters which causes them to look back at the lonely figure, so confirming in him the desire to turn once more to God. Similarly, Gyburc does not only possess compassion within herself, but like these other women, she has also the ability to impart it to others. There is, however, a significant difference: whereas the women in *Parzival* give to the hero a sense of the need for compassion simply by their example, Gyburc, in accordance with her more active rôle, actually spurs the men to mercy by her speech. That her words have borne fruit is clear at the end of the work, as Willehalm gives his orders for funeral arrangements befitting the heathen dead. Gyburc's rôle in this gesture by her husband is explicit:

> wir sulen si werdeclîcher habn
> durch die diu von in ist erborn.   (462,24-25)

Whatever the further course of events might have been, this act stands as an affirmation of Gyburc and the message she bears.

The virtue of *triuwe*, of steadfast devotion, which is so vital an attribute of the women in *Parzival*, is extolled and exemplified in *Willehalm*, too, but again the manifestation is different. Herzeloyde, Sigune and Condwiramurs are all steadfast in their devotion to their loved ones, and so Herzeloyde and Condwiramurs play a large part in sustaining their husbands, who are both conscious of the selfless devotion of the women at home. Sigune's love brings her to the point where her life is itself absolute devotion to God, and Repanse de Schoye demonstrates another aspect of *triuwe* in her devoted service to the Graal. In *Parzival*, then, *triuwe* finds expression in selfless service and the readiness to wait, but Gyburc is called upon to provide also active support of her husband, and her *triuwe* is tested to the full in her defence of Orange. As well as fighting on behalf of her husband, she is defending the cause of both of them, and this is possible only because she has faith in it, because she has faith in God: her *triuwe* is directed both towards Willehalm and towards God. The faith which radiated from Sigune in her lonely cell, and which, in the Pilgrim's daughters, inspired Parzival with a new longing for God, fills the whole being of Gyburc. As with Sigune, faith, which is basically the love of God, is seen as the natural development of human love, and goes hand-in-hand with it. Foreshadowing Gyburc is, of course, Belakane, who, after Gahmuret had left her, declared that she would gladly have accepted baptism for his sake. Once more, Gyburc is shown as the active character, for she is able to do what was denied to Belakane, to adopt the faith of her husband through her love for him, and even to fight for it.

Although Belakane does not achieve the stature of Gyburc, she is nevertheless clearly the forerunner of the heroine of the later work. Wolfram's recognition of the rights of *gotes hantgetât*, no matter what their creed or colour, is revealed first in this woman, who is shown to possess virtues equal to those of the white, Christian heroines, and whom Gahmuret never really forgot, despite his union with Herzeloyde. Wolfram's respect for the feelings of all human beings is shown also in his refusal to allow Repanse de Schoye to return as the wife of Feirefiz, until the news has come of the death of Sekundille, but it is above all in *Willehalm* that his tolerance is shown. He is always just in his treatment of the heathens, acknowledging their prowess and virtues equally with those of the Christians, yet nowhere does he express this so perfectly as in the figure of Gyburc, who, despite her colour and lineage, is a truly noble woman, an appropriate wife for Willehalm and worthy to be exalted as a saint. To Gyburc alone among his heroines Wolfram gives the name of *heilic vrouwe* (403,1).[6] She does not live a life of ascetic privation as Sigune does, yet, while Wolfram prizes Sigune very highly, he reserves for Gyburc the direct designation of saint. The reason is not hard to find, and it rests on Wolfram's concept of life and his assessment of human achievement: Sigune reaches her highest point when she has withdrawn from the world, but Gyburc does not look to withdrawal from the world as her means to salvation. In accordance with the rest of her character, which is active and positive in every way, she is best able to demonstrate her love and faith in action, and her principal appearances are active demonstrations, in which faith and love dominate her being, radiating from her and governing all she does. In the active expression of her faith through suffering would seem to lie for Wolfram the formal sanctity which he denies to Sigune.

At a time when women were being accepted increasingly in the religious orders,[7] it was perhaps to be expected that a great thinker like Wolfram should approach a comment on the trend by means of one of his greatest characters. Gyburc emerged, then, as the bearer of the religious message of the work, equipped with a knowledge of her faith and alone in the work to express it.[8] The very idea of allowing a woman to dominate the religious thought of a work was a new one[9] but perhaps Wolfram points also to a contemporary problem when he depicts Gyburc as a woman who is very much in the world, able to do good by being an active and truly fervent member of society.[10] This would seem to be his ultimate feeling on the subject: that the way to true spiritual greatness lies through the world, not away from it. In *Parzival*, also, he had shown his greatest knight as a member of society, active in the world, courageous in battle, esteemed by his fellow-men, a good husband and a father. While in no way underestimating Trevrizent and Sigune, he nevertheless allows the supreme honour to one who has combined faith in God with an active existence in the world. Gyburc is the counterpart of Parzival, then, exalted by Wolfram to the status of a saint in the world, just as the earlier hero had achieved the highest honour of Christian knighthood.

Gyburc's predecessor in the *Aliscans* was a fairly slight character, the wife of Guillaume and the reason for the conflict, but in no way actively involved in the main events. While following his source closely at many points, Wolfram chose a completely new emphasis for his work: he points to the power of love and the futility of killing, ideas which were barely implicit in the French version. The woman who bore the great message of the work could not remain on the edge of the action, so Gyburc comes forward, to endure the full impact of grief, yet at the same time to know the privilege of calling for universal love and mercy. In the suffering she must bear, and in the manner of her bearing it, Wolfram gave her the means to sanctity.

Thus, as in *Parzival*, it is a woman who is shown to endure the most profound suffering, yet like Herzeloyde, Sigune, Condwiramurs, Belakane, Repanse de Schoye and Jeschute, Gyburc suffers as the direct result of love, and, like them, she finds the strength to endure suffering because she sees it as the inevitable companion of love.[11] Moreover, as was clearly seen in the case of Sigune, perfect human love finds favour with God, and so is strengthened by divine Love, thus bringing those who know it to a strong faith. Herzeloyde's heart breaks when Parzival leaves her, but Sigune and Gyburc, in whom the element of faith is so strong, are given the strength to carry on through their grief. Sigune still has an important task to accomplish when Schionatulander dies, and Gyburc, too, finds strength in her purpose, the active defence of Orange. Like Condwiramurs, who, during the years of Parzival's absence, gave birth to their sons and educated fitting heirs to Parzival's greatness, Gyburc sustains her husband's city and thus ensures their future together.

Gyburc must endure discomfort and the threat of attack, and the absence of her husband, but more profound suffering is forced upon her by the hatred of both Christians and heathens. Of this she is deeply aware, without being able to do anything about it:

> si sprach 'der tôtlîche val
> der hiest geschehen ze bêder sît,
> dar umbe ich der getouften nît
> trag und ouch der heiden,
> daz bezzer got in beiden
> an mir, und sî ich schuldic dran.   (306,12-17)

This hatred she returns with love, most positively expressed in her great plea for reconciliation, for love is the supreme response to hate, although only a person of Gyburc's strength is capable of giving it. Once more, Gyburc's position affects the quality of her suffering, for she must observe death and suffering on both sides, while being bound equally in love to each. The grief which she suffers as a result of the deaths on both sides is expressed in her reaction to the death of Vivianz, and the powerful and moving expression of sorrow at his death suggests the culmination of her distress, which now finds utterance in mourning this one noble young Christian (101,27-102,20). Vivianz stands for all the noble men, whether Christian or heathen, who have died in the conflict, and for whom, in her grief, Gyburc declares that she would gladly have died herself. Death, however, is not given to Gyburc: rather does her martyrdom fulfil itself in a life lived in anguish at the suffering of others, and in the knowledge that she is the cause of it. Once more, in this respect, Gyburc is linked with Sigune, but there is a difference, for Sigune is conscious of her actual guilt and seeks to atone for it in a lifetime of devotion, while Gyburc cannot regret the original act, though she must grieve for its widespread effects. Her act was a good one, committed in the full consciousness of what she was doing, while Sigune must suffer for a moment of folly, the surrender to a mere whim. She makes what she considers to be a just compensation for her act, but there is no question of compensation in the case of Gyburc.[12]

Very early in the work, Wolfram asserts the innocence of his heroine:

unschuldic was diu künegin   (31,4)

and he goes on to explain that Gyburc deserves only praise and reward because she must endure suffering for the sake of Christ:

> swer sich vinden lât durh in in nôt,
> der enpfæhetn endelôsen solt.   (31,12-13)

Gyburc's desertion of her husband and her family is the inevitable result of her baptism, and, like the war between Christians and heathens, it is something over which she has no control. It is part of the suffering which she must accept in consequence of her conversion, but this does not mean that Gyburc has not suffered deeply at being separated from her family. It is true that Wolfram says nothing of such suffering, but by the time the work opens she has presumably overcome her immediate distress. She has achieved, with what struggle one can only imagine, a state of harmony in which all suffering appears to her as a result of her love for God and for Willehalm, and therefore endurable:

> der des alles hât gewalt,
> gein dem schaden bin ich palt:
> der mac michs wol ergetzen
> unt des lîbes armuot letzen
> mit der sêle rîcheit.   (216,25-29)

Nevertheless, her marriage to Willehalm has meant sacrifice for her, however gladly she may have made it. It is notable that she never accuses her former husband: on the contrary, she praises him:

> Tybalt von Arâbî
> ist vor aller untæte vrî.   (310,15-16)

She was loved in her heathen kingdom (310,9), and she left her children there (310,11), and one cannot see this sacrifice as a trivial one. Yet she has reached now that high point of achievement when she can look beyond the present towards the ultimate. As with other women in Wolfram's works, love leads to the highest bliss, but only by its passage through grief.

In the case of Feirefiz, love for a human being leads to a willing acceptance of faith in God; Sigune's steadfast devotion to a human loved one strengthens and develops into the love of God; the love of Parzival and Condwiramurs deepens until it can bring them both to the highest Christian office. The faith of Gyburc is intimately bound up with her love for Willehalm, and inextricable from it. Their love is a wonderful example of Wolfram's statement in *Parzival* that 'reht minne ist wâriu triuwe' (532,10), extending his meaning even beyond the example of the love of Parzival and Condwiramurs, for not only are Gyburc and Willehalm devoted in love for one another, but devoted also to the God from whom their love stems.[13] They are both conscious of the divine nature of their love: thus Willehalm can plead with God:

> stêt dîn tugent vor wanke blôz,
> du solt an mir niht wenken
> und mîne flust bedenken,
> sît entwarf dîn selbes hant
> daz der vriunt vriundinne vant
> an dem arme sîn durch minne   (456,6-11)

and Gyburc can reject the accusation that she has caused all this distress for the sake of human love and even for physical desire:

> Ich diene der künsteclîchen hant
> für der heiden got Tervigant:
> ir kraft hât mich von Mahumeten
> unders toufes zil gebeten.
> des trag ich mîner mâge haz;
> und der getouften umbe daz:
> durh menneschlîcher minne gît
> si wænent daz ich fuogte disen strît.   (310,1-8)

70

She takes upon herself the guilt, but it is a guilt which she is proud
to bear for the sake of God and of Willehalm:

> ich trag al ein die schulde,
> durh des hœhsten gotes hulde,
> ein teil ouch durh den markîs.   (310,17-19)

These lines suggest the extent to which the two are linked in her
mind, for, after all, her knowledge of God coincided with her acquaintance with Willehalm, and in remaining true to their love she
is remaining true also to her faith.

Through their great, mutual love, which they know to come from
God, Gyburc and Willehalm are given strength to comfort one another, despite the burden of grief from outside. Although Wolfram
has stressed so deliberately the suffering and loss caused by the battle, he is still able to say that the love of Gyburc compensates
Willehalm for what he has lost:

> Gyburc mit kiuscher güete
> sô nâhe an sîne brust sich want,
> daz im nu gelten wart bekant:
> allez daz er ie verlôs,
> dâ für er si ze gelte kôs.   (280,2-6)

The power of her love inspires Willehalm as he rides forth to Orleans, and the extent to which they are dependent on one another
is expressed in the notion of the exchange of hearts, the familiar
mediæval idea employed by Wolfram with such vivid effect:

> beide er bleip unde reit:
> in selben hin truoc Volatîn,
> Gyburc behielt daz herze sîn.
> ouch fuor ir herze ûf allen wegen
> mit im: wer sol Oransche pflegen?
> der wehsel rehte was gefrumt:
> ir herze hin ze friwenden kumt,
> sîn herze sol sich vînden wern,
> Gyburge vor untrôste nern.   (109,6-14)

71

Truly does Gyburc ride with him, for it is she who prompts his every action, the memory of her sustaining him, causing him to refrain from fine food and from kissing other lips until he has released her from distress. As Parzival never forgot Condwiramurs in all his years of absence, so does Willehalm have Gyburc constantly in his thoughts:

> swie balde er von Gyburge streich,
> sîn gedanc ir nie gesweich:
> der was ir zOransche bî. (111,27-29)

The love of Parzival and Condwiramurs is echoed in the love of Gyburc and Willehalm, but the issue is a wider one, and their marriage may justly be described as the 'Höhepunkt der einzigartigen Eheauffassung Wolframs'.[14] In *Willehalm* the future of many people is at stake, symbolized in the heathens who must be shown the way to faith by mercy, and the Christians who must not risk their Christian honour by the senseless slaughter of the spiritually weaker. Their salvation depends on the strength of the love of Gyburc and Willehalm, and its ability to spread to those on both sides of the conflict.

To the vital power of love and faith in Gyburc is added another, which links her all the more closely with the great heroines of *Parzival*. This is the virtue of humility, which, in Gyburc as in Herzeloyde, reveals itself in *armuot*. Gyburc accepts poverty and is glad to accept it, when she becomes a Christian, and what Terramer sees as a degradation, when his daughter abandons her heathen kingdom with its vast wealth (354,16-22), she herself sees as an elevation. Herzeloyde was also prepared to give up wealth, rank and physical comfort for the sake of a principle, but in *Willehalm* the sacrifice represents more, for through it Gyburc indicates her total acceptance of Christianity. It is significant that she ends her *Religionsgespräch* with the words

> und lâz mich mit armuot lebn. (221,26)

She desires, not to live *in* poverty, but *with* it, suggesting a way of life, rather than an accessory to a chosen mode of existence.[15] Poverty does not represent only the absence of riches, although in Gyburc's case baptism has meant the loss of wealth and power, but rather a life lived in the spirit of poverty, which comes close to one lived in humility: like Herzeloyde, and the later Sigune, Gyburc achieves this way of life through her devotion to a single cause. Her repeated references to her poverty (215,27; 216,28; 262,19) suggest that she regards it as a positive quality in her existence.[16] She sees the poverty which she endures on earth as a means to God:

> der mac michs wol ergetzen
> unt des lîbes armuot letzen
> mit der sêle rîcheit.   (216,27-29)

Moreover, like her love for Willehalm, it is a means which God has given to her:

> Durch den hân ich mich bewegen
> daz ich wil armüete pflegen,
> und durch den der der hœhste ist.   (216,1-3)

From these words it is clear that Gyburc desires the poverty which her conversion has imposed on her: it is not merely that she passively accepts it, but that she actively desires it and seeks to maintain it. Werner Schröder[17] ignores the spiritual significance of *armuot* as Gyburc uses it: he rejects the view that her sanctity lies to a large extent in her poverty and remarks: "Sie ist keine heilige Elisabeth. Wolfram sagt nichts davon, daß sie höfischen Prunk abgelehnt und sich von dem schönen Schein höfischen Daseins distanziert habe, noch läßt er sie jemals auch nur erwägen, ihre fürstliche Stellung an Willehalms Seite mit dem Leben einer poverella, einer Bettlerin, zu vertauschen."[18] All this is true, but a literal sacrifice of wordly goods is not necessary in this woman who has shown herself capable of forsaking all that was once of value to her and is now ready to accept suffering and privation for the sake of her faith. For Gyburc, as, on a different level, for Herzeloyde, poverty entails not only a lack of possessions, but also a lack of attachment to worldly possessions, and this enables each to accept gladly the material deprivation which is the companion of a much greater spiritual gain. The relative material poverty which her conversion has brought to Gyburc is far exceeded by the spiritual wealth which she sees in her new faith. It is the total absence of a desire for wordly goods which Wolfram extols in her, and so, as with Herzeloyde, *armuot* is very close to *diemuot*. The humility which can bring Parzival to the Graal Kingship, can also ensure eternal bliss for Herzeloyde, and sanctity for Gyburc. Each woman, moreover, is motivated and given strength by the great virtue of *triuwe*, Herzeloyde by love for her child and Gyburc by *triuwe* in its ultimate form, when it becomes faith in God.

In her character, Gyburc fulfils the promise of the heroines who precede her in Parzival, then, for she possesses the virtues which, in them, were shown to be the essence of womanhood. Yet in the context of a work such as this, the rôle of Gyburc is necessarily different from that played by the earlier women. Their significance lay often in their very presence: they were important for what they *were*, whereas Gyburc is important both for her essential being and for her active rôle in the work. The second depends, it is true, on the first, for only because she is a truly noble woman, embodying all the qualities which Wolfram extolled in her predecessors, can she assume the rôle of Wolfram's mouthpiece. In her unique situation she becomes a unique heroine, in many ways continuing and confirming the ideal already depicted, yet at the same time representing a totally new aspect of it which was never approached in the earlier work. She is indeed Wolfram's most complete demonstration of his ideal, womanhood realized to its utmost limits, and his presentation of her is consequently different from that of his other heroines, in some ways an intensification of it, in other ways a departure from it, in accordance with her essentially active rôle.

There is, in relation to this basic difference, an important point which should not be overlooked. Belakane, Herzeloyde and Condwiramurs are all mothers and reach their peak in motherhood, when, passively and by their very nature as women, they fulfil themselves in their children. This is not the case with Gyburc, whose moment of fulfilment comes, surely, when she is called upon to defend her faith actively. Although it is mentioned that Gyburc has children in the kingdom she has forsaken, she is not remembered primarily as a mother. This may seem strange, in view of the high place which Wolfram gives to Herzeloyde by virtue of her motherhood, yet the omission is perfectly in accordance with the new aspect of womanhood which he offers in the person of Gyburc. In the active rôle which she must play in *Willehalm*, there is no place for the passive and restful picture of motherhood. Her rôle is not to impart her virtue to a single being, but to inspire whole armies with her spirit of love and faith. The scale and tempo have changed since *Parzival*, and the passive heroine must be replaced by a new one, no less virtuous, but capable of fulfilling herself in an active and, in Wolfram's work, unprecedented manner. Thus, to a considerable extent, the more intimate qualities of the women in *Parzival* are omitted in Gyburc. It is as though she has risen above them, in transcending the traditional rôle of woman. Yet it is as Werner Schröder says, "Gyburc ist . . . zunächst und vor allem ein liebender und leidender Mensch,"[19] and occasionally Wolfram allows her to betray touches of her nature which remind one of the woman she is, rather than of the saint whom he sees in her. Her kindness to the unhappy Rennewart is inspired not only by the barely conscious feeling that they are related, but also by compassion for the suffering of another human being in a situation which bears close resemblance to her own. Her personal attentions to Willehalm when he returns to Orange the first time echo the devotion of the women in *Parzival*. She removes his armour for him and tends his wounds, and one is reminded of Belakane's eagerness to serve Gahmuret, of the small service which Cunneware performs for Parzival as he departs, and of Bene's attention to Gawan's comfort. Despite her personal state of distress and privation, Gyburc readily offers to feed the great army encamped about the city, recalling how Parzival and Condwiramurs were left to share the crumbs after feeding the starving people of Pelrapeire. Such slight indications of kindness and selflessness give depth to the picture of the saintly Gyburc and make of her a figure perfectly in accordance with the picture so fully presented in *Parzival*. Wolfram has time also to show in his great and courageous heroine a woman who is not untouched by grief and strain. She faints when she realizes that it is Willehalm, after all, who is returning, and not the enemy. She who has been prepared to defend the city with her sword falters now, when relief is at hand (228,26-229,2). At times, too, Gyburc gives way to her grief and expresses it in tears, which suggest, not her weakness, but her true nature as a woman, which, for most of the work, she is required to transcend.[20] Her sanctity consists, it is true, in her ability to do so, but it rests on her nature as an ordinary human being, as a suffering and loving woman.

Thus, when Willehalm leaves her on his journey to Orleans, Wolfram allows her to remember, for a moment, that she is a woman parting from her husband and to ask him to remain true to her, for the sake of his own honour and in remembrance of the sacrifice she has made for him (104,1-30). This idea, and Willehalm's response that he will eat no food other than bread and water until he has released her, are present already in the *Aliscans*, but the changes which Wolfram has made are in accordance with the new conception of the relationship of the couple. Though Gyburc speaks at some length of the beauty and attractions of the French women whom her husband will encounter (104,8-17), her request that he remember her and remain true to their love is made in the consciousness that this love is secure, whereas Guibourc betrays for a moment her real fear that the beautiful French women may take her husband from her.[21] Willehalm vows that he will remain in grief until he has freed her from suffering:

Er gap des fîanze,
daz diu jâmers lanze
sîn herze immer twunge,
unz im sô wol gelunge
daz er si dâ erlôste
mit manlîchem trôste. (105,1-6)

He does not expand, as does Guillaume,[22] on how this grief and discomfort will reveal itself, and his later refusal to kiss anyone other than Gyburc is not, as is the case with Guillaume, in direct loyalty to a vow made to her, but his own interpretation of his promise to remain in sorrow.

The picture which Wolfram draws of Gyburc is based, then, on that of her predecessor in the *Aliscans*, but with a totally new conception of her rôle in the work. She thus becomes a highly complex character, with an essential duality resultant from her situation as a heathen woman who has become a Christian, a Moorish princess who has become the wife of a Christian Margrave. Part of the duality of Gyburc, as re-created by Wolfram, lies also in the fact that she is very human, with the emotions and reactions of the heroines of *Parzival*, yet that she is called upon to suppress these at some points and to behave quite unlike these other heroines. Her ability to do so is not in spite of her greatness as a woman, but because of it. This Wolfram makes clear when he shows her to possess to the full the virtues which he prizes in his other women characters; but he makes it clear also that what makes Gyburc a saint in his eyes is the extension of their virtues, to meet a situation which she alone is required to face.

NOTES

1. Unless otherwise indicated, all references in this chapter are to *Willehalm*.
2. See B. Mergell (*Wolfram von Eschenbach und seine französischen Quellen, I—Willehalm*, Münster, 1936-42. Also: B.

de Kok: *Guibourc et quelques autres figures de femmes dans les plus anciennes chansons de geste*, Paris, 1926.

3. J. Bumke (*Wolframs Willehalm*, p. 149).

4. Compare 248,23-249, 15 and 248,4-8.

5. cf. H. B. Willson: 'Einheit in der Vielheit in Wolframs *Willehalm*,' ZfdPh, 80, 1961, pp. 40-62.

6. See J. Bumke (*Wolframs Willehalm*, p. 145.).

7. See E. Werner: 'Zur Frauenfrage und zum Frauenkult im Mittelalter: Robert von Arbrissel und Fontevrault,' *Forschungen und Fortschritte* 29,9, 1955, pp. 269-276.

8. For example, 306,29ff; 309,7ff.

9. cf. J. Bumke (*Wolframs Willehalm*, pp. 143-144).

10. J. Bumke (ibid. p. 143 i) describes Guibourc as 'eine Randfigur,' but this is not entirely just: within the framework of the *Aliscans*, she has considerable importance, though this is clearly limited in comparison with the rôle of Gyburc.

11. See, for example her words 310,1-6; 310,17-20. On the basis of such assertions, J. Bumke may justly say 'Ihre Liebesfrömmigkeit ist zugleich eine Leidensfrömmigkeit' (ibid. p. 148).

12. On the question of Gyburc's 'guilt,' see Fr. Maurer (*Leid*, Bern and Munich, 1951, p. 192ff.).

13. cf. Marlis Schumacher (p. 143ff.).

14. G. Meissburger (p. 86).

15. J. Bumke (*Wolframs Willehalm*, p. 146) describes the poverty of Gyburc justly 'als Triebfeder, als Kennzeichen ihrer Haltung.'

16. J. Bumke (ibid. p. 159ff.) sees in Gyburc's attitude towards her poverty and her emphasis on it the influence of St. Francis and his principle of *sancta paupertas*. It is interesting also to recall that St. Dominic, when he died in 1221, is said to have left his followers with the instructions 'Ayez la charité, gardez l'humilité, possédez la pauvreté volontaire' (M.-H. Vicaire: *Histoire de Saint Dominique*, Paris, 1957, p. 326). The positive nature of poverty is evident.

17. 'Armuot,' pp. 523-524.
18. Compare with this the argument of J. Bumke (*Wolframs Willehalm*, p. 146) who asserts rightly: '*Armuot* ist für Gyburc ein religiöser Wert.'
19. 'Süeziu Gyburc,' p. 69.
20. For example, 268,3ff; 102,21ff; 105,17. G. Meissburger (p. 82) ignores the significance of the tears of Wolfram's other heroines when he sees them as a sign of her weakness. There are numerous examples in *Parzival*, but see 28,14-15; 272,7ff; 729,20ff.
21. *Aliscans*: Kritischer Text von E. Wienbeck, W. Hartnacke, P. Rasch, Halle, 1903: line 1974. B. de Kok (pp. 33-34) observes: 'Voilà donc que cette femme forte qui poursuit toujours son but sans hésiter, devient une pauvre créature tremblant pour son bonheur.' At no point could this apply to Gyburc. Marlis Schumacher (pp. 146-147) discusses the scene in detail and considers that there is a contradiction here of the early impression of the secure relationship between Gyburc and Willehalm. My own view is that this is precisely *not* the case: she is fully aware of his love for her and trusts him implicitly. Wolfram has a shrewd understanding of feminine psychology, and he certainly knows that no woman would put into words her awareness of the attraction of other women, if she were not fully confident that it represented no threat to her.
22. *Aliscans* ed. cit. 1987ff.

PART II

CHAPTER FIVE

Belakane

WOLFRAM'S VIEW OF WOMAN is established beyond doubt by his four central heroines, but he does not leave it at that. Supporting this central core, affirming and extending the picture which they give, are all his other women characters. Of these many are vivid and full of significance, although they may appear dwarfed in comparison with Herzeloyde and Sigune, Condwiramurs and Gyburc. Whereas the three heroines of *Parzival* are present throughout the work, whether actually or as a very potent memory, and Gyburc dominates the whole of *Willehalm*, the scope of these other women is more limited, confined as they often are to a passing stage or an isolated event. Yet once more the skill of Wolfram is apparent, for they, too, stand out as individuals, while being at the same time perfectly integrated into the entire and completely consistent picture.

One of the foremost of these somewhat slighter women characters is Belakane. Although she vanishes from the work after her brief appearance in the first book, she nevertheless stands among the most noble of Wolfram's heroines, embodying above all that capacity for love which he prizes so highly. It is in connection with Gahmuret that Belakane enters the story of Parzival, and when their short-lived marriage comes to an end, she withdraws from it. There remains, however, a powerful symbol of the union, Feirefiz Anschevin, who in his very name combines equally the elements of heathendom and Christianity which were the ingredients of the fleeting romance of Belakane and Gahmuret. In his nature, too, are blended the noblest elements of his parentage, so that he alone is a match for Parzival. The encounter between Parzival and Feirefiz is a final, superb affirmation of Belakane, the woman whom Gahmuret never really forgot, and whom Wolfram himself treats with admiration and respect. His depiction of Belakane is one of the most remarkable: although in many of her qualities she anticipates later, more dominant heroines, there are nevertheless in her the depth and individuality which Wolfram manages to impart to almost all his women characters. With masterly economy, he creates here a woman who remains in the mind of the reader throughout the work, so that the re-appearance of Feirefiz comes, not as a contrived echo from the past, but as a fitting conclusion to a story which formed an impressive and deeply poignant opening to the whole work.

Save for the brief period of happiness in marriage to Gahmuret, Belakane is remembered as a woman grieving for the loss, first of her lover, and then of her husband. Her appearance is framed by these two bereavements, and it is ironical that Gahmuret, who alleviates the grief of the first loss, also inflicts the second. The intensity of her love is matched by the intensity of her grief, for in her is illustrated the truth of Wolfram's observation:

> ôwê unde heiâ hei,
> daz güete alsölhen kumber tregt
> und immer triwe jâmer regt! (103,20-22)

These words are used in reference to Herzeloyde, but they are equally applicable to Belakane, as to all women, who, with the capacity for love, must endure the inescapable burden of grief. That Wolfram regards as a supreme feminine virtue this capacity to love with an intensity which must ultimately bring sorrow, is clear, both from his numerous examples of it in other heroines, and from the explicit statement, in reference to Belakane, that 'wîplîcher sin in wîbes herze nie geslouf' (28,12-13). This he says when Belakane is grieving for her dead lover, Isenhart: her devotion to him

84

is the highest proof of her womanhood. Later Wolfram remembers
her in this state of steadfastness and perfect virtue when he recalls
that

> de küngîn Belakâne
> was missewenden âne
> und aller valscheite laz,
> dô si ein tôter künec besaz.   (337,7-10)

In fact it is her devotion to Isenhart which attracts Gahmuret to
her, and it is in his mind that Wolfram places the observation that
never did more womanly devotion find its way into the heart of a
woman. He falls in love with her at their first meeting, observing
her dark beauty certainly, but sensing also the great virtue which
prompts her to grieve for the dead knight.

There is no suggestion that the love of Belakane for Isenhart
precludes another love, nor that the love of Gahmuret and Belakane is lessened by her earlier devotion to another man. Gahmuret
comes to her by chance, thrown up by a storm on the shores of her
land, and he comes, as though drawn by fate, when she is in the
most dire distress and danger. In spite of the gravity of the situation, Belakane is well able to note the handsome man who has
come to her rescue, and in spite of her grief at the loss of her lover,
her heart is stirred by a new love:

> der küneginne rîche
> ir ougen fuogten hôhen pîn,
> dô si gesach den Anschevîn.
> der was sô minneclîche gevar,
> daz er entslôz ir herze gar,
> ez wære ir liep oder leit:
> daz beslôz dâ vor ir wîpheit.   (23,22-28)

From this beginning, the course of the relationship seems to be pre-
ordained. Ironically, it is when Belakane is lamenting the death of
Isenhart that Gahmuret realizes her worth, her perfect purity and

the great capacity for love, both of which are revealed in the tears which he sees as a substitute for baptismal water (28,10-19). Of this virtue he is aware 'swie si wære ein heidenin' (28,11) and from this early encounter he is filled with a love for Belakane which transcends the difference in race and creed. Wolfram has shown in one clear stroke how a new love came to Belakane the moment she saw Gahmuret, and now he tells how Gahmuret himself is stirred by the thought of the Queen:

> in brâhte dicke in unmaht
> diu swarze Mœrinne,
> des landes küneginne.
> er want sich dicke alsam ein wit,
> daz im krachten diu lit.
> strît und minne was sîn ger. (35,20-25)

The story of their romance begins, then, very like that of Parzival and Condwiramurs, for that too begins with an act of rescue and is based upon a mutual and spontaneous love. Gahmuret and Belakane, like Parzival and Condwiramurs, seem destined for one another, yet this earlier marriage is tragically brief. The desire for knightly fame, which exerts such a powerful influence over the men and so often outweighs the claims of the strongest love, brings to an abrupt end the marriage of Gahmuret and Belakane. Thus Belakane, who was won by an act of knightly valour, becomes the victim of chivalry and joins the long line of women who are left alone when their husbands, their sons and their lovers can no longer withstand the pull of the knightly life. Gahmuret himself puts into words the irony of the fate of Belakane, when he is warning Herzeloyde against imposing restrictions on his activities:

> lât ir niht turnieren mich,
> sô kan ich noch den alten slich,
> als dô ich mînem wîbe entran,
> die ich ouch mit rîterschaft gewan.
> dô si mich ûf von strîte bant,
> ich liez ir liute unde lant. (96,29-97,4)

When Parzival takes leave of Condwiramurs, Wolfram contrasts her perfect contentment in love and marriage with the restlessness of her husband, who, though he loves her deeply, cannot resist the call of the knightly life. Yet she, like Herzeloyde before her, knows that this zest for adventure and combat is an essential part of the make-up of the man she loves, and that to quell it would be to weaken their love, even to destroy it. The tragedy of Belakane is that she is never given the chance to release her husband, for Gahmuret prefers to go away in secret, rather than face a reproachful or a pleading wife. Yet surely in this he underestimates her, for she, who has lost one lover in combat and been won by a second through knightly prowess, must understand very well the power of chivalry, and in her love for Gahmuret, she would never have refused him the freedom to practise this, to him, essential art.

That this was, in fact, his motive in leaving his first wife is clear from the conditions he imposes on the second, and from these conditions is clear, too, his sense of guilt towards Belakane. The whole incident is a stain on the otherwise faultless character of Gahmuret, as Feirefiz tells Parzival (750,20-21), and it is one which is difficult to explain or excuse. In this one must, as often, be guided by Wolfram's own attitude: even when Gahmuret is leaving Belakane and her unborn child, he describes him as 'der werde man' (55,11), where there is no reason to suppose that he is using the adjective ironically. The qualms which Gahmuret later suffers help to soften what appears otherwise as a brutal act. Possibly at the time he thought he was doing the best thing in sparing Belakane—and, incidentally, himself—the pain of parting. The excuse, that the difference in religion takes him from her is quite unconvincing, since it has not so far presented itself as an obstacle, and one doubts that he would now see it as one. In discussing what is a considerable problem in view of Gahmuret's otherwise exemplary character, Friedrich Panzer offers this explanation: "Aber er nennt im Briefe gerade jenen in Wahrheit unmaßgeblichen Grund, weil seine *zuht* ihm nicht gestattet, die Frau durch den Hinweis auf das körperlich Trennende oder auf die Tatsache, daß sein Mannessein

nicht aus der Liebe allein sich nähren kann, zu verletzen."[1] The latter reason certainly seems likely, and it has the advantage of explaining his action as misguided kindness, rather than brutal negligence.
It does, however, point to Gahmuret's rather immature misjudge-
ment of the woman he professes to love, for he should know that
she would grant him leave to go on knightly expeditions, as Herzeloyde does after her. That it is 'das körperlich Trennende' which
drives him from her is surely incredible, since her black skin represents from the start no barrier to him. He himself later denies that
this was the reason for his desertion of her:

> nu wænt manc ungewisser man
> daz mich ir swerze jagte dane:
> die sah ich für die sunnen ane. (91,4-6)

On several other occasions her blackness is mentioned, but always
coupled with an expression of his love for her, suggesting that, far
from representing a barrier to him, it enhances her beauty and is
part of what he loves in her. Wolfram says, for example, that Gahmuret is troubled by thoughts of 'diu swarze Mœrinne' (35,21),
and later he deliberately tells how a black hand removes his armour
for him (44,18-19). It is as though Wolfram wishes to stress the
difference in colour from the beginning, precisely to make it clear
that it is not important to Gahmuret, so that he can say, even when
Gahmuret is about to leave Belakane:

> Doch was im daz swarze wîp
> lieber dan sîn selbes lîp. (54,21-22)

Clearly, then, the difference in colour is not the reason for Gahmuret's departure. Although the reason which he leaves behind in
his letter, that the difference in faith takes him from her, is scarcely
more credible, Belakane nevertheless accepts it as his real motive,
showing her trust in the husband she has never had cause to doubt.
It leaves her, however, not only with sorrow at her loss, but also

with remorse that it could have been prevented, and to this she gives
expression in a most poignant cry:

'. . ôwê lieplîch geselleschaft,
sol mir nu riwe mit ir kraft
immer twingen mînen lîp!
sîme gote ze êren', sprach daz wîp,
'ich mich gerne toufen solte
unde leben swie er wolte.'   (57,3-8)

In this, Belakane anticipates Gyburc, who comes to a knowledge of
God through Willehalm, and so, by perfect human love, like Sigune, comes to know divine Love. Again, though, Belakane is not
given the chance which is given to a later heroine, and she is not
able to fulfil the readiness which she expresses here. Only in her son
is her desire for baptism to be fulfilled: significantly and very ap-
propriately, Feirefiz accepts baptism in order to marry Repanse de
Schoye, whom he loves deeply. Belakane herself is an essentially
tragic figure, and so she is left to grieve over her loss, with the last
words of Gahmuret's letter ringing with tantalizing cruelty in her
ears:

frouwe, wiltu toufen dich,
du maht ouch noch erwerben mich.   (56,25-26)

One of the memorable things about Belakane is the manner of
her grief. When she reads Gahmuret's letter, she reacts with a
stoicism which makes her very fit to be the mother of the brave and
noble Feirefiz. Despite the last words of the letter, which seem to
hold out the hope of Gahmuret's return if she becomes a Christian,
there is a dominant note of finality: the fact that he gives details of
the lineage of their unborn child hardly suggests that he expects to
return, and certainly Belakane herself does not appear to think he
will.[2] Yet she is not seen to swoon as Herzeloyde does when she
learns of the death of Gahmuret, nor is her grief manifested in the
violent weeping of Herzeloyde and Sigune. Wolfram compares her

grief with the lonely longing of the turtle-dove which has lost its mate, and he does so in a beautiful, poignant picture which remains to epitomize the tragedy of Belakane:

> ir freude vant den dürren zwîc,
> als noch diu turteltûbe tuot.
> diu het ie den selben muot:
> swenne ir an trûtscheft gebrast,
> ir triwe kôs den dürren ast. (57,10-14)[3]

This second occasion may well be contrasted with her grief at the death of Isenhart, when her tears had borne witness to her love, and she had been able to put into words her love for him. There is in her sorrow now a hopelessness which cannot find expression in words or gestures, and this softer, yearning grief dominates the reader's remembrance of Belakane, even after Feirefiz tells that, in fact, she died of grief (750,24-26).

When the child is born, his skin displays the equality of the elements which gave him life, and Belakane, whose love for Gahmuret has not lessened, kisses him on the white parts which are all that remains to her of her husband. Not until the marriage of Feirefiz with the Bearer of the Graal is the harshness of Belakane's fate softened, for the elevation of the son to the position of such honour and happiness contains adequate, though belated, compensation for the sorrow and ill-treatment of the mother. That this posthumous compensation should come through the love of her son and Repanse de Schoye is apt; and apt too is the fact that the recognition of Parzival and Feirefiz, which leads to his acquaintance with the Graal, with Repanse de Schoye and so with God, takes place because Feirefiz, in humanity and generosity, refuses to fight with a disarmed opponent. The irony of the incident is intensified by the fact that Feirefiz tells Parzival that he has not yet forgiven his father for the desertion of his mother (750,20-23): he has come in search of him now, acknowledging his reputation as a knight, yet regretting this single blemish on it. That reconciliation takes the place of reproach would surely have accorded with Belakane's wish, for, in her, when Gahmuret has left her, is no trace of bitterness or reproach, only of sorrow and regret.

After his desertion of her, Gahmuret suffers pangs of conscience and grief, and his thoughts are constantly with her, so that he is distracted and unable to join in any joy:

> umb unvergolten minnen gelt
> wart ez ein künec âne:
> des twang in Belacâne.   (61,10-12)

Thus, when he first sees Herzeloyde, though he is much attracted by her, the memory of Belakane still hovers in his mind and forms an obstacle to this new love:

> wan daz grôz jâmer under sluoc
> die hœhe an sîner freude breit,
> sîn minne wære ir vil bereit.   (84,16-18)[4]

He is possessed by a sense of guilt about his desertion of her:

> mich tuot frô Belakâne
> manlîcher freuden âne:
> ez ist doch vil manlich,
> swer minnen wankes schamet sich.   (90,25-28)

Nor does he ever move from his insistence that he loves her, despite his undeniable attraction to Herzeloyde:

> dô sprach er 'frouwe, ich hân ein wîp:
> diu ist mir lieber danne der lîp. . . .'   (94,5-6)

Herzeloyde, ironically, uses the same argument to him as he used in his letter to Belakane, that a marriage to a heathen cannot bind him, but it is not until it is pointed out to him that it is his duty to marry Herzeloyde that he submits, for the code of knighthood, which demanded that he should leave Belakane in order to take part in the pursuit of chivalry, now demands that he should keep the bond which governed the tournament. The place of Belakane in society is usurped, then, by Herzeloyde, but this happens only because in the mind of Gahmuret his knightly honour is stronger than the claims of love. And, with a kind of poetic justice, the love of Herzeloyde and Gahmuret is fated, too, for in insisting that he marry her, she brings upon herself the stipulation that he must be free to practise his chivalry.

What unites Herzeloyde and Belakane is their love for Gahmuret, and the perfection of their womanhood. Wolfram's talent for creating individual characters is apparent once more in these two, who, with so much in common, emerge as such very different people. The difference rests very largely on the difference in environment of the two women, and the difference in the rôles they are called upon to fulfil. When Gahmuret first learns of the existence of Belakane, she has already suffered the loss of Isenhart, and remorse from knowing that she was the unwitting cause of his death. In this she is to be compared with Sigune, who, when Parzival first meets her, is suffering from frenzied grief over the lover she drove to his death. Yet behind Sigune is the memory of *Titurel*, with its picture of the youth and carefree happiness which are the prelude to the present sorrow. Such development is absent in the case of Belakane, for she first appears as a woman who has known bereavement and grief and now faces an acute physical threat. Her speech to Gahmuret, when she tells him how she came to be in this danger, is an account of profound suffering, and it reflects a mature, perhaps premature, awareness of the nature of human life:

> ir ieweder innen wart
> eins spers durh schilt und durh den lîp.
> daz klag ich noch, vil armez wîp:
> ir bêder tôt mich immer müet.
> ûf mîner triwe jâmer blüet. (28,4-8)

It is true that she refers to a young, irresponsible love, when she delighted at the power she exerted over her lover and sought to try

it (27,11-14), but all this is in the past, and in the present are sorrow
and danger.

In this situation, Belakane comes closest to Gyburc, for Gyburc
too has a past which has given rise to the present, and for both the
present contains suffering and peril, with the added grief of knowing themselves hated for what they have done, that through their
love they have brought suffering and even death on others.[5] Both
are mature women, aware of the basically harsh nature of human
experience. Gahmuret saves Belakane from her peril: Herzeloyde
he wins in a tournament arranged at the caprice of one who is still
a true lady of the court. Later, in Gyburc, Wolfram was to combine
perfect femininity with the capacity to act like a man in time of
need. Belakane anticipates Gyburc in this, too, although her courage is not tried so hard as Gyburc's. Of Belakane Wolfram says:

> si hete wîplîchen sin,
> und was abr anders rîterlîch   (24,8-9)

and this striking description of the earlier heroine links her most
firmly with the later one, who stands with sword uplifted and declares herself ready to defend Orange. Wolfram may already have
had Gyburc in mind when he chose to make a black woman the wife
of his noble Gahmuret, or it may have been yet another occasion
of his tolerance, which is most fully demonstrated in *Willehalm*.

What is absent in Belakane, yet present in almost all the other
women, is, of course, faith in God, for she does not know Him, although her statement after reading Gahmuret's letter comes close to
being a baptism of desire, though one which is not fulfilled in her.
Again, however, Wolfram sees beyond the belief she professes, the
race to which she belongs, to her essential virtues as a human being,
and in these she is not lacking. From the start she is, for him, 'diu
süeze valsches âne' (16,8), of whom he has said

> ir kiusche was ein reiner touf,
> und ouch der regen der sie begôz,
> der wâc der von ir ougen flôz
> ûf ir zobel und an ir brust.   (28,14-17)

These words gain in significance when one finds them echoed, so much later in the work, in reference to Feirefiz, who has just learnt both the identity of his opponent and of the death of his father:

> er lachte und weinde tougen.
> sîn heidenschiu ougen
> begunden wazzer rêren
> al nâch des toufes êren.
> der touf sol lêren triuwe,
> sît unser ê diu niuwe
> nâch Kriste wart genennet:
> an Kriste ist triwe erkennet. (752,23-30)

The capacity to love, which Wolfram had seen to combine with purity of mind and body to make Belakane a Christian in spirit, is bequeathed also to her son, for whom baptism will become a reality. Late though it comes, this is the perfect culmination to Wolfram's depiction of Belakane.

NOTES

1. F. Panzer: *Gahmuret: Quellenstudien zu Wolframs Parzival*, Heidelberg, 1940, p. 9.

2. cf. 57,1ff.

3. A. B. Groos (" 'Sigune auf der Linde' and the Turtledove in *Parzival"*) links Wolfram's treatment of Belakane with his treatment of Sigune, showing how the symbol of the turtledove which Wolfram uses explicitly to describe Belakane is implied also in his depiction of Sigune grieving over her dead Schionatulander. He draws attention, too, to the fact that Wolfram introduced the proverb 'den dürren ast kiesen' into Middle High German literature.

4. Coupled with his grief at his departure from Belakane is, of course, the sorrow at the recent news of the death of his brother.

5. Condwiramurs, too, causes great conflict by refusing to marry Clamide.

CHAPTER SIX

Repanse de Schoye

THE FIGURE of the Graal Bearer, present already in *Le Conte del Graal* but not yet developed as a character, makes a vital contribution to Wolfram's picture of woman, yet once more his technique of characterization is different and the figure he creates unique. In fact, Repanse de Schoye stands alone among the women of Wolfram's creation. This is inevitable in one who occupies her unique position, for as Graal Bearer she partakes of the mystery which surrounds the Graal itself. Thus, although in beauty and virtue she resembles other women in the works she nevertheless possesses as her chief quality a remoteness from reality, which keeps her aloof from women such as Herzeloyde, Condwiramurs and Gyburc. Although Wolfram represents them as supreme in virtue and although in love they come close to the Eternal and the Divine, they are essentially of the world of reality, fulfilling themselves as wives and mothers of real, if exceptional, men. As the wife of Feirefiz, Repanse de Schoye will certainly tend this new object of her devotion with the same constant care, and as his wife and the mother of the famed Prester John, she will rank with Herzeloyde and Condwiramurs; but her marriage to the noble half-brother of the noblest of all knights is the culmination of her years of service to the Graal, and it is primarily as Graal Bearer that she is significant in the work.

Repanse de Schoye makes two appearances in *Parzival*, when Parzival first comes to the Castle and neglects his duty there, and when he returns as the acclaimed King. On each occasion, the Graal is brought forth, and with it comes Repanse de Schoye. She is inseparable from the stone itself, and her nature is inextricably linked with its nature. Thus we are told of the purity which is demanded of the one who may bear the Graal:

> wol muoser kiusche sîn bewart,
> die sîn ze rehte solde pflegn:
> die muose valsches sich bewegn.   (235,28-30)

Later Trevrizent says, in explanation to Parzival, that

> der stein ist immer reine.   (471,22)

Moreover, Wolfram links the Graal even more closely with its Bearer by endowing the stone with the power to choose the one who may bear it:

> sich liez der grâl, ist mir gesagt,
> die selben tragen eine,
> und anders enkeine.   (809,10-12)

In the hands of others, it assumes a weight which makes it impossible to lift:[1] Repanse de Schoye alone fulfils the requirements of the Graal, and so she may succeed Schoysiane, the virtuous mother of Sigune, and the first Bearer of the Graal.

It is the purity of Repanse de Schoye which fits her for her particular rôle, and the word kiusche is used repeatedly as her outstanding quality.[2] Purity, of mind and body, is a quality essential in a virtuous woman, and the women of Wolfram's creation possess it to the full. Most particularly, he refers on several occasions to the kiusche of Belakane, and this emphasis points not only to his indisputably high opinion of her as a woman, but also to his view of the virtue itself. In Belakane, kiusche can act as a substitute for baptism,[3] and in Repanse de Schoye it can make a woman fit to bear the Graal, which, whatever its precise nature, is a supreme spiritual goal and an object sacred to Christians.

One of the clearest indications of the religious nature of the Graal comes with the baptism of Feirefiz, which results in his ability to see it. He desires to be baptised because he is assured that he will then be able to marry Repanse de Schoye, and he makes no secret of the fact that she is his reason for accepting baptism (818,1-12). Nor does Wolfram suggest that there is anything inferior in the Christianity which Feirefiz thus assumes, for, as so often, he clearly regards their love as the apt means to divine Love. Feirefiz is attracted at once to Repanse de Schoye by her great beauty, and he immediately desires to win her, consumed as he is by a love which replaces and far exceeds any he has ever known. Her beauty Wolfram represents as a radiant light (235,16-17), and, as so often in his work, this is his manner of implying inward virtue. Her beautiful appearance is the reflection of her great virtue, and the two are juxtaposed to make her the object of the most perfect love Feirefiz has ever experienced:

> ir herzen was vil kiusche bî,
> ir vel des blickes flôrî.   (809,13-14)

It is perfect because it is the means to his conversion, and for a Christian such as Wolfram this fact needs no expansion.

Only in Feirefiz does Parzival ever encounter a true rival, and only with the beauty of Repanse de Schoye can that of Condwiramurs find real comparison (811,1-3). The two couples are perfectly matched. Wolfram could provide no clearer affirmation of the nobility of Feirefiz than by allowing him to marry the woman who alone may bear the Graal, nor could there be a more fitting culmination to the devoted life of Repanse de Schoye than her marriage to the son of Gahmuret and Belakane. Comparison between Repanse de Schoye and Condwiramurs is inevitable, for both achieve supremacy in Wolfram's estimation. He himself compares them in beauty, and he allows Parzival too to reflect on the likeness between his wife and the woman he sees bearing the Graal:

> wan stüende ir gemüete
> daz si dienst wolde nemn!

> des kunde mich durch si gezemn,
> und doch niht durch ir minne:
> wan mîn wîp de küneginne
> ist an ir lîbe alse clâr,
> oder fürbaz, daz ist wâr.　　　　　　(246,16-22)

Yet, in these words, Parzival rejects the thought of a relationship of *minne* between Repanse de Schoye and himself, desiring only to serve her. Even apart from the fact that he wishes for no other love than that of his wife, it would seem that he has observed in Repanse de Schoye that remoteness from reality which makes her the object of respect and service, rather, at this stage, than of love. Anfortas explains to Feirefiz that she has been kept from the love of men by the power of grief which binds her to him (811,21-30), for the life she leads is one of absolute devotion, to her brother and to the Graal: side-by-side with the *kiusche* which Wolfram prizes so highly in her is her *triuwe*. She is bound to Anfortas by the ties of love, and by compassion for the suffering of a fellow-being, which, in Wolfram's view, is one aspect of the great virtue of *triuwe*.[4]

Until the time when these two virtues will be made manifest in Parzival himself, Repanse de Schoye must tend the Graal. Meanwhile, the link between them is implied by Wolfram and sensed by Parzival. They are linked from the moment of his entry into the Castle, when a cloak is brought to him. Clothes were normally provided for a guest, so in itself the gesture is a traditional one. However, it goes deeper than that, for the chamberlain informs Parzival that it is the cloak of the Queen, Repanse de Schoye, and he adds that Parzival is fit to wear it since he recognizes in him a worthy man (228,13-20). At this stage, Parzival is not conscious of a deeper significance in the gesture, but he is conscious of the link which is thus established between himself and the Queen. On various occasions, he recalls this link: as he watches Repanse de Schoye during his first visit:

> dez mære giht daz Parzivâl
> dicke an si sach unt dâhte,

diu den grâl dâ brâhte:
er het och ir mantel an.   (236,12-15)

When he awakes on the following morning, his thoughts fly to her:

hât dirre wirt urliuges nôt,
sô leist ich gerne sîn gebot
und ir gebot mit triuwen,
diu disen mantel niuwen
mir lêch durch ir güete.   (246,11-15)

Later he asks Trevrizent:

'wer was ein maget diu den grâl
truoc? ir mantel lêch man mir.'   (500,24-25)

Always, then, he recalls that this mysterious queen gave him her cloak, and he senses vaguely that she is in some need. However, it is left for Trevrizent to point out that it was no mere gesture but a deliberate act:

sine lêch dirs niht ze ruome:
si wând du soltst dâ hêrre sîn
des grâls unt ir, dar zuo mîn.   (500,28-30)

Not until he meets Trevrizent can he come to an understanding of what he has seen, and so to the irony of the fact that he does wrong when he believes he is doing right is added the irony of his pondering on a circumstance to which he lacks the key, for he remembers how Repanse de Schoye lent him her cloak, without appreciating that the act must have its particular meaning. It is characteristic of Parzival's youth that he registers the fact that he is wearing her cloak yet is still unable to interpret its significance, or even to realize that it has a significance. Similarly, he is conscious of the suffering of Anfortas and feels pity for him, but he lacks the power to express it, or, rather, the discernment to see that this is an occasion when he should not feel bound by the courtly convention of reticence. For the development of Parzival it is important merely that the memory of Repanse de Schoye remains with him for a long time. After a troubled night at the Graal Castle, he awakes with the desire to help the suffering King and the woman whose cloak he wears, but the means to do so does not present itself, so he leaves the Castle, having failed in his mission.

The link which is thus established between them on this first occasion is indicated quite emphatically by Wolfram himself, in two closely similar passages, where not only the cloaks echo one another, but also the beauty of the two faces:

> alt und junge wânden
> daz von im ander tag erschine.
> sus saz der minneclîche wine.
> gar vor allem tadel vrî
> mit pfelle von Arâbî
> man truoc im einen mantel dar:
> den legt an sich der wol gevar.   (228,4-10)

and

> nâch den kom diu künegîn.
> ir antlütze gap den schîn,
> si wânden alle ez wolde tagen.
> man sach die maget an ir tragen
> pfellel von Arâbî.   (235,15-19)

The virtue which she possesses and which fits her for her office is reflected in her radiant beauty, and Parzival has the same kind of beauty, the outward sign of the same virtue, which will fit him for his destined rôle. The cloak itself is a symbol of his connection with the Graal Family through Repanse de Schoye, who clearly glimpses in him the hope of salvation. In allowing the cloak to be given to him, she not only demonstrates her recognition of his nobility, as the chamberlain tells Parzival, but also offers him a share in her responsibility for the Graal she bears. Nor is she mistaken in her assessment of him, for it is only actual knowledge, the fruit of experience, which is lacking in him, and what she recognizes is the basic sensitivity and nobility which fit him for the Graal Kingship.

With the cloak of Repanse de Schoye may be linked the cloak which Trevrizent gives to Parzival at his hermitage. Again, this may be regarded as a traditional gesture of hospitality, but it would seem to be more than that, particularly in view of the previous occasion. With the cloak of Repanse de Schoye, Parzival was offered the opportunity to achieve the kingship which is his destiny; the cloak of Trevrizent, himself the brother of Repanse de Schoye and deeply involved in the fate of the Graal Family, represents an unconscious renewal of the offer, as Parzival stands on the threshold of a great new period in his life, when his return to faith in God will bring him once more to the Graal Castle, and to success where he failed before. The sword which Anfortas gives to Parzival is, like the cloak, an expression of the confidence which the suffering man places in the youth who has come to him. Wolfram says that the sword is a sign to Parzival to ask the question which will release Anfortas and the whole kingdom from suffering (240,6). Like the cloak, it is also symbolic of the willingness to transfer the responsibility for the rule of the Graal to this young man who is recognized as the future King. Just as he fails to perceive the significance of the gift of the cloak, he fails also to appreciate the depth of significance in the gift of the sword, although as he rides away he is thinking of the sword and wishing that he might earn it by aiding the suffering King. Both Anfortas and Repanse de Schoye see in Parzival the hope of release from their grief and express this hope in the two gifts. It is left for Trevrizent to explain the circumstances of the Graal Family, and so to give to Parzival the key to an interpretation of his experience there. Anfortas and Repanse de Schoye are linked with one another in their intimacy with the Graal itself, and it is not for them to instruct Parzival in the way that Trevrizent may instruct him: Trevrizent, like Sigune, has withdrawn from the Graal, despite his deep concern for it, and in this remoteness lies his ability to guide Parzival. The question which will bring release

101

must be spontaneous, so all that Anfortas and Repanse de Schoye may do is prompt him to speak with their two gifts.

Surrounded by the mystery which pervades Munsalvæsche, and raised to such a peak of virtue, Repanse de Schoye becomes the embodiment of perfect womanhood, passive in a way in which none of the other women may be called passive. Hers is not the passivity which is present in Herzeloyde, Condwiramurs, Belakane and Sigune, and is an aspect of the harmony and self-sufficiency which Wolfram sees as the nature of woman. Rather does Repanse de Schoye possess the static quality of a symbol, in which a number of attributes combine and rest, transcending change and comparison. This symbolic quality is possibly best conveyed in Wolfram's memorable picture of her:

> diu maget mit der krône
> stuont dâ harte schône.   (236,21-22)

Here she appears almost as the archetype of queenly dignity and beauty, and the significance of the lines is strengthened when one recalls that the Middle Ages saw the Virgin Mary as a Queen, and that artists of the 12th and 13th centuries almost always depicted her wearing a crown.[5] It is very likely that in his picture of this pure woman Wolfram was recalling the purest of all women, who at this period was occupying an increasingly prominent place in the minds of Christians. To take this point too far would be a mistake, for Wolfram does not stress it, but the fact remains that to Repanse de Schoye, the pure maiden, is given the supreme task of bearing the sacred object, and that, for Feirefiz, she acts as intermediary between man and God. Like Mary, she is a woman of perfect purity and charity, initiated into the mystery of the Divine, yet deeply involved with mankind, devoted to an object which is the physical expression of an abstract spiritual goal, yet personally afflicted with the grief of the world.

Repanse de Schoye is indeed unique among the women of Wolfram's works, and his treatment of her is correspondingly unique.

It is striking, and in accordance with his conception of her nature, that she never speaks: even this link with reality is kept from her. With Parzival's accession to the Graal Kingship and the release of Anfortas from suffering, Repanse de Schoye is no longer needed as Graal Bearer: Condwiramurs, her only rival in beauty and virtue, will tend the Graal with Parzival, and Repanse de Schoye may go with her husband to his Eastern Kingdom. Yet although Wolfram allows her to marry, the child of the marriage is Prester John, the mysterious Eastern King, who is himself the centre of legend and speculation. Moreover, an essential feature of the legends which surround him is his propagation of Christianity in the East. The influence of Repanse de Schoye widens, and she disappears from the work, but she who for so long has tended the Christian Graal will now extend the knowledge of the Christian faith through her son. She who has brought relief to Anfortas in his suffering will now bring joy—as her name suggests[6]—to many people.

NOTES

1. 477,15-18. See F. Ranke: 'Zur Symbolik des Grals bei Wolfram von Eschenbach,' *Trivium*, 4, 1946, pp. 20-30.

2. For example, 235,28; 477,14; 809,13.

3. See 28,14 and p. 86 above.

4. Cundrie reproaches Parzival for his lack of *triuwe*, which would have revealed itself in his ability to express *erbarmunge* (316,2-3).

5. See E. Mâle: *The Gothic Image* (Originally *Religious Art in France: XIII Century*) translated by D. Nussey, 1913, reprinted London 1961, pp. 231-258.

6. cf. M. O'C. Walshe: 'Notes on Parzival Book V,' *London Mediaeval Studies*, Vol. I, Part 3, 1939. B. Mergell suggests as a translation of the name 'Freude Verbreitende' (*Der Gral in Wolframs Parzival*, Halle, 1952, p. 78).

CHAPTER SEVEN

Jeschute

JESCHUTE BELONGS essentially to the youth of Parzival. She is the first person he meets after he has left his mother, and she is the victim of his inexperience of a world to which she belongs but of which he has no knowledge as yet. She marks the point of his departure from the close circle of his boyhood into the world outside. When he first encounters her, his knowledge is still limited to the bare precepts of his mother; he employs this knowledge, but in the broad context of the world beyond the seclusion of the forest his actions based on it prove disastrous. Like Ither, Jeschute is a victim of Parzival's ignorance, but whereas nothing may be done to compensate for the death of Ither, Parzival is later able to set right the wrong done to Jeschute, even though he cannot eradicate her year of suffering. Although she is not a major character, Jeschute is significant, like Liaze and Cunneware, in the growth of Parzival. Between his first encounter with her and his second lies one of the most important periods of his formation, a period during which he not only acquires the experience which would tell him of his mistake in his treatment of her, but also gives him the means to right it. Although Chrétien also has two encounters with his Jeschute-figure, there is less idea in *Le Conte del Graal* of crime and atonement. Perceval defeats li Orgueilleus de la Lande, who then agrees to restore his wife to favour.[1] There is no idea here, as there is very strongly in *Parzival*, of atonement on the part of the hero. The ring which Parzival takes from Jeschute he returns, as a symbol of this atonement, while in Chrétien's version, although Perceval takes the ring, he does not return it. Clearly, then, for Wolfram, the incident has considerable significance, beyond that of his source.

When Parzival comes upon Jeschute in the forest, he possesses two things: his natural inheritance from his parents, and the brief, ambiguous instructions given to him by Herzeloyde. Only with experience is he to come to an interpretation of these instructions which will be in accordance with life as he must live it. Meanwhile, in remembrance of his mother, and with perhaps even a vague stirring within him of the chivalry which made Gahmuret beloved of three women, he is attracted to Jeschute, first by the rich splendour of her tent, and then by the ring on her finger, which reminds him of the instructions of his mother, that he should take the ring of a good woman, if he encountered one. That it is the ring which attracts him and brings about Jeschute's grief is apparent, for Wolfram has described at length the beauty of the woman as she lies there, and only when Parzival catches sight of the ring does he leap on to her bed. His violent kiss and embrace, quite meaningless in themselves, reflect, too, his exact obedience to the words of his mother:

> du solt zir kusse gâhen
> und ir lîp vast umbevâhen:
> daz gît gelücke und hôhen muot,
> op si kiusche ist unde guot.   (127,29-128,2)

The fact that the whole incident echoes Herzeloyde's parting words so closely, points to the absolute innocence of Parzival, who obeys his mother to the letter, unaware that even obedience to her must be qualified by other considerations. He appears not to notice Jeschute's beauty, which Wolfram stresses all the more because it plays no part in the reaction of his hero.[2] That Parzival is so little concerned with the beautiful woman he has in his power, and that he is very much a boy still, Wolfram shows in the slight touch, amusing in its incongruity, of the sudden hunger which overtakes him. Without ceremony, and with considerably more enthusiastic attention than he has paid to his hostess, Parzival consumes the meal obviously intended for Orilus. While intent on the food, he completely forgets Jeschute.

Throughout the incident there is the contrast, amusing at times despite its seriousness, in the reactions of Jeschute and Parzival. Here is a boy for whom the sight of a beautiful woman is no match for a brace of partridges, and Wolfram himself points out with some surprise that the son of Gahmuret might have been expected to find some other attraction in the sight of a beautiful woman alone (139,15-19). As Parzival rides on, Wolfram refers to his act as 'ein tumpheit' (139,14) since, though it was indisputably a stupid deed, it has no further, more sinister implication. For Parzival, the incident has no meaning, so that when he next meets Jeschute he has genuine difficulty in remembering her.[3] For her, on the other hand, it represents the destruction of all happiness, since the motives of her assailant make no difference to her alarm and grief, nor to the anger of her husband when he returns to find that she has had a visitor in his absence. For her, Parzival's coming is a tragedy, the more poignant because her virtue is complete at all times, and because she has no defence in the face of a furious husband, who, regarding the evidence and hearing her innocent but, in the circumstances, ambiguous, references to the beauty of her assailant (133,18; 133,21-22), refuses to listen to the protests of his wife.

In Jeschute, Wolfram shows a woman who is perfect in chastity and loving devotion. Her very beauty reflects, as so often in Wolfram's works, the inner beauty of true virtue. Yet it is precisely her chastity and love which are doubted by her undiscerning husband, who is enraged by what he considers to be a stain on his honour, and acts without thought for the nature of his wife. Although his treatment of her is ruthless, Wolfram excuses him to some extent by suggesting that he must defend his honour where he considers it challenged (264,1-11). Certainly Jeschute herself never blames her husband; unlike the counterpart figure in *Le Conte del Graal*, who is bitter and resentful, she bears his injustice with patience. She is generous, also, in her treatment of Parzival when they meet again, for she tries to save him from the wrath of Orilus and finds herself in inner conflict when, watching the combat, she feels no bitterness towards either of the opponents in spite of the sorrow which each has caused her (262,28-29).

During the first encounter with Parzival, Jeschute behaves with perfect decorum, resisting him with all the strength she possesses. The injustice of Orilus is increased, then, because she has fought with all her might against the crude advances of the boy. Nevertheless, she is fearful, lest her husband should return, and her fear is not only for herself, but for her assailant too. Possibly, like everyone who meets Parzival at this stage, she is attracted by his good looks, in which she sees innate nobility. Her explanation to Orilus, that it was a fool who was passing by, is perfectly feasible, too, since his quite senseless attack on her must have appeared the act of a madman, and in this supposition she is supported by his attire. When they next meet, he is in the dress of a knight, and experience has done much to change him. In the knight who approaches her with courtesy and solicitude, she nevertheless recognizes the source of her sorrow. Since they last met, she has grown wretched with grief and neglect: he, on the other hand, has developed in knightly bearing which enhances the handsome features of his youth. Moreover, between the meetings lies for her over a year of despair and hardship, riding on a nag and estranged from the love of her husband: she has cause to remember Parzival. He, for whom the incident was a passing one, does not recall the early experience, which has been succeeded by so many of note and consequence.

Jeschute may well be compared with Cunneware, for both women suffered on account of Parzival, though without his intention. However, whereas he saw Cunneware's suffering and determined to right it one day, the suffering of Jeschute was unknown to him. As soon as he does learn of it, at their second meeting, he is ready to make amends. He is able to repair the damage he did to both women, but this he can do only as a knight. Thus, just as he is prevented from throwing his javelot in defence of Cunneware, he does not learn of the wrong done to Jeschute until, as a knight himself, he may rightfully enter into combat with Orilus. By making Cunneware the sister of Orilus, Wolfram links the two women, who are already linked by what befalls them, and a further link is established when Parzival makes it a condition of sparing the life of Orilus, not only that he should be reconciled with his wife, but also that he should go to Cunneware and offer her his service.

Incredible though this may seem, it is ignorance which allows Parzival's attack on Jeschute, and it is due to a total ignorance of standards in the world that he does not know the grief this must cause her. Yet he leaves Jeschute and immediately comes upon Sigune, and the juxtaposition of the two meetings is significant. He expresses pity for Sigune, and a readiness to help her, for ignorant though he may be, he recognizes grief and suffering, and he feels pity. This response to Sigune's anguish seems strange in the boy who has so recently brought a woman to grief and shame, but the incidents thus juxtaposed reflect the basic nature of Parzival's youth, in which elements of intuition and knowledge are still separate. Once more, this represents a significant divergence from Chrétien, who leaves the one encounter with the grieving cousin until after the visit to the Graal Castle. Wolfram, who stresses the importance of compassion in Parzival, brings the two meetings, with Jeschute and with Sigune, close, and so achieves added effect by the comparison. When he desires to aid Sigune, Parzival feels for his javelot and finds also the ring and the brooch which he took from Jeschute. Once more, then, the two encounters are brought together, since the second brings this reminder of the first, and in his genuine wish to help Sigune, he now forces the audience to remember the harm he did to Jeschute. Moreover, the javelot and the jewel are also juxtaposed, the unknightly weapon with which he is to kill his kinsman, and the spoil of his first unchivalric act of violence. Strangely, too, the brooch which he has taken from Jeschute leads him to King Arthur, when the fisherman accepts it in payment for directing him.

That this unknightly deed does, in this way, help him to the seat of knighthood is not so incongruous, however, if one considers that only the knowledge of the ill-deed is lacking in him, and this is to come when he has a knowledge of true courtesy.

The second meeting with Jeschute is carefully positioned, too, for Parzival now has considerable command of the art of chivalry: he has learnt readily the lessons of Gurnemanz, and through Condwiramurs he has come to know love and real happiness. Yet, already, too, he has come to the Graal Castle and neglected his duty there, and, although it remains for Cundrie to reduce him to near-despair, he is already aware from Sigune of his failure. Thus, when chivalry has brought him both joy and sorrow, he comes upon Jeschute, who still rides as the victim of his ignorance, when as a boy he went his way with single-minded determination. The time-lapse is evident.[4] Not only has time produced a change in Jeschute, who is worn and ragged, but Parzival stands before her as a man now, who has come a long way since they last met, but who now approaches the greatest experience of his life. He has proved himself as a knight, though he has failed in the task set him as the future Graal King. The world of chivalry has accepted him, but his greatest test remains. It is impossible, then, for Wolfram to leave him at this point with the stain of the wrong done to Jeschute, and it is apt that he should have this chance to right it, before he must apply himself with all his might to the achievement of the highest goal of Christian knighthood.

At Trevrizent's hermitage, he reconciles the couple by his solemn oath freely given, and so here he atones for the first crime of his youth. Almost five years later, he is to return to the hermitage and, guided by Trevrizent, to atone for the greatest sin of his life, his bitter rejection of God. The years of his grief and lonely wandering stand between these two events, and the return after so long echoes the earlier occasion and stresses the time and experience which lie between.

Thus, just as the meetings with Sigune reflect the passing of time and the changes it has brought about in Parzival, so too do the two encounters with Jeschute, placed at such vital points in his development, reflect a little of his early growth, from a gauche boy into a man with sensitivity and compassion, authority and mercy. More than this, Jeschute herself is important as the first woman Parzival meets when he has left his mother. She is to be followed by Liaze, who awakens in him the awareness of the nature of woman and the hope of love which leads to Condwiramurs. His experience with Jeschute cannot even be described accurately as physical attraction, since he overlooks her beauty in his desire for her ring, which represents womanhood to him. Throughout what is a fairly brief description, Wolfram refers repeatedly to this beauty, which is wasted on the boy. By such observations as

> der knappe klagete'n hunger sân.
> diu frouwe was ir lîbes lieht.   (131,22-23)

Wolfram not only makes the scene amusing, despite its disastrous end, but also suggests the unconcern of Parzival for Jeschute as a woman: Orilus has nothing to fear from this youth. In general Wolfram refrains from detailed description of the beauty of his heroines: he takes it for granted. In the case of Jeschute he gives more elaborate details, to draw attention to the lack of response in Parzival and so indicate the nature of the encounter.

However, beauty is often seen by Wolfram as the outward expression of inward virtue, and this is the case also with Jeschute. Since human virtue partakes of divine perfection, Wolfram naturally sees beauty itself as a divine creation, so that Parzival praises God for the beauty of Condwiramurs (283,2-9) and, in describing Jeschute, Wolfram observes that her beauty is the product of God's art:

> si was geschicket unt gesniten,
> an ir was künste niht vermiten:
> got selbe worht ir süezen lîp.   (130,21-23)

110

As she lies asleep, her beauty is concentrated in her red lips, which
Wolfram uses as symbols of her power to love and to be loved:

> si truoc der minne wâfen,
> einen munt durchliuhtic rôt,
> und gerndes ritters herzen nôt.
> innen des diu frouwe slief,
> der munt ir von einander lief:
> der truoc der minne hitze fiur.
> sus lac des wunsches âventiur.   (130,4-10)

Even when she next meets Parzival and is herself torn and ragged,
her lips glow brightly:

> swiez ie kom, ir munt was rôt:
> der muose alsölhe varwe tragen,
> man hete fiwer wol drûz geslagen.   (257,18-20)[5]

The suggestion is, surely, that her love for Orilus has not grown
less through the months of hardship imposed by him. As with Condwiramurs, Wolfram pictures Jeschute's beauty as a combination of
red and white, the colours of beauty and purity, love and sorrow.
Moreover, he allows an echo of the beauty of Condwiramurs when
he speaks of her teeth as snow-white (130,11), for the mention of
snow brings with it the memory of Parzival transfixed on the plain
of Plimizoel by the remembrance of the pure beauty of his wife.

Jeschute's love for Orilus allows her to accept his unjust treatment of her without bitterness and with no lessening of this love.
Her almost incredible forebearance is reminiscent of the patience
of Grizelda, but even more closely does she resemble Enite, who
was also subjected to cruelty and degradation by her husband. Both
women are reduced to the status of servant, estranged from the
favour of their husbands, yet both endure hardship and humiliation
for the sake of their love. They have in common the patience and
ability to suffer selflessly which both Hartmann and Wolfram re-

111

gard as a feminine attribute. When Parzival encounters Jeschute
on the second occasion, he notes that she is unused to caring for
horses, and one remembers Enite struggling to lead eight horses,
and the boy who is so distressed by her predicament.[6] This inability
to care for horses, a task not expected of a lady, is one manifestation
of the perfect gentility of Jeschute. Her treatment of Parzival on
both occasions reflects this too, and he recognizes it despite her
wretched appearance, for nobility transcends the external.[7] Above
all, it is virtue which shines forth from this woman who is half-
naked, and this Wolfram symbolizes in the whiteness of her skin as
it is seen through the knotted rags. The juxtaposition of such poverty and such virtue is striking, and Wolfram takes advantage of
the opportunity to point out that wealth is not all-important, hinting at the falsity beneath the splendid apparel of some women:

> doch næme ich sölhen blôzen lîp
> für etslîch wol gekleidet wîp.　　　(257,31-32)

Because of her great love, which links her with the great heroines, Jeschute is able to bear the indignity which Orilus imposes on
her, and because of it, too, they are able to be reconciled at a place
sanctified by faith and love of God. Once more, the divine nature of
perfect human love is suggested, for the choice of Trevrizent's hermitage places a blessing on their love. Thus their love, like that of
Herzeloyde and Gahmuret, Sigune and Schionatulander, Willehalm
and Gyburc, Parzival and Condwiramurs, comes to joy through sorrow, and Wolfram interprets the tears of Jeschute as the product of
joy:

> ouch ist genuogen liuten kunt,
> weindiu ougn hânt süezen munt.
> dâ von ich mêr noch sprechen wil.
> grôz liebe ist freude und jâmers zil.　　　(272,11-14)

The tears of Jeschute are for Wolfram proof of her womanhood,
as they are with Belakane, Gyburc, Antikonie and Orgeluse:

> dô lac frou Jeschûte
> al weinde bî ir trûte,
> vor liebe, unt doch vor leide niht,
> als guotem wîbe noch geschiht.   (272,7-10)

Jeschute is remembered, then, despite the brevity of her appearance, as one of the most emphatic examples of that love and chastity which are the basic virtues of Wolfram's ideal heroines.

NOTES

1. ed. cit. 3944ff.
2. 130,3-25. Although Wolfram allows Parzival to kiss Jeschute twice (131,13; 132,20), the kisses mean little, especially if contrasted with the seven kisses (some MSS have twenty) of Chrétien's story, where they were accompanied by amorous, though youthful, speeches from Perceval (ed. cit. 723-728).
3. L. P. Johnson ('Characterization in Wolfram's *'Parzival,'* *Modern Language Review*, Vol. 64, no. 1, 1969, pp. 68-83) attributes Parzival's non-recognition of Jeschute to her own physical condition, rather than to Parzival's spiritual state (p. 80). It is true that Wolfram stresses her wretched appearance, but it is in accordance with Wolfram's concept of the significance of the two meetings that there should be a deeper factor as well.
4. Note, moreover, the careful symmetry in the two pairs of encounters: on the first occasion Parzival meets first Jeschute, then Sigune, on the second, first Sigune, then Jeschute.
5. Chrétien, on the other hand, who is not concerned with giving the impression of a woman filled with a deep and enduring love, says that she is drained of colour: ed. cit. 3746.
6. Hartmann von Aue: *Erec*, ed. A. Leitzmann, Tübingen, 1963, 3580ff.
7. See, for example, 257,6-7, and compare Wolfram's words 3, 21-24.

CHAPTER EIGHT

Liaze

PARZIVAL'S ACQUAINTANCE with Liaze is brief, but it is also very significant in his development. Bodo Mergell is surely right in his assessment of the episode: "Die Liaze-Episode, in ihrer stillen Verhaltenheit eine der zartesten des deutschen Gedichtes und ohne Entsprechung in der Quelle, ist mehr als höfisches Zwischenspiel und muß von Parzival aus verstanden werden."[1] Liaze belongs to that group of people whose influence accompanies Parzival, extending beyond a short appearance in the work, and, like Cunneware, Jeschute and Gurnemanz, for example, she is able to exert this influence because Parzival meets her at a particular period in his life and at a particular stage in his development.

When Parzival rides to the castle of Gurnemanz, he has advanced some way since he left his mother. He has reached Arthur's Court and now wears knightly attire. However, in coming thus far, he has also brought upon himself the burden of two offences, of which he is as yet unaware. His abuse of Jeschute and his killing of Ither are serious mistakes in terms of ordinary humanity, but they represent also sins against the code of chivalry. Knighthood is concerned with two main issues: the art of courtly love and the art of knightly combat. Jeschute's grief and degradation and Ither's death demonstrate Parzival's ignorance of both aspects of knightly behaviour. They are the victims of his ignorance which Gurnemanz and Liaze now remedy to some extent, with instructions ranging from lessons in specific techniques of chivalry to more abstract precepts for life. From Gurnemanz, Parzival learns to honour women and to desire

114

that perfect love in which man and woman are one; and with this introduction to the notion of love, Parzival is introduced too to Liaze, who arouses a new emotion in him.

Since he left Jeschute, Parzival has acquired some knowledge of the world. The son of Gahmuret must surely have observed a little of the behaviour of the knights at Arthur's Court, and now he has learned something about courtly demeanour from Gurnemanz. His approach to Liaze shows, then, just how far he has come since his invasion of Jeschute's tent:

> der gast begunde sich des schemn,
> Iedoch kuster se an den munt.   (176,8-9)

The comparison, which must be apparent to the reader, is emphasized by Gurnemanz, who recalls Jeschute:

> ouch solt an iuch gedinget sîn
> daz ir der meide ir vingerlîn
> liezet, op siz möhte hân.
> nune hât sis niht, noch fürspan:
> wer gæbe ir sölhen volleist
> so der frouwen in dem fôreist?   (175,29-176,4)

The boy who kisses Liaze is shy, for he is vaguely aware now of the serious nature of relationships between men and women, and he approaches the new experience with diffidence. Liaze is the perfect companion for this youthful experience of love. From the stress which Wolfram lays on her nearness to Condwiramurs, it is clear that she comes very close to his ideal of womanhood. She does not, however, quite reach it, for perfection is to come with Condwiramurs, who may well be regarded as a heightened Liaze. Because she must play a subordinate, yet essential rôle, Liaze remains a slight character, a charming picture of youth which will grow into perfection and maturity. This maturity we are not to see, however, for that is not Wolfram's intention in creating this character.

The alterations and additions which Wolfram makes to his source are usually very significant, and Liaze is an important example of such an addition. In Chrétien's version, Perceval passes from his assault on the girl in the tent to acquaintance with Blancheflor. Wolfram found such a transition displeasing, unlikely perhaps, and his conception of the perfect love and marriage of Parzival and Condwiramurs needed a firmer basis than the boyish and unthinking attraction to Jeschute, whose partridges were as inviting to him as she herself. Liaze supplies the link, leading from the physical, and for Parzival meaningless, encounter with Jeschute, to the deep and lasting emotion of his love for Condwiramurs. What Liaze gives to Parzival is the first realization of the relationship possible between a man and a woman. Yet with this realization comes too the vague awareness that his feeling for her is not real love, or perhaps that he is not yet ready to settle down. He rides away from her,

> der meide sælden rîche,
> diu im geselleclîche
> sunder minn bôt êre.　　　　　　　(179,27-29)

It represents no fault in Liaze that she does not achieve the stature of Condwiramurs. Of necessity, she must remain a less prominent character, for Parzival is not ready for love. The reason he gives to her father is that he must prove himself worthy of her and then return to ask for her hand in marriage. In this he is certainly sincere, for it is not in him to say what he does not mean, but he is prompted by other considerations, too, the same desire for action and fame which drew Gahmuret first from Belakane, then from Herzeloyde, and perhaps a feeling, scarcely definable at this stage, that Liaze is not the woman for him. Even with his still incomplete understanding he senses, surely, that she cannot give him that perfect love which he recognizes at once in Condwiramurs.

However, the two women are cousins, and with Wolfram's strong sense of relationship they are thus immediately linked, with the sug-

gestion of a similarity between them. As Parzival rides away, he
is troubled by a longing:

> ôwê wan daz in ruorte
> manec unsüeziu strenge.   (179,16-17)

This is interpreted as a longing for Liaze, but it may as easily be a
longing for the perfect love which is to come to him soon. Possibly
both sensations are within him, and their mingling suggests, too,
how closely the women are linked. This is more powerfully expressed when Parzival is actually brought face to face with Condwiramurs, and his first impression is that here is Liaze once again:

> 'Lîâze ist dort, Lîâze ist hie.
> mir wil got sorge mâzen:
> nu sihe ich Lîâzen,
> des werden Gurnemanzes kint.'   (188,2-5)

There are similarities, of course, as Wolfram intended to imply in
making them cousins, and to Parzival's inexperienced eye the beauty
of Condwiramurs is reminiscent of that of Liaze. Wolfram, however, adds his own comment, for Condwiramurs must be supreme
in beauty as in all else:

> Lîâzen schœne was ein wint
> gein der meide diu hie saz,
> an der got wunsches niht vergaz.   (188,6-8)

Nevertheless, Parzival's reaction indicates the extent to which his
attitude towards women was established by his relationship with
Liaze, and how, in introducing him to the notion of the companionship of women, she inevitably established herself as his criterion
of womanhood. Like all his early experiences, however, this is
merely a stage in his development, and Liaze's place in his scale of
values is taken by Condwiramurs.

Liaze's is a passive rôle, and she influences Parzival simply by her presence. Her passivity may be seen in contrast to Sigune, who, although she, too, is a passive character in some ways, actively influences Parzival by her words and guidance. Just as in a heightened degree Condwiramurs is later to be the goal of Parzival's striving, and Gyburc the impulse to Willehalm's actions, so, by her very nature as a woman, does Liaze inspire Parzival, prompting him to achievements which will make him worthy of her, now that he has glimpsed the love which is the reward of the noble knight:

> er wolt ê gestrîten baz,
> ê daz er dar an wurde warm,
> daz man dâ heizet frouwen arm.
> in dûhte, wert gedinge
> daz wære ein hôhiu linge
> ze disem lîbe hie unt dort.   (177,2-7)

It does not detract from his intention at this point that Parzival is never to return to Liaze. In riding away from her, he outgrows her, yet it remains as a compliment to Liaze that it is Condwiramurs, her cousin and so like her in many ways, who supersedes her in Parzival's affections, for this implies, not a rejection of her, but an affirmation of her significance in his life.

As Wolfram says (179,24-25), it is as the son of Gahmuret that Parzival rides away from the castle of Gurnemanz, for, in acquaintance with Liaze, he has found within him the power of love which is fitting in the son of a man who loved, and was loved by, three noble ladies. Just as Gahmuret was troubled by the memory of Belakane, so is Parzival unable to forget Liaze, although he who never knowingly did wrong is not oppressed by the sense of guilt which marred the joy of Gahmuret. The situation is not the same, however, and Belakane and Liaze, although there is a slight echo, are not parallel figures: one is less conscious of a great loss in the case of Liaze, who was, after all, never married to Parzival, and in fact Wolfram gives no evidence of her loving the young knight. Although Parzival had promised to return when he had proved him-

self worthy of Liaze's love, it is clear that Wolfram does not blame
him for his marriage to Condwiramurs. For Parzival, in his early
development, there is no going back: his relationship with Liaze
marks one stage in his development, and he passes on to his meeting
with Condwiramurs.

Yet the impact of this early experience is a considerable one, and
Parzival does not forget Liaze, any more than his father forgot Belakane, though deeply in love with Herzeloyde. When Condwiramurs
is telling Parzival of her distress and the threat of Clamide, she
happens to mention Liaze, with no more subtle reason than to iden-
tify Schentaflurs for him (195,2-6). Parzival's immediate reaction
is grief at the memory of the girl he had loved yet left behind. He
agrees to help Condwiramurs, and he does so for the sake of Liaze,
whose brother was killed by the present antagonist of Condwiramurs. Later, when Parzival has Clamide in his power, he remembers
how Gurnemanz, the father of Liaze, urged him to be merciful towards his captives:

> dô dâhte der den sic hât
> sân an Gurnemanzes rât,
> daz ellenthafter manheit
> erbärme solte sîn bereit.
> sus volget er dem râte nâch:
> hin ze Clâmidê er sprach
> 'ine wil dich niht erlâzen,
> ir vater, Lîâzen,
> dune bringest im dîn sicherheit.' (213,29-214,7)

Once more, then, it is the memory of Liaze which prompts him to a
fine action, so that she, like Cunneware and Jeschute, exerts a distant influence over this man who remembers her with gratitude and
affection for the part she played in his early life.

She belongs, too, to the line of those who take up the work of
Herzeloyde, instructing and guiding Parzival, whether deliberately
or more indirectly, by the very impact of personality. Herzeloyde

119

had given Parzival some very brief and ambiguous instructions on
behaviour towards women, and these had led to the tragedy of Jeschute. Now, at Gurnemanz's castle, his learning continues, with the
wise old knight to instruct him in the courtly arts, and Liaze, by her
very presence, to allow him to glimpse the joys of knighthood. Only
a woman of her virtue can do this, and Liaze's virtue is revealed,
as so often by Wolfram, in outward appearance:

> Liâzen lîp was minneclîch,
> dar zuo der wâren kiusche rîch.　　　(176,11-12)

Like Condwiramurs, Liaze is seen to be a very fit companion for the
young Parzival, matching him in nobility and good looks.[2] Those
who see him ride to the castle see in Parzival the hope of the end
of the grief of Gurnemanz, with the prospect of a match for his
one remaining child. This, combined with the likeness to Condwiramurs, serves to fill in a little of the character of Liaze, who is otherwise left as a rather shadowy figure. Possibly Wolfram did not wish
to endow her with too much individuality, lest Parzival's break from
her appear too callous, but it is possible also to see her as an almost
abstract personification of womanhood, not, like Herzeloyde and
Sigune, the ideal of womanhood, but rather the embodiment of a
notion which comes to Parzival at this time, of the existence of
woman, and the idea of love.

Together, Liaze and Gurnemanz initiate Parzival into the world
of chivalry, yet in doing so they bring upon themselves the grief
of his departure, for what they reveal to him combines with his innate nobility to take him from them. In leaving Liaze, Parzival
shows his awareness of the meaning of chivalry, and of this chivalry, his personal aim, she is both the impulse and the goal. The situation is frequent, an inevitable product of the knightly order, as
has been seen, that the woman who is won by knightly strife becomes too the goal of all striving for the man who has won her, and
she is herself forced to accept that the man she loves must constantly

Conciencia

prove himself worthy of her love, even if in doing so he must die. Thus Liaze, by arousing in Parzival the first awareness of the power of courtly love, must lose him, when, in his attempt to be worthy of her, he finds a more perfect goal in the person of Condwiramurs.

NOTES

1. *Wolfram von Eschenbach und seine französischen Quellen, II—'Parzival,'* p. 64.
2. 176,26. This has an echo in Wolfram's later description of the perfect match of Parzival and Condwiramurs as they sit together (187,24ff.).

CHAPTER NINE

Cunneware

CUNNEWARE IS ONE of the most interesting women in this group, a figure subtly drawn who increases in depth with closer acquaintance. Like the others, she possesses two levels of significance, one in her own right and the other as a factor in the growth of the hero. The second is dependent on the first, because it is as a highly individualized heroine, who shares some of the qualities of the central women characters, that she is able, like Liaze and Jeschute, to make use of her contact with Parzival in order to influence him and help him to the highest goal of knighthood.[1]

Central to Cunneware's rôle in *Parzival* is the mysterious power she possesses of recognizing the greatest of all knights.[2] The laughter which breaks also the silence of Antanor has been prepared for already, for it is important both to Wolfram's picture of Parzival and of Cunneware herself. Angry with Jeschute and indignant at her supposed infidelity, Orilus refers to his prowess in jousting which he undertook for her sake and which should therefore endear him to her, and, with no apparent necessity, he refers to his sister, the sweet Cunneware:

> ir munt kan niht gebâren
> mit lachen, ê si den gesiht
> dem man des hôhsten prîses giht.   (135,16-18)

The effect of this information, irrelevant at the time, is the immediate realization of the significance of Cunneware's later reception of

Parzival. Moreover, when Orilus tells of the condition on his sister's laughter, Parzival has just committed, in his assault on Jeschute, the first serious crime of his youth. He is far, as yet, from the knightly supremacy which the maiden's laughter is to prophesy.

Even when he arrives at Arthur's Court, he is totally unversed in the art of chivalric behaviour.[3] Only Kei, outspoken and ruthless, gives expression to his indignation and astonishment at Cunneware's verdict on this gauche youth (152,7-12), but he is surely not alone in his surprise at her reaction. Yet Cunneware is unerring in her judgement, and from this moment she becomes involved in Parzival's growth towards the ideal of chivalry which she here predicts for him. It is essentially a case of growth towards the ideal, of course, and hers is not a reasoned verdict, based on observation and judgement, but a mysterious, almost magic, power. This becomes even more apparent, when, in his next act, the senseless killing of Ither, Parzival again commits a serious crime against the unwritten code of humanity and the code, unknown to him, of knightly conduct. How far does he now appear from the ideal knight, and how unlikely Cunneware's intuitive prediction!

Just as he had previously shown his natural compassion in his ready sympathy for Sigune, Parzival again feels pity, this time for the suffering of Cunneware and Antanor, and his grief is intensified by his awareness that he is responsible for their suffering. The incident, then, is comparable too to Parzival's encounter with Jeschute: in both cases he is the cause of suffering, unintentionally in both cases, but the difference lies in the fact that he is conscious of his responsibility here, whereas only much later is he to become aware of his injustice to Jeschute. At this stage, he does not know how to avenge Cunneware: his reaction, unschooled as he is, is to seize his javelot, but Cunneware is not to be avenged with an unknightly weapon. Because the crowd is so dense around the Queen, Wolfram says, he does not throw it (153,19-20), and in this way he is saved from a further crime, as well as from further impairing the honour of Cunneware. It is a stroke of good fortune that he is prevented

from hurling the only weapon he possesses, for his revenge is thus
postponed to a more fitting occasion, when, as a knight, he is able
to punish Kei for his abuse of a lady. What matters at this point is
that he is ready to act in the defence of Cunneware. Like Sigune,
she is the object of his pity and his youthful eagerness to act in the
aid of a fellow-being. The two women receive his natural compassion, which, by an all too literal interpretation of the teaching of
Gurnemanz, he is so fatefully to suppress later.[4]

The relationship between Parzival and Cunneware is possibly a
unique one in Middle High German literature: it is based on admiration and mutual respect, friendship without the complexity of
minne. Parzival is indebted to her, both because she saw in him potentially the noblest knight and because she suffered for his sake.
The second reason places him under a courtly obligation to avenge
her, but the first binds her close to him in affection and gratitude.
Once he has avenged her, their relationship may develop into the
deeper one of friendship, without the unbalancing influence of obligation. His spontaneous, youthful desire to take his revenge on the
man whom he has seen maltreating the lady is perfectly in accordance with his later sense of knightly obligation to avenge her: what
was then a human hatred of injustice and brutality is supported
when, as a knight, he is required by the code of chivalry to avenge
a wrong committed because of him. The memory of the wrong still
not righted accompanies Parzival for a long time, until at the Plimizoel he is able to injure Kei:

> sus galt zwei bliwen der gast:
> daz eine leit ein maget durch in,
> mit dem andern muoser selbe sîn.   (295,28-30)

Until that time Parzival never forgets his duty towards Cunneware,
and the interval is punctuated by incidents after which he sends
his defeated opponents to serve Cunneware. Thus, in their turn,
Kingrun, Clamide and Orilus (198,23ff; 214,30ff; 267,10ff) all
journey to Cunneware with the message, of which they are the liv-

ing proof, that the Red Knight has not forgotten her, nor the wrong he has yet to right.

Assured by Gawan that it was indeed Kei whom he injured, Parzival can leave aside the qualms which made him hesitate to come before Arthur, and so he meets once more the lady who recognized his innate greatness. It is a joyful reunion, sealed by honour reestablished on both sides, and Cunneware welcomes him as her knight (305,16-17). In his constancy to her, she sees the beginning of a justification of her prediction for him:

> 'Got alrêst, dar nâch mir,
> west willekomen, sît daz ir
> belibt bî manlîchen siten.
> ich hete lachen gar vermiten,
> unz iuch mîn herze erkande,
> dô mich an freuden pfande
> Keie, der mich dô sô sluoc.
> daz habt gerochen ir genuoc.
> ich kust iuch, wære ich kusses wert.' (305,27-306,5)

The gesture of drawing a cord from her own dress to tie his cloak suggests a seal on the bond which exists between them (306,18-20). The scene is notable for the joy and the sense of well-being which pervade it. Parzival has reconciled Jeschute and Orilus and thus repaired this destructive act of his youth, and now he has also taken his revenge on Kei. Accepted within the assembly of the Round Table and acclaimed by the Lady Cunneware, he walks between her and King Arthur. Of Cunneware, Wolfram says

> diu was dô trûrens worden vrî   (310,12)

and the simple statement is full of meaning, suggesting not only that she is happy now that Parzival has avenged her for the physical wrong done her by Kei, but also that he has begun to prove her right in her recognition of his potentialities and that she herself is freed from a life without laughter.

125

Into this scene of rejoicing, Cundrie breaks, with the news which is to bring about the destruction of Parzival's joy. In this new phase of Parzival's experience, Cunneware plays her part, too, for she who has asserted his future supremacy as a knight is now his companion in grief.[5] She is the first to weep at the sorrow and dishonour which Cundrie has brought upon him, and her distress is the sign to the other ladies of the court:

> Cunnewâr daz êrste weinen huop,
> daz Parzivâl den degen balt
> Cundrîe surzier sus beschalt,
> ein alsô wunderlîch geschaf.
> herzen jâmer ougen saf
> gap maneger werden frouwen,
> die man weinde muose schouwen.   (319,12-18)

Her rôle in his sorrow is not a passive one, however, for she comforts him with her presence when he prepares to depart. In the simple gesture of taking him by the hand (331,19-21), she pledges her support in his trial. It is she who puts on his armour, performing one last service of friendship towards the man who is to wander friendless for almost five years. She tells him that she will share in his sorrow until it comes to an end, even though she now has cause to be happy in her marriage to Clamide (332,24-30).

The marriage of Cunneware and Clamide is a strange one, in some ways, since Clamide's forceful wooing of Condwiramurs places him in an unfavourable light from the start. Cunneware is too significant a figure, however, for Wolfram to have arranged her marriage lightly,[6] and so it is perhaps preferable to accept the marriage and draw conclusions about the character of Clamide from the fact that Wolfram allows him to marry the virtuous Cunneware.[7] Moreover, Parzival himself actually helps to arrange the match (327,15-30), and in his affection and esteem for Cunneware, he would never have consented to a marriage with an unworthy man. There remains, however, always the memory of Condwira-

murs threatened by the powerful Clamide, and as excuse for him
one can only offer the explanation that his love for her was so great
that it overcame his sense of justice and proportion. That he loved
her is clear from his grief when he loses her, and he does not pre-
tend that his love for Cunneware is as strong as that which he bore
Condwiramurs. Cunneware represents for him a compensation,
though incomplete, for the woman he lost, as he explains to Parzival:

> ob ich an freuden sol genesen,
> sô helft mir daz si êre sich
> sô daz ir minne ergetze mich
> ein teil des ich von iu verlôs,
> dâ mich der freuden zil verkôs.   (327,8-12)

Quitar merito

Thus Cunneware is linked with Condwiramurs by means of Clamide. Yet already the two women are linked, for Parzival has a
deep affection for Cunneware, though without the abiding passion
which exists in his love for his wife. When she bids Parzival farewell, she is acting in the place of his wife, and, like Condwiramurs,
she shares in his grief.[8] The two loves can exist side-by-side, neither
detracting from the other, and this harmony is shown in the incident on the Plain of Plimizoel, when Parzival is transfixed by the
sight of the blood in the snow, which reminds him of his wife, yet,
jolted by the chance movement of his horse out of this state of sense-
lessness, he is able to deliver the blow which avenges Cunneware,
before returning to his former state, obsessed by love for his wife.
In Parzival's affections, as in Clamide's, then, Cunneware is second,
and this is to be expected, for Condwiramurs must remain supreme,
in beauty, virtue and in love. For Cunneware, too, Clamide is clearly
second to Parzival, to whom she is devoted: as a married man he is
lost to her, yet Clamide tells how she refuses the service of all other
knights in her devotion to this one (327,1ff).

That Cunneware is linked with Condwiramurs as she is, is evidence of her perfection. She possesses the power to love with con-

stancy, and, in her grief at Parzival's degradation, is revealed the compassion which is an essential human virtue. As with Condwiramurs, there is little elaboration on these virtues, however, for it suffices that she is loved by Parzival, and that to her is given the honour of being with him as he embarks on the quest which will bring him at last to the achievement which she has predicted for him.

NOTES

1. Although the original idea of the maiden who laughs for the first time when she sees Perceval is Chrétien's (ed. cit. 1035ff), Wolfram develops her as a character far beyond his source.

2. This is clearly a fairy-tale motif, though in *Parzival* there remains little of the fairy-tale character about Cunneware. See Grimm: *Kinder- und Hausmärchen*, Große Ausgabe, Berlin, 1890, p. 22ff. 'Der gute Handel' and p. 196ff. 'Die goldene Gans.' In the latter story it is a 'Dümmling,' too, who succeeds in making the princess laugh. See also M. Ramondt: "Zur Jugendgeschichte des Parzival,' *Neophilologus* 9, 1924, pp. 15-22.

3. See, for example, 148,19; 149,25-150,2; his unprovoked attack on Ither; his desire to defend Cunneware by hurling his javelot.

4. The desire to avenge the wrong done to the lady is absent in *Le Conte del Graal* where, with less stress on compassion in the whole work, the boy now rides away:

> Einsi cil crie et cele pleure
> Et li vallés plus ne demeure,
> Ains s'en retourne sanz conseil
> Aprés le Chevalier Vermeil. (ed. cit.1063-1066)

Rather as Chrétien allows Perceval to see his mother lying dead and to ride on, he here permits him to place his own purpose before the need of others.

5. This aspect of her rôle is, of course, absent in Chrétien's story, where *la pucele qui rist* is not endowed with the same significance. M. F. Richey points out the essential difference between the two women ('The Independence of Wolfram von Eschenbach in Relation to Chrétien de Troyes as shown in *Parzival* Books III-VI,' *Modern Language Review*, 47, 1952, pp. 350-361): in particular p. 361.

6. It is not like the marriages at the end of Book XIV, for example, where one feels that Wolfram is at pains to supply a happy conclusion to the light-hearted Gawan episodes.

7. Wolfram's obscure reference to Cunneware as 'lôs' (284,12) has no apparent textual justification. Martin's explanation of the line is unconvincing, although it is difficult to find another: 'Vielleicht verdiente Cunneware diesen Vorwurf insofern, als sie gefährliche Kämpfe veranlaßte, weshalb auch Orgeluse *lôs* heißt 711,19. (E. Martin: *Parzival und Titurel: Zweiter Teil, Kommentar*, Halle, 1903).

8. M. F. Richey ('The Independence of Wolfram von Eschenbach. . . . ,' p. 361) also notes this link between Condwiramurs and Cunneware when she speaks of 'a new symmetry of design in Wolfram's presentation of Condwiramurs and Cunneware, the two women to whom Parzival is most attached, the one his wife and queen, the other his most devoted friend.' Of Cunneware she says: 'She is the last to be with him before he leaves, her bodily presence a support to him then as well as the unseen presence of Condwiramurs.'

   In Parzival's farewell from Cunneware as he sets off on a vital new stage in his career there is, moreover, perhaps also an echo of his departure from his mother.

CHAPTER TEN

Cundrie

CUNDRIE IS AN outstanding example of Wolfram's ability to enlarge a single incident, and to endow a relatively minor character with a new and profound significance. In *Le Conte del Graal*, the *pucele laide* came to reproach the hero for his failure at the Graal Castle, and she left, never to reappear. Her act, then, was a destructive one which, owing to the unfinished state of the work, was never repaired or justified. Nor is it likely that Chrétien ever intended to vindicate her action, for she is a very minor character, her rôle a purely functional one and she herself lacking in human individuality. Her speech to Perceval is a much more objective accusation, without the deeply felt anger of Cundrie which needs to be vindicated.

Cundrie upbraids the hero even more violently than her predecessor and casts him into despair, but Parzival is to come through despair and emerge a more complete being for having done so. This emergence culminates in his call to the Graal Kingship, and to Cundrie is given the honour of bringing him the news. The perfect symmetry is in itself an indication of Wolfram's conception of the character of the Graal Messenger, for she makes two very similar appearances at Arthur's Court, one marking the beginning of Parzival's lonely wandering and the other marking his emergence from grief. The first thrusts him into the greatest sorrow that exists for a Christian, the rejection of God, and the second raises him to the peak of earthly happiness. The link between the two is to be found in Wolfram's words after Cundrie has finished her first fateful speech to Parzival:

> und dennoch mêr im was bereit
> scham ob allen sînen siten. (319,6-7)

Side-by-side with the despair and shock which she has produced in him is this vital sense of 'shame,' which, according to Wolfram, will save him from real wrong-doing (319,8-10). *Scham* is a concept closely linked with *diemuot* which, as both Trevrizent and Anfortas explain, is essential in the Graal King (798,30; 819,18-19): only now does Parzival become fully conscious of his failure, and only this consciousness of failure can bring to the fore the *scham* which will enable him to strive unceasingly from the moment of realization. The way to the Graal lies through *scham* to true humility, and Cundrie, in evoking the first, has set him on the long and arduous path towards his goal. From this moment, then, she becomes deeply involved in his destiny and instrumental in bringing about his success: the part which she plays is later confirmed unambiguously in the fact that she is the one who leads him to his kingdom.

For the first appearance of Cundrie, Wolfram is indebted to Chrétien. Her ugliness and the violence with which she reproaches Parzival even exceed the description of the source. Like Chrétien, he describes the Graal Messenger in extravagant terms, giving the impression of a creature barely human:

> über den huot ein zopf ir swanc
> unz ûf den mûl: der was sô lanc,
> swarz, herte und niht ze clâr,
> linde als eins swînes rückehâr.
> si was genaset als ein hunt:
> zwên ebers zene ir für den munt
> giengen wol spannen lanc.
> ietweder wintprâ sich dranc
> mit zöpfen für die hârsnuor. (313,17-25)[1]

Significantly, however, Wolfram omits one observation of Chrétien's:

> Onques rien si laide a devise
> Ne fu neis dedens enfer   (4617-4618)

for it is important that Cundrie should not be linked with the powers of hell. In other respects, Wolfram has done nothing to soften the impression of evil which is dominant also in Chrétien's work. In remaining loyal to his source in this case, he has acted against his normal custom of announcing virtue by external beauty, for it is essential to his concept of the character of Cundrie that she is virtuous and well-intentioned, despite the immediate effect of what she says.

Certainly the impact of her words is made all the greater by her terrifying appearance, and the terror which she inspires combines with the harshness of her pronouncement to cast Parzival into a state of rebellion and humiliation. Yet only thus is he to come to true happiness, so that, by what appears to be a destructive act, Cundrie is able to produce a wholly salutary issue. Even at this early stage, then, when all else is overwhelmed by the violence of her words to Parzival, and by her appearance of evil, Wolfram anticipates the happy end and hints at the essential goodness of Cundrie. He introduces her as 'ein magt gein triwen wol gelobt' (312,3), and when she has finished speaking she weeps, for

> die maget lêrt ir triuwe
> wol klagen ir herzen riuwe.   (318,9-10)

In view of the importance which Wolfram attaches to *triuwe*, there can be no doubt that at this point he is wishing to indicate that, despite her awful appearance and the harshness of her attack on Parzival, this woman is in no way evil, since she possesses the supreme virtue of loyalty. It is loyalty to Anfortas and to the whole of the Graal Kingdom which prompts Cundrie to upbraid Parzival for his failure at Munsalvæsche, and, as later events show, she is also demonstrating her loyalty to Parzival himself, since in pointing out his negligence she prompts him to the quest, which will bring him to the Graal. Her anger is the result of a profound sense of grief and disappointment, for Cundrie is herself deeply involved in the fate of the Graal Family: unlike the *pucele laide*, who does not express personal sorrow, Cundrie weeps when she has finished her speech to Parzival:

> Cundrî was selbe sorgens pfant.
> al weinde si die hende want,
> daz manec zaher den andern sluoc:
> grôz jâmer se ûz ir ougen truoc.   (318,5-8)

On many other occasions, Wolfram has allowed tears to demonstrate love and loyalty in a woman, and in this early expression of her grief, Cundrie, too, is shown to possess the virtue which Wolfram has already praised in her and which is subsequently to be revealed to the full.

The *pucele laide* reproaches Perceval for not enquiring why the lance bled, nor whom the Graal served (4652ff): his lack had been one of observation and curiosity. Cundrie, on the other hand, sees in his silence a lack of compassion for the suffering of a fellow-being (315,26-316,3). His failure, then, becomes a failure in human feeling, and so Wolfram endows his coming to the Graal, his failure there and his return, with a deeper significance. Like everything appertaining to Wolfram's Graal, the character of Cundrie is deepened, too, in comparison with the ugly messenger of Chrétien: Cundrie comes not only to tell Parzival of his failure, but also to make him aware of the seriousness of his neglect, which is the disregard of his responsibility towards his fellow-men. She thus becomes concerned in his growth, from the time when she must point out his failure to the time, more than four years later, when she is given the honour of leading him to the highest goal of knighthood. The tears she sheds in her grief at the harsh words she must utter and at the circumstances which make them necessary, are an indication of her personal concern for the tragedy of the Graal, but Wolfram supplies a further cause of grief, for he allows Cundrie to lament that the son of Gahmuret and Herzeloyde should have transgressed in such a way and that she should have the task of making it known. She is conscious of the irony of such loss of knightly honour in the son of the noble knight, and astonished and grieved that the gentle and deeply sensitive Herzeloyde should have borne a son who has failed to display his pity for human suffering (317, 11-318,4). From this point of view, too, Cundrie is personally disappointed by Parzival's failure: not only her link with Anfortas and the Graal, but her link also with the parents of Parzival contributes to her grief, and her loyalty belongs both to the kingdom which she serves, and to the child of the noble and virtuous Gahmuret and Herzeloyde. Thus Wolfram motivates the anger of Cundrie by means of the *triuwe* which he has previously praised in her, and thus also does he succeed in softening the figure of the Graal Messenger in anticipation of her second appearance.

Between the two principal appearances of Cundrie there are, however, several brief mentions of her which make her into a fuller character and serve also to strengthen the initial impression of good despite apparent evil. Her close relationship with the Graal is emphasized when Sigune tells Parzival that Cundrie brings her food from the Graal (439,1-5). Her hideous physical appearance is explained when Malcreatiure comes as messenger to Gawan. There follows the strange explanation of the lack of control of the daughters of Adam which produced strange, misshapen beings, of which Cundrie and her brother are examples (518,1ff). By once more introducing Sekundille, who sent the strange pair to Anfortas, Wolfram explains, too, how the servant of the heathen Queen becomes the messenger of the Christian Graal. This explanation of her origin serves also to explain the list of talents, which Wolfram, unlike Chrétien, had attributed to her at the first encounter (312,19-25).[2] She also possesses a knowledge of medicine, a talent constantly linked with a knowledge of magic: this Wolfram reveals when Arnive tells Gawan of the special ointment which Cundrie brings her from the Graal, where it is used to ease the wound of Anfortas

(579,23-580,1). By explaining Cundrie's origin in this way and linking her with the less familiar learning of the East, Wolfram has supplied an explanation of much which would otherwise seem strange in her. She is a woman with extensive and unusual knowledge, the legacy of her birth and the years she spent in the heathen kingdom of Sekundille; her appearance is explained by Wolfram and, though it is true that his explanation is a strange one, it is as if he sought to explain it in order to show that Cundrie is a real human being, rather than the inhuman creature which some have found her to be.[3]

The splendour of her attire, which is in itself in such striking contrast to her ugliness, also belongs to her Eastern origin,[4] for she comes from the court of Queen Sekundille, in whose country, Wolfram says, the mountains were all of gold and the rivers carried down precious stones instead of grit (519,14-17). When she comes to Arthur's Court for the second time, her appearance is, if anything, even more spectacular. The rich, hooded cloak which she wears hides her identity, so that she can plead with Parzival for forgiveness before she reveals herself. Güntert sees in her a type of *Frou Werlt*, disguising her true ugliness in a splendid exterior,[5] but here he is surely overlooking an essential feature of Wolfram's concept of the figure of Cundrie. In her, true goodness is hidden beneath the ugliness of her exterior. Far from disguising it, the spectacular attire exaggerates it, and so she becomes an even more terrible figure than Chrétien's *pucele laide*, whose physical appearance was not made worse by incongruous apparel. It is true that when Cundrie comes for the second time she is disguised by her splendid clothes, but this is to conceal her identity, not her ugliness. The comparison with *Frou Werlt*, with inner corruption hidden by a beautiful exterior, cannot be sustained, then, since in Cundrie Wolfram is attempting to show the reverse, one in whom goodness belies an evil exterior. There is evidence in Wolfram's work of his dislike of the deceit of some women, who attempt to disguise their true appearance. In the Prologue he observes that some women are praised for their beauty, but that what matters is the virtue beneath, without which they will not receive his praise (3,11-24). In describing Jeschute he takes the opportunity to point out that he prefers her, a pure woman though in rags, to many a well-dressed woman, with the implication that beneath the elaborate dress there may be falsity and evil (257,31-32). Here, surely, would be the type of *Frou Werlt*, but in Cundrie is found the opposite: her clothes, exaggerated and spectacular as they are, must surely be taken as an aspect of her hideous appearance, which is in complete contrast to her inner goodness.[6]

The reader does not immediately gain a full insight into the virtue of Cundrie, however. Apart from Wolfram's repeated references to her *triuwe* and the tears of sorrow which she sheds, there is, after her first appearance, no firm proof of her goodness. The next mention of her is as the one who sent Parzival in search of the Graal with her harsh words:

> ich meine den werden Parzivâl,
> den Cundrîe nâch dem grâl
> mit unsüezen worten jagte. (433,9-11)[7]

She is still associated only with his grief and lonely wandering and, at this stage, when he seems so far from success, the positive, constructive result of her words is obscure. As time passes, however, she becomes more closely associated with the Graal, and instances are given of her charity and service. It is Cundrie, as we have seen, who supplies Sigune with food (439,1-5) and Cundrie who provides the salve which eases the pain of Anfortas (579,23-30). Thus by the time she comes to Arthur's Court for the second time, Wolfram has prepared in some measure for the good news she bears. The contrast with the previous occasion is most striking. Her coming had then been 'daz siufzebære zil' of Parzival's joy (312,1), but now she is greeted with enthusiastic welcome:

> wol dem künfteclîchen tage! (778,13)

136

Her tidings then had been the source of grief to many people (312, 5) but now they are sweet tidings (778,14-15). The astonishment of the onlookers is no less this time, but it lacks that sense of fore- boding which characterized the earlier occasion, when Wolfram had hinted in advance at the disastrous content of Cundrie's message (312,5; 312,30; 313,14-15; 314,12; 314,22). Her first action now is to go to Parzival and beg his forgiveness. Only then does she reveal her identity, and still Wolfram does not spare the details of her ugliness:

> ir ougen stuonden dennoch sus,
> gel als ein thopazîus,
> ir zene lanc: ir munt gap schîn
> als ein vîol weitîn.   (780,19-22)

Even before she reveals her identity, she is explicitly 'diu werde, niht diu clâre' (780,2), for in her Wolfram has created a figure unique in his work, in whom great worth is not accompanied by beauty.

The news which she brings raises Parzival to great joy, and she leads him with Feirefiz to Munsalvæsche. Yet even though she is the bearer of glad tidings, she thanks King Arthur and Feirefiz for intervening on her behalf to gain forgiveness of Parzival 'nâch grôzer schulde' (780,5). Clearly, she considers herself guilty for having reproached him so fiercely before, but if she was indeed guilty, then it was a guilt incurred without intent. The implication from Wolfram seems to be that any guilt she may bear lies in her allowing her anger to gain control over her.[8] She is like Signune in this respect, for both of them express in forthright terms their disgust at Parzival for his failure, but both are prompted by their innate virtue. Moreover, both produce a wholly desirable effect in him, so that Parzival can later look with gratitude upon these two women who first made him aware of his mistake and so spurred him to make amends. Wolfram's affirmation of the rôle of Signune comes in Parzival's own desire to visit her again in her cell. His affirma-

tion of the rôle of Cundrie comes when she is Parzival's companion
on his great journey. Moreover, with them on that journey goes
Feirefiz, the man who had loved Sekundille, the former mistress of
Cundrie: Cundrie is the heathen messenger of the Christian Graal
and linked equally with the two sons of Gahmuret.

NOTES

1. cf. *Le Conte del Graal*, ed. cit. 4614-4637. In some ways Cundrie suggests the female counterpart of the strange creature
   whom Kalogreant, like Calogrenant, encountered in the forest. Hermann Güntert (*Kundry*, Heidelberg, 1928), discussing the ugly appearance of Cundrie, points to Celtic traits and
   supplies a number of examples of hideous apparitions in Celtic stories (p. 21ff). The whole problem of the possible fore-
   runners of Cundrie has been disregarded in this examination,
   which intends to view her as a human being, as Wolfram un-
   doubtedly saw her, and in relation to the other women in his
   works. Some interesting ideas on the subject are contained in
   the work by Güntert and in an article by P. Ackermann: 'Who
   is Kundrie—What is she?' *The Literary Review*, Fairleigh
   Dickinson University, Teaneck, New Jersey, Vol. 2, no. 3,
   1959, pp. 458-468.

2. H. Güntert (p. 35) points out that the Eastern lands were renowned for astrology, mathematics and philosophy, and that,
   since Eastern learning was connected also with the idea of
   magic, Wolfram gave Cundrie the additional name of *la sur-
   ziere*.

3. Wagner found in her 'ein wunderbar weltdämonisches Weib'
   (Letter to Mathilde Wesendonck, 1st August 1860). Güntert
   (p. 25) suggests that she is a ghost, coming from the *Toten-
   reich* where women are kept prisoners. G. Ehrismann ('Märchen im höfischen Epos,' *Beiträge zur Geschichte der deut-*

schen Sprache und Literatur, 30, 1905, pp. 14-54) also sees her as a being from the land of the dead (p. 47ff).

4. In spite of the reference to the French fashion of her cloak (313,8), the brilliant colours and elaborate style of her clothes seem to point to Eastern influence.

5. p. 34 and p. 42ff.

6. cf. also E. Martin p. LXI.

7. Although the effect of her speech is to send him off in search of the Graal, it cannot have been her intention, since she believes, like Sigune and Trevrizent, that the Graal is not to be found by the one who seeks it.

8. See his statement 312,3-4.

PART III

CHAPTER ELEVEN

The Pilgrim's Daughters

THERE IS ALSO in Wolfram's works a small group of women who exemplify a vital feature of his view of woman. These are the young heroines, Obilot, Alyze and the Pilgrim's daughters, in whom he shows the beginnings of perfect womanhood. They anticipate the mature heroines, but Wolfram shows also the particular power which is theirs by virtue of their youth.

The two daughters of the Pilgrim whom Parzival meets on Good Friday are in one respect unique among Wolfram's women. Their very brief appearance and the lack of deliberate characterization would perhaps lead them to be included among his minor heroines, yet the rôle which they play is by no means minor and causes them to rank rather with the central heroines.

There can be little doubt that Wolfram intended to show that these two young women are instrumental in Parzival's return to faith, hence are vital in his eventual achievement of the Graal Kingship.[1] The encounter occurs when Parzival has come very close to Munsalvæsche, yet failed to reach it. Though physically he was very near to it, his spirit was not in accord with the spirit of the Graal: his unrepentant state is made clear when Wolfram draws attention to the difference in apparel between the Pilgrim and the knight:

> in selhem harnasch er reit,
> dem ungelîch was jeniu kleit
> die gein im truoc der grâwe man.   (447,5-7)

143

The group of pilgrims will ultimately bring Parzival to a new assertion of his faith, and they are themselves the embodiment of faith, walking as they do, barefoot, despite the cold and their noble birth. As the embodiment of faith which has its source in love, the group of pilgrims becomes a symbol, and the two unnamed maidens are to be seen as the epitome of womanhood, recalling in their very brief appearance the virtue and the powers shown at greater length in the principal heroines. Above all, it is love which they represent, and the episode reveals love in its various manifestations. As they journey barefooted and wearing only rough cloaks on the bitterly cold Good Friday, their faith, the love of God, radiates from them and finds expression in the beauty of their faces (446,18). The strength of this love allows them to pay no heed to the cold or to their high social rank, and thus they journey in true humility, united with Herzeloyde and Gyburc in a love which transcends the material.

In their treatment of Parzival, they reveal that depth of human love which is both the beginning and the manifestation of true Christianity. Like Gyburc and Sigune, they possess such intense love that they are able to impart it to others. It is above all their compassion for the lonely knight which leads them to suggest to their father that he is being too harsh and that he should offer hospitality and warmth rather than reproaches. They seek to show him the path to Christianity, not with cool moral instruction, but with a practical demonstration of Christian love. Their words inspire their father to a gentler approach and to an offer of hospitality for the sake of Christ (449,19-20). Without the urging of the two women, the Pilgrim, despite his worthy intentions, would have failed to offer this simple Christian gesture which actually produces in Parzival the desire to return to God. As the girls look with such kindness upon Parzival, he notes the redness of their lips:

> Parzivâl an in ersach,
> swie tiur von frost dâ was der sweiz,
> ir munde wârn rôt, dicke, heiz.   (449,26-28)

144

In this single description of their physical appearance, Wolfram includes a wealth of significance, for wherever he mentions red lips, it is to suggest the power of love of their bearer.[2] He does not, therefore, exclude from this encounter the element of mutual human attraction between the young man and the two women, but more important to him is the spirituality of their love. Parzival is impressed by their beauty and, on the deeper level, recognizes it as the revelation of their love of God, yet he feels that he must decline their offer of hospitality, because he does not share this love (450, 14-20). Nevertheless there can be no doubt that their compassion has moved him, and he rides from them with grateful thanks for their kindness (450,27-29). The knight who now rides away is truly the son of Herzeloyde: in him lie latent the virtues of his mother, and these are now stirred for the first time for many months:

> hin rîtet Herzeloyde fruht.
> dem riet sîn manlîchiu zuht
> kiusch unt erbarmunge:
> sît Herzeloyd diu junge
> in het ûf gerbet triuwe,
> sich huop sîns herzen riuwe.　　　　(451,3-8)

Because he is the son of Herzeloyde, the virtues of compassion and repentance are hidden within him, and these virtues are aspects of the love and humility which he has seen personified in the Pilgrim's daughters. Thus these two young women arouse in him the virtues which he possesses as the son of Herzeloyde, and womanhood personified in them joins with that of his mother to direct him to Trevrizent.

Parzival's own parting words to Gawan echo in this sudden change of heart, though not in the way he intended them. Woman, now that he has reached his lowest ebb of grief and desolation, is not a substitute for God, but a means to Him. In the radiant faith of the Pilgrims, but above all of the young daughters, he has glimpsed the way to true happiness and is almost prepared to try to find it for himself. Prompted by a longing for that same goal which they have attained, he turns and looks at them, and Wolfram says that it is the *triuwe* of the maidens which prompts them, too, to follow him with their eyes (451,26-27). Parzival sees the beauty in them which is both physical and the revelation of their inner beauty, and with this last look he rides away, longing to find himself the God whom they worship.

Nowhere is the spirituality of Wolfram's concept of womanhood so powerfully or succinctly expressed as in this, one of the central scenes in *Parzival*. Here is implied the nature of perfect womanhood, with its principal virtues of love and humility, and the power to impart these virtues. Herzeloyde gave to Parzival the sensitivity without which their influence would not have been felt; Condwiramurs sustained him with her love until he came to meet them; Sigune, in directing him as she thought towards the Graal, directed him towards them. Three noble women, then, have made this encounter possible, and the nobility of the two young girls now ensures that it is a fruitful one. Though their appearance is brief, the rôle of the Pilgrim's daughters is vital, both to the theme of the work, and to Wolfram's whole concept of womanhood.

NOTES

1. Though Perceval, too, encounters a group of pilgrims (ed. cit. 6217-6330), the tone of Chrétien's episode is very different. It is not love which they show to Perceval, but indignation at his lack of respect for the Holy Day. There are not two virtuous young girls, but ten ladies, and the incident lacks the delicate charm of Wolfram's, where the perfect womanhood of the two sisters is shown as instrumental in Parzival's return to faith.

2. For example, 130,4-10; 176,10; 187,3; 405,19.

CHAPTER TWELVE

Alyze N⁰

ALTHOUGH FOR the character of this young heroine Wolfram is indebted very largely to his source, he presents in her a woman who is perfectly in accord with the whole picture of womanhood in his works. As in the *Aliscans*, her rôle is twofold, for she is seen both in her relationship with Rennewart and as mediator between Willehalm and her mother. Alyze as she emerges in Wolfram's work is different, however, from Aélis in the *Aliscans*, and the difference is a very subtle one. The love of Aélis and Rainouart was happy in its outcome: they are able to marry when Rainouart accepts baptism. The episode is completed. Wolfram's Rennewart was a mysterious character, and the end of the story was to remain uncertain. Consequently the story of Alyze is left also without an end, and she herself is an almost mystical figure.

Despite the brief appearance of Alyze, she cannot be placed, with Bene and Itonje for example, among the minor characters. Rather does she belong with those of Wolfram's heroines who embody the virtues which he sees as the essence of womanhood. She has not the stature of Herzeloyde or Sigune, Condwiramurs or Gyburc, for her rôle clearly does not demand it, yet, like Obilot, she possesses the same virtues as they do.

Little has been written about Alyze, perhaps because the young heroine is overshadowed by the significance of Gyburc, but Dietlinde Labusch touches on a vital aspect of the nature of the young girl when she says "eine magisch-natürliche Wirkung geht von Alyze aus. . . . Ihre Jugend und Schönheit sind ein Wert, ein Mys-

147

terium."[1] It is in the ability of Alyze to calm the rage of Willehalm and to reconcile him with her mother that this almost supernatural power is seen most clearly. There is only a slight change from the source, but the change is vital to Willehalm's concept of her power. In the source, too, Guillaume's anger had faded in the face of the beauty and pleading of his niece.[2] The impression is more striking in *Willehalm*, however, where the very entry of Alyze causes Wille-halm to regret what he has done:

> Dô kom des küneges tohter
> Alyze. done mohter
> sîne zuht nimmêr zebrechen:
> swaz er zornes kunde sprechen,
> der wart vil gar durch si verswign.
> swes ir muoter was bezign
> von im, wærz dannoch ungetân,
> ez wære ouch dâ nâch fürbaz lân.   (154,1-8)

For a long time Alyze remains silent, while Wolfram describes her great beauty, which is accentuated by the magnificence of her attire (154,1-156,30). The description is matched, in length and enthusiasm, by no other in all the praise which Wolfram gives to his heroines. He achieves by this means a unique impression of Alyze at her first appearance, and he succeeds in focusing complete attention on her, as indeed must the attention of the whole court rest on her as she stands there. His description shows the extent to which he sees beauty as the reflection of virtue, and the beauty of Alyze is, above all, the reflection of her power to heal and to reconcile. Thus Wolf-ram says of her:

> man möht ûf eine wunden
> ir kiusche hân gebunden,
> dâ daz ungenande wære bî.   (154,21-23)[3]

and

148

si gap sô minneclîchen schîn,
des lîhte ein vreuden siecher man
wider hôhen muot gewan.   (155,4-6)

and again

ir lîp was wunsch des gernden
und ein trôst des vreuden wernden.
swem ir munt ein grüezen bôt,
der brâhte sælde unz an den tôt.   (155,9-12)

Once more he sees the beauty of a woman as a radiant light:

von der meide kom ein glast   (155,13)[4]

and it is likely that he once more had the Virgin Mary in mind, when he wrote of this young girl, with her power to reconcile and to atone for the wrong of another woman.[5]

With the humility which Wolfram sees also as essential in a noble woman, Alyze falls at the feet of Willehalm, a silent gesture which moves him no less than her subsequent pleas (155,27-156, 3). When at last she begins to speak, Alyze weeps, linked with the whole group of women, whose perfection is revealed by Wolfram in their tears. In her speech, Alyze touches the heart of Willehalm by two distinct approaches. She begs him to spare her mother for her sake, and she points out that in punishing the Queen for her misguided words he will bring shame upon their whole family (157,15-24). Finally, she beseeches him for mercy for the sake of his mother and his wife (157,25-30). Her mention of Gyburc is a poignant one, for it brings with it a sudden reminder of the real cause which is at stake:

diust mir leider nu ze verre komn.   (157,30)

Like Obilot, who will be 'kranz aller wîplîchen güete' (*Parzival* 394,12-13), Alyze possesses the power of the young woman to reconcile and to bring love where hate has been. It is a power which Wolfram gives most emphatically to these two, and the implication is surely that their very youth gives them a clearer insight and a greater ability to perceive the essentials which elude their more complex elders.

In this first and most impressive appearance of Alyze, youth and beauty do indeed amount to 'ein Mysterium,' and the remainder of what Wolfram tells of her is fittingly somewhat remote and uncertain. The love which has grown up between her and the young Rennewart is revealed only indirectly, when Wolfram relates the history of the heathen boy (284,1-30). Even so, the intensity of their love is felt:

> ir zweier liebe urhap
> volwuohs: die brâhtens an den tôt
> und liten nâch ein ander nôt   (284,14-16)

and some of the pain of parting is contained in Wolfram's casual explanation:

> der künec wolt in hân getouft:
> er was von Tenabrî verkouft:
> des wert er sich sêre.
> dô muos er von der êre
> Alyzen gesellekeit
> varn: daz was ir beider leit.   (284,17-22)

Only now is realized the true significance of the kiss which Alyze gave to Rennewart when he left (213,21-28). What had seemed little more than a courteous leave-taking is now seen as a farewell between two secret lovers who may never meet again. The marriage which closes their story in the *Aliscans* is not even anticipated in *Willehalm*, where Rennewart is driven into battle by his love for Alyze and is never seen to emerge from it:

> Alyzen minn die von im brach
> dar nâch in kurzen zîten
> in tôtlîchen strîten.   (285,20-22)[6]

Thus Alyze remains a figure of great virtue and a certain mystery, linked with Repanse de Schoye by the stress on her virginity and her pure goodness which still permits of a chaste capacity for passion. The conversion of Feirefiz to Christianity through his love for Repanse de Schoye is not, however, echoed in a similar conversion of Rennewart. The happier tone of *Parzival* allowed such a conclusion, but *Willehalm* does not, so that the story of Alyze remains incomplete, and she herself is denied the fulfilment which in another context might have been hers.

NOTES

1. p. 155, note 144.
2. cf. B. de Kok, pp. 103-104.
3. In the healing power of her beauty and virtue, Alyze recalls the young girl in *Der arme Heinrich*.
4. Compare also *Willehalm* 200,12-16.
5. Compare in particular Wernher's *Maria* (ed. cit. 4150-4151):

> dâ lac diu maget reine
> in einem grôzen liehte.

His description of Alyze is comparable with that of Herzeloyde (64,4-6); Repanse de Schoye (235,15-18); Condwiramurs (186,19-20).

6. The love of Alyze and Rennewart resembles that of Sigune and Schionatulander. In both cases Wolfram shows the power of a very youthful love, and both loves are kept secret. cf. L. Wolff ('Der Willehalm Wolframs von Eschenbach,' *Deutsche Vierteljahrsschrift* 12, 1934, pp. 504-539). He speaks of the love as "jene früh erwachende Liebe, die Wolfram auch im Schionatulander behandelt hat' (p. 536).

CHAPTER THIRTEEN

Obilot

OBILOT IS a less complex figure than her elder sister, Obie. In her there is no such development as one sees in the older girl. She is as she appears to be, a little girl content to play childish games on the one hand, yet conscious already of her nature as a woman. It is precisely this fusion in her of the child and the woman which Wolfram uses and so endows her with a particular power which links her with Alyze, and both of them with the great adult heroines of his creation.

B. Q. Morgan finds Obilot a less successful figure than her counterpart in *Le Conte del Graal*. He even goes so far as to say that "for the first time we have to report a relative failure as compared with Chrétien."[1] Surely, however, in saying this he is disregarding the different aims of the two writers in their treatment of the younger sister. Chrétien shows a child whose actions are those of a child, precocious in some ways, although this same precocity does not make her any less credible or any less fitted to the rôle she is required to fulfil in *Le Conte del Graal*.[2] Wolfram has done more, however, than present, as Chrétien does, a charming picture of a young girl who seeks and finds in Gauvain a knight who is willing to avenge the wrong done her by her spiteful elder sister. Wolfgang Mohr suggests that Wolfram thinks of his Obilot as a little older than Chrétien's *pucele as manches petites*, consequently as a little wiser.[3] Perhaps this is true; certainly Wolfram anticipates in Obilot the woman she is to become and this is basic to his depiction of her.[4]

In Chrétien's version, the two sisters are sharply differentiated:

152

they are clearly separated by age and personality. The blow which the elder sister gives to the younger divides them completely, and Gauvain is called upon to avenge it. No such distasteful incident occurs in Wolfram's version. It is true that the sisters are opposed in their opinions regarding Gawan, but since Obie's is governed by her love for Meljanz, the requital of this love causes her anger to subside and the rift between herself and Obilot disappears.[5] Unlike Chrétien, then, Wolfram sees the two sisters not in opposition, but rather partaking of the same qualities of love and charm. Obviously, this is not evident throughout in Obie, although the end of the episode hints at a similarity between the two girls which is suggested already in the similarity of their names.

In the near-tragedy of the love of Meljanz and Obie, Wolfram shows the power of the convention of courtly love, its potentiality for harm. Obie is conscious of her power as a woman to command her lover, but Obilot is not less conscious of the power in herself. Both sisters employ this privilege, the one ruthlessly and dangerously, the other with wisdom and with a happy issue. Nor is there anything unlikely in the fact that Obilot is aware of her power as a woman to offer her love to a man in exchange for his service. In the society of *Parzival*, a young girl would certainly be familiar with the courtly code, and she would not need to be precocious in order to possess an awakening sense of her own place in this society. B. Q. Morgan's objection lies in what he considers the precocious nature of her speech to Gawan. Of it he says: "In fact, it must be admitted that her conversation with Gawan is not appropriate to her age or character; into her mouth are put worldly-wise utterances quite out of keeping with the rest of her story."[6] If one examines the conversation, one finds, however, a number of fairly conventional phrases, which admittedly sound strangely adult, but which may well have been culled from speeches overheard, or even from actual instructions received from the teacher she mentions (369,9-10). It is true that she shows a familiarity with courtly language,[7] but she does not necessarily know what it means, rather as her proud promise to give Gawan a favour ends when her young play-mate reminds her that she has only dolls to offer him (372,18). This incident, delightful in itself, serves also to show the juxtaposi-tion in Obilot of the child and the adult. It has a precedent in the occasion when Lippaut comes upon his daughter playing with her friend at the game of rings: asked what she is doing there, she re-plies that she has come to ask Gawan to serve her (368,10-18).[8]

Even though she may not understand the full implication of *minne*, Obilot is nevertheless sincere when she chooses Gawan as her knight, and the relationship is an important one for her. The whole episode is pervaded with the sense of her childlike earnest-ness, and Gawan responds with gentle charm. His first reaction is to reject her offer, which represents a temptation to offend against his *triuwe*, as he has already explained to Lippaut (366,20-367,2; 370,8-12). However, remembering Parzival's parting words to him, he sees that perhaps it is right for him to trust this child, who has the makings of the woman whom Parzival praised above God:

> nu dâhter des, wie Parzivâl
> wîben baz getrûwt dan gote:
> sîn bevelhen dirre magde bote
> was Gâwân in daz herze sîn. (370,18-21)

The reference at this stage to the words of Parzival in his desola-tion is certainly not a chance one.[9] Rather does it suggest that Obilot, young as she is, has the beginnings of purity and womanly good-ness. The suggestion recurs more explicitly later in the assertion by Meljanz:

> Obilôt wirt kranz
> aller wîplîchen güete. (394,12-13)

Gawan agrees to fight for Obilot's sake, though having previously voiced the objection that she is too young to offer love (370,15-16). He accepts her sleeve as a token and fights for her with character-

istic valour. Afterwards he gallantly hands over to her his captives
(394,4-10). All this he does with perfect regard for the conventions of chivalry and with an earnestness which echoes her own. He
does not, however, deceive her, for he has already made the position clear to her, and for him the episode resembles a game, played
in all sincerity, yet with the awareness throughout that it is un-
real.[10] Wolfram reminds his audience of this when he speaks of the
kiss which Gawan gives to Obilot:

> er dructez kint wol gevar
> als ein tockn an sîne brust.   (395,22-23)

The comparison of Obilot with a doll at this point breaks the illu-
sion and prepares for the end, when Gawan takes his leave. Obilot,
who has become involved in the relationship as a child often does
in a game, is not prepared for it to end:

> Obilôt des weinde vil:
> si sprach 'nu füert mich mit iu hin.'   (397,15-16)

Gawan grieves, too, for perhaps he also has played the game a little
too earnestly and has become a little involved himself, as Wolfram
knew was possible.

In her relationship with Gawan, then, Obilot anticipates the woman she is to become. This is not the whole of her rôle, however,
and in the other aspect of it, too, are seen those qualities which allow
her to rank among Wolfram's ideal women. When Obie accuses
Gawan, saying that he is a merchant, Obilot is indignant, not because she is herself actually involved with Gawan at this point, despite the attraction she may already feel towards him, but because
the suggestion is clearly an unjust one:

> du zîhst in daz doch nie geschach:
> swester, des mahtu dich schamen:
> er gewan nie koufmannes namen.
> er ist sô minneclîch getân,
> ich wil in zeime ritter hân.   (352,20-24)

155

Young though she is, she immediately recognizes Gawan for the noble knight he is. She behaves at this stage with much greater wisdom and control than Obie, for—and here one must clearly follow Wolfram's example in excusing the elder sister—she is not swayed by the power of love. She is outraged by her sister's abuse of her privilege to command her lover:

> 'unfuoge ir dennoch mêr gebôt:
> geim künege Meljanz von Lîz
> si kêrte ir hôchverte vlîz,
> dô er si bat ir minne.
> gunêrt sîn sölhe sinne!'   (353,18-22)

Not out of spite for her sister—spite is certainly alien to her nature —but from a mixture of the desire to have this knight as her own and perhaps a childish desire to compensate him for the abuse of her sister, Obilot resolves to ask him to serve her:

> sîn dienst mac hie lônes gern:
> des wil ich in durch liebe wern.   (352,25-26)

Only later does she learn that her father has asked Gawan to aid him but has not received a definite reply from him (368,19-21). Her request is the same when she finally puts it to Gawan, knowing now that it is in her father's interest for her to succeed in gaining Gawan as her knight, and she is sincere when she ends her plea:

> sît och mîn vater helfe gert
> an friwenden unde an mâgen,
> lât iuch des niht betrâgen,
> irn dient uns beiden ûf mîn [eins] lôn.   (370,4-7)[11]

That Obilot's appeal to Gawan has the consequence of his fighting for Lippaut is interesting, for it links her once more with Alyze, whose appeal to Willehalm to control his temper succeeds because of the charm with which she delivers it: the result in that case, with control restored on both sides, is that Willehalm is given the military support he requires. Neither Obilot nor Alyze acts deliberately as a strategist: each behaves with feminine grace and so produces a favourable reaction in the man in each case. Even more apparent is the resemblance between Obilot and Alyze in their rôles as reconcilers. Alyze reconciles her mother and her uncle; Obilot brings Obie and Meljanz together. Only because she sees, in her wisdom, that the two must be reconciled and that it is in her power to reconcile them, are the lovers reunited. When Meljanz offers his pledge to her, she gladly transfers it to her sister:

> Meljanze si dâ nâch gebôt
> daz er sicherheit verjæhe,
> diu in ir hant geschæhe,
> ir swester Obîen.
> 'zeiner âmîen
> sult ir si hân durch ritters prîs:
> zeim hêrren und zeim âmîs
> sol si iuch immer gerne hân.
> ine wils iuch dwederhalb erlân.'   (396,10-18)

Wolfram comments that God is speaking from her young mouth (396,19), for hers is indeed the rare and divine gift of peacemaker.

In Alyze and Obilot, then, two not very prominent characters, Wolfram shows the qualities of the ideal woman already in a young girl. His picture of Obilot, like that of Alyze, is a delightful one, of purity,[12] love, wisdom and grace, giving promise of the mature womanhood of Herzeloyde, Condwiramurs and Gyburc, yet enhanced by the youth and freshness which were already present, though not fully developed, in the younger sister of Chrétien's creation. Speaking of Obilot, W. Stapel observes: "In diesem Kinde ist die Funktion des Weibes metaphysisch vertieft. In ihrem lyrischen Zauber ist sie nur mit einer Gestalt wie der Mignons zu vergleichen. Was ihren metaphysischen Gehalt betrifft, so verweise ich auf die Bedeutung Gretchens am Schlusse des *Faust*."[13] What he says may be extended also to Alyze and the Pilgrim's daughters, for all these young heroines possess a particular distinction among Wolfram's women characters, combining the power of their youth and sweetness with the power which they already possess and share with the great heroines. Wolfram and Goethe do indeed join in this view of the nature of woman, and her rôle in the life of man.

NOTES

1. p. 189ff.
2. For a detailed account of her rôle in *Le Conte del Graal* see Martin, pp. 281-282.
3. W. Mohr ('Obie und Meljanz. Zum 7. Buch von Wolframs Parzival' in *Gestaltprobleme der Dichtung. Günther Müller zu seinem 60. Geburtstag am 15. Dezember 1955*, Bonn, 1957, pp. 9-20). Wolfram does not actually say how old Obilot is, although 370,16 offers a hint; but she is probably about eight, at the most ten.
4. This does not necessarily mean that he thought of her as older, but that it was more fitting to the rôle she was to play that she should possess already the first traces of maturity. cf. X. von Ertzdorff ('Fräulein Obilot: Zum siebten Buch von Wolframs Parzival,' *Wirkendes Wort*, 12, 1962, pp. 129-140): 'Fräulein Obilot ist kein Kind mehr wie die Pucelle as manches petites, sondern eine, wenn auch noch ganz junge, höfische kleine Dame' (p. 129).
5. See p. 175 and p. 178 below.
6. p. 191.
7. See, for example, 369,22-27; 371,1-8.
8. The game of rings is known from *Willehalm* 327,8 to have been a game for children. E. Martin (on line 368,12) suggests how it was played.
9. It is interesting, moreover, that in following the advice of Parzival, Gawan actually incurs the risk of killing him.

10. It seems reasonable to interpret Gawan's behaviour in this way, although one may not disregard the fact that, for him too, there is some genuine attraction: 370,20-23; 372,9-12. cf. X. von Ertzdorff (p. 133): 'Aber die Begegnung mit Obilot ist für ihn eine Begegnung in der Form höfischer Minne, eine Begegnung, die er sehr ernst nimmt, die ihn aber nicht für dauernd bindet, weil er ein anderes Ziel vor sich hat.' W. Mohr (p. 15) sees the whole episode as a time of 'Entpersönlichung' for Gawan. The notion is clearly prompted by Obilot's remark: 'ir sît mit der wârheit ich' (369,17). Mohr is unable to accept that Gawan can enter into this relationship in normal circumstances: 'Aber er kann von sich selbst frei werden, indem er Obilots abstraktes Spiel mitmacht und sich durch die Verwandlung in 'Obilot' der Minne schlechthin anheimgibt.' This seems an unnecessarily elaborate interpretation. H. Sacker (p. 78) also speaks of the relationship as a game. It is important, however, to see that this is not how Obilot herself sees it.

11. W. Mohr (p. 14) interprets this as cunning on the part of Obilot and adds: 'Sie formuliert dies doppelte Anliegen energisch genug am Ende ihrer Rede.' Once more, he seems to misjudge her.

12. Purity does not exclude a certain incipient sensuality, however.

13. W. Stapel: 'Wolfram von Eschenbachs Parzival,' *Wolfram Jahrbuch*, 1955, pp. 9-27.

PART IV

CHAPTER FOURTEEN

Ampflise

FOUR OF Wolfram's heroines represent an aspect of mediæval life which he could hardly ignore. These are Ampflise, Obie, Antikonie and Orgeluse, the court ladies of his works, and they are basically unlike the other women of his creation. In them he depicts a different level of human associations from the deep and spiritual relationships of his other heroines, yet close study shows that, ultimately, they resemble these other heroines to some extent. These four are linked with one another by the courtly code, which placed the lady in a position where she might demand the service of her knight, and reject or reward him as it pleased her. Ampflise is the true liege-lady of Gahmuret; Obie and Orgeluse wield their power over Meljanz and Gawan; even Antikonie, whose relationship with Gawan is different, nevertheless belongs to this group of women, with their more superficial, courtly relationships. Yet they diverge from the prototype of the court lady and become integrated into Wolfram's picture of womanhood.

Ampflise is a most intriguing figure. She never actually appears in the work, and her relationship with Gawan is revealed only /hmuret? gradually and never fully. Thus Wolfram has created a figure of some mystery, who remains in the background as a powerful force in Gahmuret's life. She is comparable, perhaps only, with Sekundille, who also never appears, but who nevertheless exercises a very great influence over Feirefiz. The love of the two women is the guiding force in the lives of their husbands, spurring them to deeds of valour, and both women have a further claim on the sympathy of the reader, since each is displaced by another love, which is to be an even greater one.

It is Ampflise's fate that she is herself the victim of the chivalry which she taught Gahmuret. His marriage to Herzeloyde is the most complete expression of the teaching she gave to him, yet though it bears witness to his loyalty to her as his liege-lady, it also brings the destruction of her hopes of marriage with him herself. Ampflise, like Sekundille, is a tragic figure. That Gahmuret loved her is evident, but such was the bond which linked them that his love could find most potent expression in his marriage to Herzeloyde.[1] Gahmuret's love for Belakane and Herzeloyde is revealed in Feirefiz and Parzival, the physical proof of his perfect union with both women. Of his love for Ampflise there is no such proof. Rather is it revealed in his own perfection as a knight, hence in the perfect chivalry of his sons. The products of the love of Gahmuret and Ampflise, then, are abstract qualities, and there is some justification for regarding Ampflise herself as an abstract symbol of knightly greatness, and the goal of his striving.

His love for Ampflise and his own conception of the bond which exists between them do not detract from his love for Herzeloyde. The two loves are different, and, for Gahmuret, they can exist side-by-side. This is shown in his words to her messengers, when he explains that in marrying Herzeloyde, he is doing his duty as Ampflise's knight, thereby manifesting his love for her:

> dô si mir gap die rîterschaft,
> dô muos ich nâch der ordens kraft,
> als mir des schildes ambet sagt,
> derbî belîben unverzagt.
> wan daz ich schilt von ir gewan,
> ez wær noch anders ungetân. (97,25-30)

For Ampflise herself, however, his action in marrying Herzeloyde is a much more final, a tragic one. In the letter she sends Gahmuret, pleading for his love and service, she appears no longer as the abstract symbol of chivalry, as the liege-lady content to be served and admired from afar, but as a woman who loves a man and who desires to marry him. The earnestness of her appeal is reflected not only in the letter but also in the desperate attempts of her messengers to persuade him (87,7-16; 97,13-24).[2] Their anger, as they depart without taking their leave, expresses the indignation of their Queen, spurned in her love by one who owes her his loyalty, but the tears of the three pages suggest perhaps more the grief of the woman who has lost her chance of marriage with the man she loves (98,13-14).

The end of the story of Ampflise, then, is rejection and disappointment. Yet, with an irony rarely equalled by Wolfram, this very rejection represents Gahmuret's most complete recognition of Ampflise and his debt to her. To understand the full implications of this culmination of their relationship, it is necessary to examine the relationship itself, as Wolfram shows it.[3]

Ampflise is first mentioned very briefly in *Parzival* as Gahmuret leaves home, setting out on what is to be a career of great chivalry:

> Als uns diu âventiure saget,
> dô het der helt unverzaget
> enpfangen durch liebe kraft
> unt durch wîplîch geselleschaft
> kleincetes tûsent marke wert.
> swâ noch ein jude pfandes gert,
> er möhtz derfür enphâhen:
> ez endorft im niht versmâhen.
> daz sande im ein sîn friundin.
> an sînem dienste lac gewin,
> der wîbe minne und ir gruoz:
> doch wart im selten kumbers buoz.   (12,3-14)

She is not yet named, for this is only a passing mention, which serves as M. F. Richey puts it "to enhance the impression of Gahmuret's compelling charm, and to bring out one of the most deeply ingrafted traits of his nature, his susceptibility to the bitter-sweet passion of love."[4] It serves also to lay the foundation for the later, more detailed references to Ampflise which Wolfram can then introduce with the words:

> Ein wîp diech ê genennet hân . . . .   (76,1)

The first reference to her looks both forward and back, then: forward to the fuller account of the relationship at the time of Gahmuret's marriage with Herzeloyde and Ampflise's public acknowledgement of her love for him, and back to the time when Gahmuret won her favour and together they laid the foundations of a relationship which was to endure for many years, until the end of Gahmuret's life, in fact. In passing quickly over his first mention of her, Wolfram founds the figure of Ampflise in the remoteness which is hers throughout. Like the great storyteller he is, he arouses interest which he will satisfy only later.

For an account of the beginnings of the relationship between Gahmuret and Ampflise, with the sequel in the gifts which Ampflise sent him, the reader must look to Gahmuret's own explanation to Herzeloyde:

> wir wâren kinder beidiu dô,
> unt doch ze sehen ein ander vrô.
> diu küneginne Amphlîse
> wont an wîplîchem prîse.   (94,27-30)

He tells of their youthful acquaintance and of the material benefits which he received from her:

> mir gap diu gehiure
> vom lande de besten stiure:
> (ich was dô ermer denne nuo)
> dâ greif ich willeclîchen zuo.   (95,1-4)

More important, however, is the knowledge of chivalry which he obtained from her:

ich brâht in Anschouwe
ir rât und mîner zühte site:
mir wont noch hiute ir helfe mite,
dâ von daz mich mîn frouwe zôch,
die wîbes missewende ie flôch.   (94,22-26)

He acknowledges her as his liege-lady both here, in his efforts to
deter Herzeloyde from her persuasion:

jâ diu ist mîn wâriu frouwe   (94,21)

and later in his message to Ampflise when he has agreed to marry
Herzeloyde. It is because of her, he says, that he is a knight and
she cannot therefore wish him to behave in a manner not befitting
a knight (97,25-30): he must abide by the code of knighthood and
act in accordance with the judgment now passed. He concludes his
message with a declaration of his lasting love for her:

ich sül iedoch ir ritter sîn.
ob mir alle krône wærn bereit,
ich hân nâch ir mîn hœhste leit.   (98,4-6)

There is some temptation to question the sincerity of such a declaration from the man who is clearly attracted to Herzeloyde, but a
similar problem arises, in any case, with Belakane, whom he also
loves very deeply, but whom he nevertheless abandons in favour of
Herzeloyde. For this Wolfram supplies an explanation, when he
refers to the fairy nature of Gahmuret which responds to the spring-
time and requires that he shall fall in love again:

sîn art von der feien
muose minnen oder minne gern.   (96,20-21)

Love is a basic requirement of Gahmuret's nature, and so he is capable of declaring, in all sincerity, his lasting love for Ampflise,
while about to enter into a marriage with Herzeloyde, which does
not detract from his love for Belakane.

Gahmuret's love for his two wives, different in each case, is different in turn from the love he has for Ampflise. His relationship with her is basically that of the knight towards his liege-lady, but the original relationship has developed into the deeper one of love, and this is clearly mutual. Hitherto, the possibility of marriage has been barred, but with the death of the King of France, her husband, Ampflise now finds herself in a position to woo Gahmuret:

> Nu was ouch rois de Franze tôt,
> des wîp in dicke in grôze nôt
> brâhte mit ir minne:
> diu werde küneginne
> hete aldar nâch im gesant,
> ob er noch wider in daz lant
> wær komen von der heidenschaft.
> des twanc si grôzer liebe kraft. (69,29-70,6)

In these lines Wolfram suggests the power of the love of Ampflise which is echoed in the desperate attempts of her messengers. As for Gahmuret, he was often troubled by love for her, but there is a suggestion that this has lost in intensity, although his reaction to her letter suggests that this is only a temporary abatement and that the memory of her can quickly stir him. Certainly he did once love her deeply,[5] and the very sight of the letter is enough to arouse emotion in him. It is significant, however, that his reaction is to bow when he sees the letter, a suggestion perhaps that contained always in his love for her is the respect due to the high-ranking lady from her knight (76,21). It is the letter which prompts Gahmuret to go into the joust:

> an disem brieve er niht mêr vant.
> sîn härsnier eins knappen hant
> wider ûf sîn houbet zôch. (77,19-21)

His sadness lifts, and he fights for his lady Ampflise:

Gahmureten trûren flôch.
man bant im ûf den adamas,
der dicke unde herte was:
er wolt sich arbeiten.   (77,22-26)

There is no doubt that his love for Ampflise has been renewed with
the arrival of the letter:

aldâ wart von Gahmurete
geleistet Ampflîsen bete,
daz er ir ritter wære:
ein brief sagt im daz mære.
âvoy nu wart er lâzen an.
op minne und ellen in des man?
grôz liebe und starkiu triuwe
sîne kraft im frumt al niuwe.   (78,17-24)

Thus with the irony which pervades so much of her story, Ampflise
has, in sending him this letter, ensured that he shall marry another
woman, for it is precisely due to these deeds of valour accomplished
for her sake that he wins Herzeloyde. Yet despite the tragic outcome for Ampflise, this joust bears witness to his love for her, rank-
ing in significance as it does with the battle between Parzival and
Feirefiz, in which each is spurred by the thought of his lady.

Like the love of Condwiramurs and Sekundille in that battle, the
love of Ampflise comes to Gahmuret across a great distance. One
of the chief qualities of her love is its power to ignore time and
space, and this impression is strengthened by Wolfram's treatment
of her, for she remains at all times a distant, vague figure.[6] Much is
implicit in this treatment, for in keeping her aloof, Wolfram stresses
her importance as a powerful, almost abstract force in the life of
Gahmuret. He suggests also something of the regality which surrounds this lady, who does not appear herself, but sends first her
treasures, then her messengers. Nor does Wolfram describe Ampflise, and this omission serves also to increase her remoteness from

reality. He does, however, allow her to point out her own beauty when she is recommending herself to Gahmuret and stressing her superiority over Herzeloyde in all respects:

> ich bin schœner unde rîcher,
> unde kan och minneclîcher
> minne enphâhn und minne gebn.   (77,13-15)

Only here does Wolfram allow a very ordinary human feeling to touch the figure of Ampflise, a womanly fear of her rival which is expressed in this boast and gives to the distant Ampflise a new warmth. Her words are matched in *Titurel*, when Herzeloyde fears that Ampflise has put the thought of love into the mind of Schionatulander, in order to grieve her through Sigune and so have her revenge (*Titurel* 122,2-124,4).

It is to *Titurel* that one must look for the remainder of the story of Ampflise as Wolfram gives it; yet even here it is not completed, for the account is brief and episodic. What matters for the story of *Titurel* is that Ampflise gave Schionatulander to Gahmuret as a page at the time when he became a knight (*Titurel* 39,1-2). Thus she is responsible, though indirectly, for the meeting of Sigune and Schionatulander, and Herzeloyde's fear that it was Ampflise who taught Schionatulander the art of love is not quite unfounded, although she allows her own dread of her rival to supply the motive. Schionatulander did act as messenger between Gahmuret and Ampflise during this period of their relationship, and he certainly did come to know of love.[7] *Titurel* treats a period in the relationship of Gahmuret and Ampflise which is not covered in *Parzival*. Though slight, the account which it gives serves to indicate the length of time of the acquaintance which began when they were children, endured through his marriage with Belakane and continued until his marriage with Herzeloyde. In the two works, Wolfram creates in Ampflise a subtle figure, enigmatic yet powerful, remote yet real, one who embodies the type of the liege-lady, and yet transcends the type and becomes an individualized woman, whose story is a strange and tragic one.[8]

NOTES

1. D. M. Blamires (p. 46) discusses the relationship between Gahmuret and Ampflise, concluding, quite rightly, 'Ampflise causes the difficulty by wishing to become Gahmuret's wife.'
2. Of the letter M. F. Richey (*Gahmuret Anschevin*, p. 37) says 'It contains, in the first place, a declaration of love, impassioned in feeling, yet restrained in utterance—a confession of thoughts that burn through the measures and ornate diction in which they are clothed.'
3. It is interesting that in her imaginative account *Herzeloyde in Paradise*, Oxford, 1958, M. F. Richey has Gahmuret reunited in heaven, not with Belakane or Herzeloyde, but with Ampflise. One may ponder in vain on this whimsical notion, but it does raise the question of just how much affinity the courtly Gahmuret had with his liege-lady.
4. *Gahmuret Anschevin*, pp. 4-5.
5. Compare the almost identical expressions of love in 12,14 and 76,24: this surely suggests a mutual love and a powerful one.
6. Added to the vagueness of Wolfram's picture of Ampflise is the fact that it is built up only gradually, a piecing together of slight information and hints. K. Kinzel (p. 55) comments of Ampflise: 'Es ist neben Sigune die einzige gestalt, welche uns so andeutungsweise bei verschiedenen gelegenheiten vorgeführt wird.' This is true, except that it ignores Sekundille, who is characterized in a very similar way (see p. 224ff). Kinzel goes on to say, however: 'Merkwürdig ist, daß in echt künstlerischer weise ganz dunkle züge erst allmählich zur völligen klärung gebracht werden.' It is exaggerating the figure of

Ampflise and also misunderstanding her significance to see her as 'völlig klar': a certain mystery is an essential feature of her character and her rôle in *Parzival*.

7. This Wolfram himself says: *Titurel* 54,1-3. cf. also M. F. Richey (*Schionatulander and Sigune*, p. 43.)

8. Her remoteness is not incompatible with individuality; in fact it is a part of Wolfram's individualization of her. The opposite view is taken by K. Kinzel (p. 57): 'Die figur der Ampflise ist einzig in ihrer art im Parzival, Wolfram führt sie uns nicht persönlich vor und hat deshalb auch keine mühe darauf verwant sie zu individualisieren.'

CHAPTER FIFTEEN

Obie

WHEN WOLFRAM came to Chrétien's story of the two sisters which forms the substance of Book VII of *Parzival*, he gave the sisters similar names and clearly wished to imply a very close connection between them. Almost certainly Obilot is a diminutive of Obie,[1] but to regard Obilot as a younger version of Obie is to misunderstand Wolfram completely. This is not the nature of the relationship between them. Rather does Obilot, the younger sister, anticipate the path which will be taken by the older girl, and in Obie herself Wolfram shows the development towards his ideal of womanhood. That Obie will approach this ideal is by no means apparent early in the story, for once more Wolfram was faced with a problem posed by his source: the events as related in *Le Conte del Graal* required an elder sister in complete opposition to Wolfram's idealistic concept. He selects a compromise solution, whereby he admits the failings of Obie but provides also an explanation of them, and so makes it possible for her to play a similar rôle in his work to the one she played in *Le Conte del Graal*, but without disturbing to any extent his own concept of the nature of woman.

Wolfram possessed a deep consciousness of the tragic in life, and above all he shows an awareness of the sorrow which is the companion of joy, and particularly of love. Repeatedly in his works he shows that this juxtaposition is innate in the demands of the chivalric life. To be worthy of the love of a woman, a man had to prove himself a noble knight, and constantly to renew his reputation in order to retain her love. There was another side to the same problem, for it meant that a woman could press her lover to extreme action, could make great, often impossible, demands on him. In the ill-fated loves of Belakane and Isenhart, Galoes and Annore, and above all of Schionatulander and Sigune, Wolfram shows the tragic results of such demands, given and accepted in love, yet paid for by the death of the man and the grief and remorse of the woman. In the love of Obie and Meljanz, Wolfram shows another incipient tragedy, which is yet averted and ends in happiness. It begins with the woman's insistence that her lover should prove his worth before he dares to ask for her love and that the outcome is, nevertheless, a happy one, accords with the more light-hearted tone which is present throughout the Gawan section of *Parzival*.[2]

In adopting the incident from Chrétien, Wolfram endowed it with greater significance, too, and he makes the reader of *Parzival* more conscious that involved here is a basic problem of the life of chivalry. In *Parzival* there is a deeper awareness than in *Le Conte del Graal* that the outcome could easily be a tragic one, for there is in Wolfram's account a desperate urgency which is not present in Chrétien's. In *Le Conte del Graal*, the unnamed elder daughter of Tiebaut demands of Melians de Lis that he should perform acts of chivalry before he can win her.[3] With her father, she arranges a tournament which will give him the opportunity to show his valour. Such a situation, which placed all the responsibility with the woman, was unpleasing to Wolfram. He diverges from Chrétien, but in doing so he widens the entire issue, and what was a courtly tournament becomes a grim battle.[4] Obie refuses to accept Meljanz until he has proved himself, and this enrages him. He turns his anger upon her father, who, he says, has taught her such arrogance (347, 7-14). The situation, then, bitter enough already, is made graver by the fact that in *Parzival* Meljanz is a powerful king and has in his service a number of knights, all ready now to join him against Lippaut.[5] An additional emotional problem arises, for Lippaut has loved and served Meljanz since the death of the latter's father, and yet he is repaid by this act of insult and aggression. Thus what was, in Chrétien, a relatively small conflict, pointless in itself but local in consequence, becomes in *Parzival* a bitter battle, with large forces on both sides and the promise of widespread disaster as its outcome.[6]

That this ominous situation is the direct consequence of the behaviour of Obie and Meljanz is more apparent in Wolfram's account, too, and the reader is never allowed to forget that their foolishness is the reason for the conflict, for mention of it occurs throughout (345,26; 346,3-347,30; 353,18ff; 365,11ff; 392,13ff). The responsibility, moreover, rests with both of them, and once more this represents a divergence from Chrétien, where it is the whim of the woman which causes the trouble. Without entirely removing the responsibility from Obie, Wolfram gives a large share of it to Meljanz, for it is he who declares war on Lippaut, as a revenge for the taunting words of Obie, and Wolfram refers often to the anger of Meljanz, clearly seeing his guilt in this lack of control (344,14-18; 347,15; 349,1). Obie's interpretation of her power as a woman to command her lover combines with his indignation and sense of slight to bring their love into peril. Although Wolfram's Obie is less objectionable than her counterpart in *Le Conte del Graal*, she is nevertheless the originator of a much more serious situation. Yet Wolfram has removed from her much which was displeasing to him in the woman of the source. Certainly, the spiteful elder sister of Chrétien's version was quite repugnant to Wolfram, and in his Obie he softens her characteristics to a considerable extent and gives to her a new emphasis. In Chrétien, the undignified bickering of the sisters is a large and unattractive part of the whole episode,[7] and it casts an ugly shadow over the figure of the elder sister. Wolfram reduces this considerably and omits the fact of the elder sister's striking the younger.[8] Such behaviour is out of the question in a heroine of Wolfram's, even if in other respects she is far from perfect.[9] Wolfram succeeds in integrating the sisters' quarrel more closely into the wider issue of the battle, subordinating the first to the second. Although this has the effect of changing the rôle of Obilot to some extent,[10] it also places Obie in a slightly better light than in *Le Conte del Graal*, where she is seen equally as the woman who inflicts hardship on her lover and as the spiteful antagonist of a much more attractive sister.

The quarrel between Obie and Obilot arises, moreover, because Obie is jealous of the evident nobility of Gawan, whereas one has the impression in Chrétien's version of an almost permanent antagonism between them. In her love for Meljanz, strangely manifested though it may be, Obie cannot tolerate that any man should rival her lover in valour and nobility. It is not until much later that Wolfram explains her behaviour with this reason, however, and at the time it certainly appears that she is simply behaving perversely, in her anger with her lover and herself. It is Gawan's misfortune that he should be the innocent victim of her anger with one man, as Wolfram himself points out (365,18-19). Foolishly she persists in her original contention that Gawan is a merchant,[11] and she pursues the notion to excess in her accusations of him, first as a cheat, then as a counterfeiter. The very idea of taking this noble knight, with his extensive reputation, for a merchant, is so ridiculous, to the mediæval audience as to the modern reader, that this whole episode takes on a rather comic tone, though, as in the whole of Book VII, there remains the awareness that comedy and tragedy are two sides of the same thing, that the one can soon replace the other.

However, it is not Wolfram's wish to make Obie suffer for her foolishness, and all turns out well for her. As M. F. Richey says: "Fortune is kinder than they deserve,"[12] and Wolfram, too, is perhaps kinder than they deserve, for he does not begrudge them their happiness. Indeed, he does his best to excuse their behaviour and gives a precise instruction to his readers not to blame Obie (366,2). From this unambiguous desire to exempt Obie from blame, it is clear that Wolfram sees her love for Meljanz, and his for her, as adequate motivation for behaviour which is far from ideal. When Meljanz offers his love to Obie, she scorns it in words which, striking as they do at his youth and inexperience, cannot fail to rouse him:

Si sprach hin zim 'wært ir sô alt,
daz under schilde wære bezalt
in werdeclîchen stunden,
mit helm ûf houbt gebunden
gein herteclîchen vâren,
iwer tage in fünf jâren,
daz ir den prîs dâ het genomn,
und wært ir danne wider komn
ze mîm gebote gewesen dâ,
spræche ich denne alrêste jâ,
des iwer wille gerte,
alze fruo ich iuch gewerte. (346,3-14)

She is guided in this by her interpretation of the privilege of the
lady over the knight. She loves Meljanz, as is clearly shown by her
subsequent behaviour, but she also knows that he loves her, and that
her attempts to urge him to deeds of valour for her sake will not be
in vain. In her immaturity, however, she goes too far: her words do
not inspire him to action for her sake, as they would if they were
words which gave promise of reward, but rather do they rouse him
to anger against her and her father, for she suggests that, even if he
had the advantages of experience and a noble reputation, her love
would still be grudgingly given.[13] It is a cruel response to the young
lover, and the uncontrolled malice of her rejection of Meljanz,
even though it represents only her immature judgement and a false
view of her power as a lady to command her lover, is matched by his
fury. He takes seriously what was intended only half in earnest, and,
like Obie, he behaves with youthful rashness and quite without
thought. He sees her rebuff as an act of treachery on the part of her
father, and, just as she does not pause to consider the possible consequences of what she is saying, he does not see the absurdity of
blaming a loyal and noble vassal for the folly of his daughter, nor
his own foolishness in expanding a personal grievance into a wide-
spread conflict. They are equally unwise, equally responsible for
what happens and equally fortunate that the end is not disaster.

   That Obie is misguided rather than ill-intentioned is evident from
Wolfram's attitude towards her. Indeed, foolishness and misguided-

ness are basic to the character as he re-creates her, for he can find excuses for a foolish woman, whereas he would be reluctant to do so in the case of a really wicked one. Compared with Chrétien, he softens the quarrel with Obilot; in her attempts to humiliate Gawan, he sees that she is thwarted, so that what could have been dangerous behaviour merely appears ridiculous; and, above all, he grants her the happiness of marriage with Meljanz at the end of the episode. The whole episode is more rounded, then, than in *Le Conte del Graal*, where the two do not marry, even though it may be assumed that they do so, and Wolfram shows here the passage of love through scorn and conflict to a happy end, in sharp contrast, above all, to the ill-fated love of Sigune and Schionatulander. One wonders why, having shown the tragic issue of love on several occasions, he chose to grant a happy issue in this case, where the lovers seem so much less deserving of happiness, so much more guilty of ill-conduct. The answer lies partly in the essentially non-tragic nature of the Gawan-action, but there is also the fact that to allow Meljanz to die as a result of such harsh words would be to inflict on Obie a grief more bitter even than that of Sigune, who, although she was responsible inasmuch as she urged Schionatulander to the action which led to his death, did not bear the added burden of the memory of spiteful words, spoken in arrogance and without thought. Such would be the burden upon Obie, and Wolfram is too gentle to permit this. However, to allow the reward of a happy marriage to two people who have behaved in a very wrongful way and whom good fortune alone has saved from disaster, was perhaps just as unacceptable to him. Moreover, the type of ruthless, spiteful woman shown by Chrétien is clearly not in accord with Wolfram's picture of woman.

Consequently, there is in *Parzival* a careful transformation of what was in *Le Conte del Graal* 'a shrill ill-tempered shrew, without a single redeeming feature'[14] into a girl who, though she may not be particularly attractive, is not wholly unsympathetic. The way in which Wolfram manages this transformation is yet another example of his subtle handling of his source and of his insight into human nature. He gives to Obie that redeeming feature which is lacking in the elder sister in Chrétien. For Wolfram, who regards love as all-important, this aspect of Obie's nature is capable of overcoming all her unfavourable characteristics. Moreover, he shows that even these are manifestations, negative though they may be, of her love. A further transformation occurs, within Wolfram's own work, as he shows how gradually the same love reveals itself in a positive way.

From the beginning, she taunts Meljanz because she loves him, but already here Wolfram supplies the key to her nature, for as Meljanz goes away she grieves that she has made him angry:

> sîn zürnen sêre wart geklagt
> von al der massenîe:
> in klagt ouch Obîe. (347,16-18)

Contained in her lament are her grief at having lost him and her regret for what she has done. It is in accordance with her youthful lack of wisdom and a part of the same obstinacy which made her reject Meljanz that she does not act on her grief, to recall him and reconcile herself with him. Instead she allows the hostility between them to grow into an extensive conflict which she can hardly have anticipated. Yet through this defence which she stubbornly maintains, Wolfram allows her true feelings for Meljanz to penetrate: eagerly she watches him from the window as he excells himself in jousting. Her delight at his success mingles with her grief and reveals itself in anger, directed first at Obilot, then at Gawan. After her unsuccessful attempts to humiliate Gawan, from no real wish to harm him and from no deep-rooted malice against her sister, Wolfram himself steps in and for the first time comments on her behaviour. His intervention is perfectly timed, for by now Obie has wrought considerable harm and with her attack on the innocent and noble Gawan, a constantly attractive character, she now runs the risk of losing any sympathy which may remain to her. In thirty lines

he excuses the behaviour of Obie and Meljanz as the product of a
very great love. From the space and time which he expends on it,
it is clearly central to his view of Obie:

> Obîe und Meljanz,
> ir zweier minne was sô ganz
> und stuont mit solhen triuwen,
> sîn zorn iuch solde riuwen.   (365,11-14)

More than of Meljanz, Wolfram seeks to explain the various aspects of Obie's behaviour. Her grief turned to anger, and this she
has vented on Gawan and Obilot:

> daz er mit zorne von ir reit:
> des gab ir trûren solhez leit
> daz ir kiusche wart gein zorne balt.
> unschuldec Gâwân des enkalt,
> und ander diez mit ir dâ liten.   (365,15-19)

In her anger she has neglected her composure as a woman:

> si kom dicke ûz frouwenlîchen siten:
> sus flaht ir kiusche sich in zorn.   (365,20-21)

In her desire for the supremacy of her lover, she has been jealous
of any rivals:

> ez was ir bêder ougen dorn,
> swâ si den werden man gesach:
> ir herze Meljanze jach,
> er müest vor ûz der hôste sîn.   (365,22-25)

Finally he gives the simple instruction:

> nune wîzetz Obîen niht.   (366,2)

This defence of Obie, which is very like his later defence of Orgeluse,[15] prepares the way for the end, when Obie is reunited with
Meljanz. In the meantime, Wolfram turns his attention to Obilot

and her relationship with Gawan, but he has succeeded in these lines in explaining Obie's behaviour, and in attributing her actions to the power of her love, he raises her above accusations of malice and wickedness. He shows how it is possible for him to allow a happy outcome, and he paves the way for the moment at the end of Book VII, when he can say:

> dâ meistert frou minne
> mit ir krefteclîchem sinne,
> und herzenlîchiu triuwe,
> der zweier liebe al niuwe. (396,21-24)

The power of love which hitherto has governed their separate actions now brings them together again. Obie's gesture in taking the arm of Meljanz suggests this coming together, and in kissing his wound she makes amends for the wrong she has inflicted on him. In these last moments which close the story, Obie is shown transformed by love and humble repentance, for it is surely an aspect of humility which allows her to kiss Meljanz before the large crowd, when even Wolfram asks "Wer macht si vor der diet sô balt" (397, 1). Now at last she shows some affinity with Wolfram's great heroines and is united with them perhaps above all in the tears which she now sheds (396,27-30). Moreover, she does not stand, as in Chrétien, in stolid opposition to her younger sister, but rather comes nearer to Obilot, of whom Meljanz has just prophesied that she will become the crown of womanly goodness (394,12-13). It is early to speak of Obie, as B. Q. Morgan does, as 'a truly noble woman,'[16] but at least Wolfram has shown her to possess those qualities which will lead her to the exemplary state already apparent in her young sister.

NOTES

1. cf. E. Martin: *Kommentar* line 345,24. Kr. Nyrop (*Grammaire Historique de la langue française*, Copenhagen 1899-1930) gives a number of examples of the suffix -ot added to

names: Bernardot, Charlot, Henriot, Georgiot etc. He comments (Vol. III, Para. 290): 'Le suffixe -ot a primitivement
une valeur diminutive et souvent caressante.'

2. cf. W. Mohr (p. 18): 'Gawans und Parzivals Wege stehn
unter entgegengesetzten Zeichen. Während Gawan, wo er hin-
kommt, unwillkürlich Ordnung schafft, bringt Parzival, ohne
es zu wollen, Verwirrung und Leid. Die Dissonanzen, die er
um sich erregt, haben tragischen Klang, sie zeigen ein zer-
störtes Verhältnis zur Welt und zu Gott an . . . Auch die Ge-
schichten von unreifer Jugendminne gehen auf der Parzival-
seite tragisch aus; Obie und Meljanz auf der Gawan-seite ist
das lustspielhafte Gegenstück dazu.' On the other hand, in the
present instance one is obliged to accept that many people die
in consequence of Obie's wilful behaviour, but it is in the nature of the Gawan-action that this fact is passed over relatively
lightly.

3. ed. cit. 4856ff.

4. It is true, however, that Chrétien himself hints that the tournament is ill-conceived: ed. cit. 4838ff.

5. In Chrétien, the power of Melians is not so firmly stressed. He
is 'uns echevaliers preus et hardis' (4826), but no mention is
made of his royal birth. His father, it seems apparent, was the
lord of Tiebaut (cf. 4842-4843). Wolfram brings the character of the father much more to the fore, stressing his kingship and the extent of his power: 344,21ff. After the death of
the father, he refers on several occasions to the kingship of
Meljanz: 344,15; 344,21; 353,19; 356,4; 384,15.

6. As well as by Lippaut's own army, Bearosche is defended by
Gawan, armies led by Lippaut's brother, Marangliez, his
brother-in-law, Kardefablet, and the two kings, Schirniel and
Mirabel, while Meljanz has as his supporters Lisavander, La-
heduman, King Poydiconjunz, Duke Astor, Meljacanz and
the 'Red Knight.' The scope of the battle is enormous, more
particularly in relation to the motive for it.

7. ed. cit. 5029ff.

8. ed. cit. 5338.

9. cf. B. Q. Morgan (p. 192): 'In Chrétien what do we find? A shrill, ill-tempered shrew without a single redeeming feature. Not a kind word does she speak and many unkind and harsh ones. . . Wolfram is not content with this: he thinks too highly of womanhood to let such a figure stand.'

10. See p. 153 above.

11. Wolfram is indebted for this idea to *Le Conte del Graal* (ed. cit. 5060), when one of the ladies watching from the window observes, quite without malice, that Gauvain is a merchant. Wolfram transfers the thought to Obie and allows her to develop it to absurd lengths.

12. *Studies of Wolfram von Eschenbach,* London, 1957, p. 119.

13. Very different is the pact between Schionatulander and Sigune: *Titurel* 166, 167,168. In the condition which Schionatulander willingly accepts from Sigune is contained the promise of lasting reward.

14. B. Q. Morgan, p. 192.

15. See p. 204 below.

16. p. 192.

CHAPTER SIXTEEN

Antikonie

THERE CAN BE little doubt that Wolfram found himself in a difficult situation when he came to his version of Chrétien's adventure of Gauvain and the lady of the castle. Aware though he was of the failings of some women,[1] Wolfram is nevertheless remarkably consistent in his depiction of heroines who conform to his high ideal of womanhood. What he found in Chrétien's unnamed figure, the predecessor of his own Antikonie, was a woman behaving in a most unbecoming manner, a far-cry from the purity and reserve of Jeschute, Liaze, Belakane, Condwiramurs. The incident in *Le Conte del Graal* is aptly and not unjustly summarized by B. Q. Morgan: "Chrétien makes Gauvain, an utter stranger, enter a castle, make love to its mistress and succeed in his suit; all within eighteen lines!"[2] Apart from the fact that the incident thus narrated detracts considerably from the nobility of Gauvain, it also places the lady in an exceedingly bad light. She offers no resistance to the rash and uncourtly advances of Gauvain; in fact, she encourages him from the moment of his entry (5808ff). She offers no opposition when he almost immediately begins to make love to her (5827ff).

On another occasion Wolfram had encountered a similar problem. Chrétien's Blancheflor also behaved in a forward, unbecoming manner, and for Wolfram this represented a more serious problem, since his concept of the nature of Parzival's wife is such a powerful element in the whole work. In that case he solved the problem by a radical re-shaping of the character in accordance with his reinterpretation of the whole work: Condwiramurs belongs to *Parzival*, Blancheflor to *Le Conte del Graal*. Such treatment was not warranted in the case of Antikonie, a relatively minor character, nor could he change her behaviour to any extent without changing the entire episode. Moreover, in the Gawan-sphere different values operate, and Antikonie cannot be judged by the same standards as Condwiramurs, any more than Gawan himself can be considered a serious contender for the Graal Kingship. Book VIII is a light-hearted episode, aptly placed before the serious and momentous events of Book IX, and its two principal protagonists are lively and very human people, whose behaviour probably delighted Wolfram's audience, and, precisely because of the context, is unlikely to have offended its moral sensibility.

Even so, the figure of Antikonie is in some ways a disturbing one, and there are indications that Wolfram himself is not entirely at ease in this episode. Although in some respects he seems to be delighting in the outrageous situation and is quite capable of showing in Antikonie a woman behaving in a bold fashion quite unlike his other heroines and appearing very attractive in the process, he does not really like this break with the ideal he has so carefully created. Perhaps his hesitation to continue with the story, once he has embarked on it, is not what it appears at first sight, a humorous narrative device to tantalize his readers, but a genuine indication of his distaste for what he is about to relate:

> welt ir, noch swîg ich grôzer nôt.
> nein, ich wilz iu fürbaz sagen.   (403,10-11)

He is at pains, moreover, to stress the virtue of Antikonie before Gawan meets her (404,24-27). Where Chrétien had concerned himself primarily with the lady's physical beauty (5820ff), Wolfram endeavours to couple beauty with virtue in his description of Antikonie. Yet there is something strangely evasive in his manner of describing her:

> was si schœn, daz stuont ir wol:
> unt hete si dar zuo rehten muot,
> daz was gein werdekeit ir guot.   (403,26-28)

In the wish he expresses, that Heinrich von Veldeke were still alive
to sing the praises of Antikonie (404,28-30), is contained perhaps
an indication of his own dislike of the task.

> der kunde se baz gelobet hân   (404,30)

says Wolfram, with a suggestion that he himself is unable to praise
her greatly, since it goes against his custom and desire to utter false
praise, or, on the other hand, to speak ill of a lady.[3] K. Kinzel is
surely right in finding the key to Wolfram's attitude towards her in
the lines:

> swar ich rede kêr ze guote,
> diu bedarf wol zühte huote.   (404,9-10)[4]

Thus Wolfram explains a certain reticence in his praise of Antikonie. Nevertheless, four lines in particular remain strangely con-
tradictory to the behaviour of Antikonie as Wolfram shows it:

> sol wîplich êre sîn gewin,
> des koufes het si vil gepflegn
> und alles valsches sich bewegn:
> dâ mite ir kiusche prîs erwarp.   (404,24-27)[5]

Following immediately on these lines, however, is his lament that
Heinrich von Veldeke should not be alive to praise her, and the
very juxtaposition suggests Wolfram's feeling that he has already
been untrue to himself in attributing womanly honour and purity
to one in whom it will be shown to be lacking.

Certainly in the early part of the account, Antikonie behaves
with a lack of reserve unexpected in the woman who has just received such deliberate praise. It is true that she is not so forward as

her counterpart in *Le Conte del Graal*.[6] Wolfram has made the incident a little more acceptable by lengthening the account, allowing the relationship between Gawan and Antikonie to develop more gradually and so improving on the impression in Chrétien of a spontaneous and most distasteful attraction, in which Gauvain demands love and the lady gives it without hesitation. Antikonie is a little more reserved: she attempts to prevent his advances, though one questions the earnestness of her objections.[7] Already with their kiss of greeting they have gone beyond the relationship of hostess and guest:

> da ergienc ein kus ungastlîch (405,21)

and Antikonie has shown little sign of objecting to it. Nor does she, the lady of the castle with the servants at her command, protest when they find occupations elsewhere and leave her alone with Gawan (406,21-26). The attraction is a mutual one, and the intrusion of the knight is a disappointment to both of them:

> von der liebe alsölhe nôt gewan
> beidiu magt und ouch der man,
> daz dâ nâch was ein dinc geschehen,
> hetenz übel ougen niht ersehen. (407,5-8)

Antikonie appears as a rather bold woman, then, whose undeniable beauty (402,22-23; 403,26; 405,19) has captivated Gawan and whose lack of reserve has encouraged his advances. He, in his turn, is the daring knight, very human and charming, but quite without the delicacy of Parzival. Yet both of them have fine qualities, as Wolfram is at pains to stress, and they are well-matched. The words of Vergulaht commending Gawan to his sister's care anticipate the relationship, and the first kiss which passes between them bears witness to a mutual attraction already present.[8]

In the remainder of the account, however, Wolfram is clearly striving to place Antikonie in a better light. He cannot excuse her

187

former behaviour as he did Obie's, but at least he can attempt to bring her into line with his ideal. Her loyalty to Gawan is a powerful redeeming factor. Whereas, in Chrétien's version, the servant accuses her of embracing the man who killed her father and continues for almost twenty lines to upbraid her (5849-5865), Wolfram does not permit such accusations of Antikonie. In a brief, much more realistic exclamation, the White Knight points to Gawan as the murderer of the King and the assailant of his daughter (407, 16-19). Antikonie is not implicated in the accusation and yet she remains with Gawan to aid him. She does not hesitate to run with him to the tower, and it is she who finds the chess-set and she who hurls the pieces at the crowd below:

> ez wære künec oder roch,
> daz warf si gein den vînden doch:
> ez was grôz und swære.
> man sagt von ir diu mære,
> Swen dâ erreichte ir wurfes swanc,
> der strûchte âne sînen danc.
> diu küneginne rîche
> streit dâ ritterlîche,
> bî Gâwân si werlîche schein,
> daz diu koufwîp ze Tolenstein
> an der vasnaht nie baz gestriten.   (408,29-409,9)

It is true that the comparison with the merchant-women hardly suggests dignity,[9] but Antikonie is acting for the sake of expedience, with no thought for what is becoming. Again Wolfram defends Antikonie, for her action is motivated by love of Gawan:

> swâ harnaschrâmec wirt ein wîp,
> diu hât ir rehts vergezzen,
> sol man ir kiusche mezzen,
> sine tuoz dan durch ir triuwe.   (409,12-15)

One is reminded perhaps of Gyburc, with upraised sword and arrayed for battle (*Willehalm* 227,12ff). Antikonie comes nowhere near Gyburc in other respects, yet the likeness here is interesting. Wolfram has no objection to displays of militant action in women, provided that the cause is a worthy one, no matter what the level.

Wolfram's final proof of the sincerity of her love comes with the tears she sheds:

> in strît si sêre weinde:
> wol si daz bescheinde,
> daz friwentlîch liebe ist stæte.   (409,19-21)

There can be little doubt now that Wolfram means to place her in a new light, redeemed by love for Gawan, though previously she revealed this without regard even for conventional restraint. Although he is indebted for the actual idea of the chess-set battle to Chrétien (5886ff),[10] Wolfram has certainly used it with a new significance, finding in it the means to raise Antikonie above the level of a shameless coquette.

To Chrétien's account Wolfram adds the inspiration which Antikonie gives to Gawan in the battle:

> Gâwânen wac vil ringe
> vînde haz, swenn er die magt erkôs;
> dâ von ir vil den lîp verlôs.   (410,10-12)

He gains strength from her physical beauty:

> swenne im diu muoze geschach,
> daz er die maget reht ersach;
> ir munt, ir ougen, unde ir nasen.   (409,23-25)

Thus does Antikonie aid and defend Gawan physically and sensually, in accordance with the nature of their relationship.[11] She shows physical courage in this defence, and in her subsequent vindication of Gawan before her brother she shows a mastery of language and an ability to turn the facts, in order to supply a satisfactory explanation:

> dô was ich âne wer ein magt,
> wan daz ich truoc doch einen schilt,
> ûf den ist werdekeit gezilt:
> des wâpen sol ich nennen,
> ob ir ruochet diu bekennen.
> guot gebærde und kiuscher site,
> den zwein wont vil stæte mite.
> den bôt ich für den ritter mîn,
> den ir mir sandet dâ her în. (414,18-26)

Only after all the arguing and conferences regarding Gawan's fate, and the decision to let him free for the sake of Antikonie (427, 5-11), does Wolfram allow himself to praise her with real enthusiasm:

> mit lobe wir solden grüezen
> die kiuschen unt die süezen
> Antikonîen,
> vor valscheit die vrîen.
> wan si lebte in solhen siten,
> daz ninder was underriten
> ir prîs mit valschen worten. (427,5-11)

Possibly one feels that this is unnecessarily enthusiastic in view of the total lack in Antikonie of that womanly purity and restraint which Wolfram is known to regard so highly. Clearly he sees her love and loyalty towards Gawan as redeeming her, and this is demonstrated by the fact that Wolfram is reserved in his praise until she has proved her love by her devotion to Gawan during the battle and later in her defence of him. It is now that Wolfram talks of her as 'vor valscheit diu vrîe' (413,2), 'diu juncfrouwe wert' (414, 13) and 'diu süeze sælden rîche' (427,19). It does not offend Wolfram's taste or his sense of what is fitting to praise Antikonie now that a new aspect of her nature has been revealed,[12] and he now has justification of the ambiguity in his own previous attitude towards her.

K. Kinzel is right when he says of Antikonie: "Zurückhaltung hat sie nicht gerade in ihrem betragen gezeigt; nur eine seite ihres weiblichen charakters stellt sich als lobenswert dar: die redlichkeit ihrer gesinnung (413,2; 427,8), die festigkeit (*triuwe*), welche sie veranlaßte, Gawan auch in der äußersten not nicht im stich zu lassen."[13] It seems, however, rather strained when he goes on to justify Wolfram's use of the word *kiusche* in relation to Antikonie (404,27).[14] Much as one would like to find an element of womanly modesty in Antikonie, her behaviour provides little reason to do so. Moreover, in these lines, Wolfram is talking about her reputation, and there is the chance of a discrepancy between reputation and reality. A final possibility remains, that the audience is meant to see in Antikonie a woman, otherwise modest and pure, but captivated by the charms of Gawan, who is known to be a noble and gallant knight. He, in his turn, is attracted by her great beauty.[15]

Wolfram allows Antikonie and Gawan to part sorrowfully, a final indication of the love between them (432,2-6). At the end, then, one has the feeling that Wolfram's sympathy is with the couple who love one another and yet must part. Such sympathy is possible, however, only because he has contrived to show both of them somewhat ennobled by the battle in the tower, when their mutual love was apparent and a decisive factor. Nevertheless, the figure of Antikonie remains rather marred by her bold reception of Gawan and her unbecoming readiness to accept his love. Gawan himself passes on to his relationship with Orgeluse, and for him the meeting with Antikonie is just a phase, though nonetheless real at the time. The story of Parzival shows a three-fold development in Parzival's relationship with women, from Jeschute, through Liaze, to Condwiramurs. Similarly, Antikonie supplies the link in Gawan's adventures between Obilot, whom he serves with no hope of reward, and Orgeluse, whom he serves and from whom he eventually receives the reward of love and marriage. In the case of Obilot, the courtly convention of service for favour is all-important, for a relationship of love is impossible. With Antikonie there exists mutual love which disregards the conventions. Only in Orgeluse do the two things combine.

Antikonie remains in one's memory as the heroine of this strange and amusing interlude. She belongs very much to the Gawan-sphere and in particular to this stage in Gawan's adventures. The difficulties in interpreting her character—and there are many difficulties—arise because Wolfram has done his utmost to reconcile his picture of her with the wider picture he gives of his ideal of womanhood. Strictly speaking, she does not fit into this picture, yet he has tried to give her a place in it. Her situation is thus an ambiguous one, and in spite of all attempts to explain her behaviour, Antikonie remains a problematical character. There can be little doubt, however, that she is more of a problem to Wolfram, who attempts to explain, excuse and redeem, by protracting the episode and thus placing more emphasis on her and the whole relationship, than to Chrétien, who had not Wolfram's consistently elevated view of woman and for whom the incident passes by without particular note.

NOTES

1. See above, p. xviiff.
2. p. 193.
3. D. M. Blamires (p. 398) has pointed to the similarity between Heinrich von Veldeke's Dido and Antikonie, and he comments: 'The significant phrase is 'baz gelobet.' In view of the parallelism existing between Antikonie and Dido one would expect a similar assessment of the moral situation. But Veldeke disapproves of Dido's *unmâze*, whereas Wolfram refrains from expressing such a view, although the situations possess the same moral elements. The purpose of the words 'baz gelobet' must then be taken in an oblique and ironical sense and mean that Veldeke *could have given a truer picture* of Antikonie than Wolfram actually does from the strictly moral

angle. Veldeke could not have presented a more lively, realistic or individualized character than Wolfram, but by this double-edged reference to him Wolfram shows that by absolute standards, i.e. by his own standard that true *minne* is consummated in marriage, the relationship between Gawan and Antikonie is imperfect. . . .' He is surely right when he sees Wolfram's mention of Heinrich von Veldeke as a subtle attempt to point out the amoral nature of the episode, so that he can continue to relate it without reference to the moral standards which are being violated. Blamires concludes his discussion of the episode thus: 'In this way the full poetic value of the story can be expressed, while the reference to Veldeke safeguards the deeper-going morality that pervades the poem as a whole as well as showing Wolfram's literary master.'

4. K. Kinzel ('Beiträge zur Erklärung und Beurteilung des Parzival,' *Zeitschrift für deutsches Altertum* 30, 1886, pp. 353-365). He interprets the words 'zühte huote' as 'die achtsame behütung ihres durch erziehung gewonnenen feinen benehmens' (p. 364). Martin, on the other hand (*Kommentar* 404, 7ff) suggests as a translation of the two lines: 'Wo ich lobe, da muβ diese (Rede) unter der Obhut der Zucht stehen—muβ (so) rein aufgenommen werden (als ich sie ausspreche).' A more satisfactory interpretation seems to be that of H. Mustard and C. Passage (*Parzival*, translated into English, New York, 1961) who render the lines '. . . . and wherever I bestow a good word it must have the guarantee of good breeding' (p. 218). This does not, in any case, contradict the statement of K. Kinzel: 'So ist es klar, daβ ein solches, uneingeschränktes Lob der Antikonie nicht zu teil werden kann.' A recent interpretation of the highly complex lines is contained in the article by J. F. Poag ('Wolfram von Eschenbach's Antikonie,' *Germanic Review*, Vol. XLI, no. 2, 1966, pp. 83-88): "Adding an explanatory clause we might restate Wolfram's comment in the following manner: 'When I begin to

say something good, then my speech requires the safeguard of propriety, of courtly conduct (because in reality I am saying something improper).' A paradoxical statement of this sort would be in keeping with Wolfram's literary style and it would, moreover, resolve the seeming discrepancy between Antikonie's actual conduct and the author's praise of her virtue. Wolfram's praise would not be praise at all." All this is feasible in the context of Poag's argument, but it is not the only way of understanding Wolfram's admittedly very difficult attitude towards this woman.

5. Poag (op. cit. p. 85) draws attention to the ambiguity of the whole episode and in relation to these lines he points out the possibility of a negative interpretation. He translates: 'If womanly honor is profit, then she has *sold* much of it (her honor) and has *committed herself* to every falseness, so that her chastity has undergone a *drawing together* (that is, her chastity has been diminished).' Throughout his article Poag indicates a meaning below the surface in most of what Wolfram says of Antikonie. He concludes: 'The whole is to be understood as a harmonious mixture of *double-entendre*, irony, parody, mock-heroics,' (p. 88). Convincing though his arguments are, they seem to disregard Wolfram's concept of the nature of woman, which even in this episode he is striving to preserve. Certainly Antikonie does not live up to his lofty ideal, but he strives to show her in a positive, favourable light. This view of Antikonie is clearly in direct opposition to that of Poag.

6. Nevertheless, her words of greeting to Gawan, for example, are deliberately capable of misinterpretation: 405,5-14. They contain more than the welcome of a hostess. As K. Kinzel observes ('Beiträge zur Erklärung und Beurteilung des Parzival,' p. 360): '. . . immerhin tritt uns Antikonie hier als ein keckes und nicht eben sehr sprödes frauenzimmer entgegen.'

7. In his desire to uphold her, B. Q. Morgan (p. 194) attributes more virtue to Antikonie than she in fact possesses: 'Chrétien makes her yield without the least hesitation. Not so Wolfram.

A virtuous woman, and Antikonie is that, is not so ready to give her love. She objects, temporizes, puts Gawan off.' This seems an over-generous interpretation of 405,2ff.

8. See in particular the words of Vergulaht (402,25-30).

9. E. Martin (*Kommentar* 409,8) says of the *koufwîp* '. . . . auf sie blickte die ritterliche Gesellschaft verächtlich nieder.' Wolfram is clearly intent on suggesting the abandoned vigour of the attack.

10. Note, however, that Chrétien does not have the detail of the woman's finding the chess-set in the first place.

11. One recalls how, on a more spiritual level, Condwiramurs and Sekundille aid Parzival and Feirefiz, and Ampflise Gahmuret.

12. cf. H. Sacker (p. 85). He compares Antikonie with Sigune and says: 'By standing by her lover in his hour of need, she has demonstrated that, as far as is required of her, she too is constant.' J. Poag, on the other hand, refuses to accept as serious the praise which Wolfram gives to Antikonie for her part in the chess-set battle, when he says (p. 88): 'It is obvious that Wolfram's description of the struggle is mock-heroic and it is almost as clear, I think, that Wolfram's references to the *triuwe* of Antikonie (who stands at Gawan's side in his hour of need) are a further contribution to the mock-heroic tenor of the whole. The few remaining isolated references to Antikonie's various virtues can easily be understood as a product of the same ironic vein.' Surely he goes too far in his desire to show Wolfram's disapproval and ignores the positive evidence on the other side, which Wolfram himself has been at such pains to furnish.

13. 'Beiträge zur Erklärung und Beurteilung des *Parzival*,' p. 364.

14. ibid. p. 364: '. . . der dichter meint also vielleicht: wahre echte *kiusche* (im umfassenden sinne von der weiblichen zurückhaltung, oder gar im engsten geschlechtlichen sinne) hat sie zwar nicht, aber sie war wenigstens ein weib von redlicher gesinnung, nach dieser seite hin zeigte sich ihre *kiusche*.'

15. cf. B. Q. Morgan (p. 194): 'His very boldness has captivated

her, and her scruples were gone in a moment of unreasoning passion.' Again (p. 195): 'And Wolfram does not forget to mention her beauty again; he realizes that this alone can explain the whole episode.' It is true that Gawan is attracted by her beauty, but this in itself is not sufficient explanation of the incident, and it is certainly not a justification, as Wolfram is well aware, hence his discomfort.

CHAPTER SEVENTEEN

Orgeluse ✗

ORGELUSE IS a strange and puzzling figure. She cannot be classed among Wolfram's ideal women, yet she is a woman of very great personality, who for a time dominates the work. She does not possess the serene virtue of her fellow heroines in *Parzival*, and only in her activity does she resemble the saintly Gyburc. Much of what she does is reprehensible, in fact, were it not for Wolfram's explicit instruction to his audience not to criticize her behaviour (516,3-14). As he does with Obie, he here takes from his source a character who is far from perfect, and, without changing her behaviour to any extent, he supplies a motive for it and so, showing it in a new light, he raises the character above criticism. In the case of Orgeluse he does more, too, for he endows her with a new significance in the whole work and allows her to transcend the relatively small rôle which Chrétien gave to her. M. F. Richey saw clearly the truth of Orgeluse when she spoke of her as 'the superb and infinitely subtle Orgeluse, with her queenly arrogance and deep-hidden springs of passion.'[1]

To see Orgeluse as 'infinitely subtle' is surely to see her as Wolfram saw her. In Chrétien's proud and spiteful woman he perceived the potentials of a tragic figure, and he sought to motivate her behaviour by supplying the details of her tragedy. Nor is it only a personal tragedy which he gives to her, in the death of Cidegast, but, in the ill-fated love of Anfortas, he unites her sorrow with that of the Graal Family and links her with the wider issue of the work. Thus, from her limited rôle in the French version,[2] she becomes in *Parzival* the woman who not only dominates the Gawan-action, but who is responsible also for the downfall of Anfortas and must share in the grief of the Graal Family. Her rôle is thus integrated into the whole work, and her significance is heightened by the new complexity which Wolfram gives to her.

Some among Wolfram's heroines develop with years and experience; new aspects of the character of others are revealed as their story progresses; some, like Repanse de Schoye, Cundrie and Ampflise, are enigmatic figures, where Wolfram's technique of characterization is one of implication and a gradual building-up of a picture. Only to Orgeluse is given the particular subtlety of a strange and complex past, coupled with a depth of passion which can express itself as powerfully in hate as in love. In this very aspect Orgeluse stands apart from the other women characters in *Parzival*, for only in her does Wolfram reveal the power of hatred, and only here does he show how a very great love can lead to an equally great desire for revenge. The other women, no less individual, possess equally deep emotions, but these reveal themselves in the constancy of Condwiramurs, the heart-break of Herzeloyde, the steadfast devotion of Sigune. These are passive manifestations of emotion, and even the active defence of Orange by Gyburc is not really comparable with the vigorous and persistent striving for revenge of Orgeluse. Once more, M. F. Richey is surely right when she says of Orgeluse: "In her hunger for revenge one sees the possibility of the same kind of tragic grandeur as in Kriemhild, but with this difference, that the possibility lies only in herself, and is not borne out in her environment."[3] This is certainly closer to the truth than the final assessment of Orgeluse by B. Q. Morgan: "But withal she remains a thoroughly worldly beauty, a coquette, and so makes a good mate for Gawan, the model of a successful but far from high-souled warrior and man of the world."[4] Such a view of Orgeluse disregards completely the subtlety of her character which is essential to an understanding of her, for it takes into account only the superficial and ignores the depths which Wolfram has been at pains to uncover. It is the depths which provide the key to the full understanding of what is on the surface, and only a view of Orgeluse which considers both can do justice to Wolfram's conception of her.

There is altogether a certain duality in the character of Orgeluse. It is reflected in the basic discrepancy just mentioned, between the superficial view of her and the deeper view, achieved by Wolfram's addition of a history which provides motivation and explanation of her behaviour. It is present in the duality of passions within her, in love which can lead to hatred and revenge, in contempt which can be replaced by love. Wolfram's first words about Orgeluse suggest a dichotomy, for she is to be both joy and sorrow to Gawan:

> da ersaher niderhalben sîn
> freude und sîns herzen pîn. (508,15-16)

The old knight warns Gawan and speaks also of the contrasting elements in Orgeluse:

> wan diu ist bî der süeze al sûr,
> reht als ein sunnenblicker schûr. (514,19-20)

Wolfram himself echoes these words, when he speaks of her as

> ougen süeze unt sûr dem herzen bî. (531,26)

Arnive describes her as 'sîner ougen senfte, sherzen dorn' (600,10). Nor is Gawan himself unaware of the negative qualities of Orgeluse, despite his attraction towards her:

> diu mir diz ungemach gebôt,
> diu kan wol süeze siuren
> unt dem herzen freude tiuren
> unt der sorgen machen rîche. (547,14-17)

Wolfram himself is deeply conscious of the incongruity of the great beauty of Orgeluse and the wrong which she does. He stresses her beauty throughout, from the moment when Gawan encounters

her for the first time. The impact of the meeting is a powerful one.
She is suddenly present before Gawan as he rides along the road,
and there is in Wolfram's description the static quality of a paint-
ing, a lovely woman in a beautiful natural setting:

> ein brunne ûzem velse schôz:
> dâ vander, des in niht verdrôz,
> ein alsô clâre frouwen,
> dier gerne muose schouwen,
> aller wîbes varwe ein bêâ flûrs.
> âne Condwîrn âmûrs
> wart nie geborn sô schœner lîp.   (508,17-23)[5]

The action pauses for a moment while Wolfram describes her, and
in this way he manages to suggest the powerful impact which she
makes on Gawan, who seems to stop short in his amazement and
admiration. No greater praise could Wolfram offer than that only
Condwiramurs exceeds her in beauty. This first impression is a forceful one, for the audience as well as for Gawan, and it has a sensual
quality which anticipates the nature of the relationship between
Gawan and Orgeluse and points to the distinction from that of Parzival and Condwiramurs, despite the comparison here. It accompanies the subsequent action, supplying ample justification for
Gawan's persistent devotion to Orgeluse, in spite of her treatment
of him, and explaining the influence which she wields over so many
knights, among them the noble and ill-fated Anfortas. Moreover,
since it is Wolfram's custom to house virtue in external beauty, the
beauty of Orgeluse suggests her essential goodness and points forward to the time when this will be revealed. Yet even this description contains an ominous indication of what is to come:

> och sagt uns d'âventiur von ir,
> si wære ein reizel minnen gir.   (508,27-28)

With his use of the word *reizel*, Wolfram suggests Orgeluse's power
to lure men and bring them to grief.[6] Of this power she is fully

aware and she even tries to persuade Gawan to turn elsewhere this desire which she describes as his 'kranke(n) gir' (510,7).

Chrétien's l'Orgueilleuse had greeted Gauvain with a flood of abuse.[7] In *Parzival* it is Gawan, ever courtly, who greets her and speaks first, giving expression to the impact she has made on him:

> er sprach 'ob ich erbeizen muoz
> mit iweren hulden, frouwe,
> ob ich iuch des willen schouwe
> daz ir mich gerne bî iu hât,
> grôz riwe mich bî freuden lât:
> sone wart nie rîter mêr sô frô.
> mîn lîp muoz ersterben sô
> daz mir nimmer wîp gevellet baz.'   (509,2-9)

Her first words are a curt and arrogant response:

> 'deist et wol: nu weiz ich ouch daz.'   (509,10)

Her words are a denial of her great beauty, and Wolfram is aware of the incongruity when he observes:

> ir süezer munt mêr dannoch sprach.   (509,12)

He uses the same expression on other occasions, conscious of the irony that such sweet lips should utter words which are far from sweet (515,12; 523,5). However, with the memory of other times when Wolfram has drawn particular attention to the lips of women and intended thereby to imply truth and loyalty and womanly virtue, comes the suggestion here that Wolfram is stressing the incongruity in order to hint that this is not the true nature of Orgeluse, that her words belie the lips which utter them and the heart which conceives them.[8]

During the early part of the relationship between Gawan and Orgeluse, however, the reader is not provided with a key to the behaviour of the lady, and he can only judge it as he sees it. She is no less arrogant than her counterpart in *Le Conte del Graal*, and no less cruel in her treatment of Gawan. Yet she possesses a great vitality and an active, if malicious, spirit, and at times Wolfram allows her to display a certain humour, though this is often sadistic. She is delighted to see Gawan puzzling how best to dispose of his own horse while he fetches hers (512,1-23). She laughs openly at the pain and discomfort of Gawan and Malcreatiure (521,15-18), and she laughs again at Gawan's grief and embarrassment when the knight goes off on his fine steed and leaves him with the nag (523,2-4). She treats him with such disdain that one wonders why Gawan persists in his devotion to her, yet, as we have seen, Wolfram has given to his Orgeluse an attraction which far exceeds that of Chrétien's Orgueilleuse. The earlier figure was a rude and arrogant woman, ruthless in her treatment of the amorous Gauvain, and quite without the vivid personality so evident in Orgeluse.[9] The beauty of Orgeluse is her immediate attraction for Gawan, but he clearly also admires her strength of character and the spirit she displays, even though she does so in a capricious and sometimes malicious manner. It is obvious that Gawan sees in her a woman who, though hard to win, would be worth the strife. She herself points to the standard of service which she demands when she says:

mîn dienst bedarf decheines zagn.　　　(511,20)

She tries repeatedly to put Gawan off, to deter him from his resolution to serve her, suggesting that love for her will bring peril and little reward (510,1-14; 511,4-10; 512-12). Yet despite her own warnings and her total lack of encouragement, as well as the sad and ominous warnings of the onlookers (513,1-16; 514,1-8), Gawan is not deterred. He is a knight of noble reputation, fearless and strong, and he is also the eternal lover, who has now met the great love of his life, as Wolfram himself says (582,5-7). From the moment he sees Orgeluse, he loves her, and he becomes so captivated by her that threats and warnings, rejection and contempt, are

all in vain. The proud determination of Orgeluse is matched by that
of Gawan, and she can invent no test which he will refuse to under-
take, and none in which he will fail.[10] Gawan looks forward in the
hope of reward, firmly believing that Orgeluse's contempt will turn
to love:

> er sprach: 'ist iu nu zornes gâch,
> dâ hœrt iedoch genâde nâch . . .'   (515,17-18)

Nor is Orgeluse slow to recognize true worth, and, as she becomes
more closely acquainted with Gawan, a new respect begins to appear in her treatment of him, although for a long time she disguises
it in the contempt which is in itself part of her method of trying
his worth. When she mocks at Gawan's horseless state, there is perhaps just the slightest trace of admiration in her words:

> 'für einen rîter ich iuch sach:
> dar nâch in kurzen stunden
> wurdt ir arzet für die wunden:
> nu müezet ir ein garzûn wesn.
> sol iemen sîner kunst genesn,
> sô trœst iuch iwerre sinne.
> gert ir noch mîner minne?'   (523,6-12)

She has witnessed his compassion and versatility, and a woman of
her resolute purpose cannot fail to be impressed by his perseverance
in his efforts to gain her love. Her enquiry, whether he still desires
her love, suggests a greater inclination on her part to accept his
service. Soon after, when Gawan is faced with the problem of riding with his equipment on the nag left behind by Malcreatiure,
Orgeluse again laughs and compares him to a merchant:

> si sprach 'füert ir krâmgewant
> in mîme lande veile?
> wer gap mir ze teile
> einen arzet unde eins krâmes pflege?

hüet iuch vor zolle ûfem wege:
eteslîch mîn zolnære
iuch sol machen fröuden lære.'   (531,12-18)

It is interesting that this was precisely the insult of Obie to Gawan,
but she was much more bitter than Orgeluse, whose words are softened by the wit with which she delivers them. On such occasions,
though Orgeluse may speak with contempt and disregard for Gawan, one is aware of the sparkling personality which captivates him
and so many knights. Hers is not the more laboured spite of l'Orgueilleuse, who lacks the grace and impelling vitality of Orgeluse.

Over all the actions of Orgeluse during the early part of her relationship with Gawan hangs the consciousness of her great beauty.
The imprint of that first picture remains, and the beauty which re-
deems her in Gawan's estimation at all times[11] serves also to soften
her behaviour for the audience, even though one is conscious of
the incongruity between her beauty and her words and actions. At
an apt moment, when her maliciousness is becoming too objectionable for the most tolerant audience, Wolfram steps in to warn his
hearers not to judge Orgeluse until they know the truth about her:

swer nu des wil volgen mir,
der mîde valsche rede gein ir.
niemen sich verspreche,
ern wizze ê waz er reche,
unz er gewinne küende
wiez umb ir herze stüende.   (516,3-8)

His reference to the state of her heart looks forward to the time
when he will tell of her love for Cidegast and later for Anfortas.
The defence of Orgeluse is comparable with that of Obie, but there
is a difference. In the case of Obie, Wolfram has already provided
the explanation of an overwhelming love which leads her to behave
in this foolish and harmful way, and now he tells his audience not
to blame her. Here he instructs his audience not to criticize Orgeluse, hinting at a revelation which is to come and which will explain

her behaviour. Meanwhile, the reader must watch as she treats Gawan with cruel disregard for his obvious devotion. Yet somehow, with his skilful depiction of the beautiful and dynamic woman, combined now with his promise of a later explanation, Wolfram has managed to quell the indignation of the reader, who can watch patiently, in the firm belief that things are not as they seem, that all will be explained.

During his adventures at Schastel Merveil, Gawan is troubled, as well as by his wound and his great peril, by the loss of Orgeluse. He sees many lovely women, but none is comparable to her (581,30-582,3). He suffers greatly because of his love and when he catches sight of Orgeluse in the magic pillar, his former passion is renewed in all its intensity:

> Gâwân sich umbe kêrte,
> sînen kumber er gemêrte.
> in dûht diu sûl het in betrogn:
> dô sach er für ungelogn
> Orgelûsen de Lôgroys
> und einen rîter kurtoys
> gein dem urvar ûf den wasn.
> ist diu nieswurz in der nasn
> dræte unde strenge,
> durch sîn herze enge
> kom alsus diu herzogîn,
> durch sîniu ougen oben în.   (593,7-18)

Still Orgeluse greets him with taunting words, but she shows some relaxation of her earlier pride when she allows him to ride with her, where previously she had insisted that he should keep some distance away from her. This is the beginning of a softening in their relationship. She tells him that he may ask for her love if he fetches a wreath from the branch of a certain tree (600,20-24). Gawan agrees with delight, and suddenly Wolfram remarks that the lovely flowers are nothing in comparison with the beauty of Orgeluse (601,1-3). It is true that her beauty has been stressed throughout, but the impact of this particular comparison is a powerful one—perhaps because it comes so suddenly, perhaps because Wolfram rarely compares human beauty with the beauty of nature—and it seems to offer a sudden hope of a happy outcome. At last, and soon after this comparison, Orgeluse shows emotion, when she weeps to see Gawan fall (602,17-18). This first display of feeling in the woman who has behaved with such determined harshness prepares the way for what is to come, for the moment when she humbles herself before Gawan, and for the entire account of her sad history.[12]

We have seen that on many occasions Wolfram shows tears to be the true sign of a noble woman, and when he allows Orgeluse to weep he gives an indication that the defence which she has hitherto maintained is broken, that with the coming of Gawan, who is willing and able to avenge the wrong done to Cidegast, she no longer needs to deny her true virtue as a woman. When Gawan returns, Orgeluse weeps once more as she kneels before him and begs forgiveness for her past treatment of him (611,23-30). As they ride away together, she is weeping for her beloved Cidegast (615,22-29), and even when, much later, she kisses Gramoflanz in sign of reconciliation, Wolfram says of her:

> dar umb si weinens luste.
> si dâhte an Cidegastes tôt:
> dô twanc si wîplîchiu nôt
> nâch im dennoch ir riuwe.
> welt ir, des jeht für triuwe.   (729,20-24)

At this point, then, Wolfram interprets her desire to weep as true devotion and thus supplies the key to her nature, for her life has for a long time been led in devotion, though very different in its manifestation from that of Sigune, the greatest personification of this virtue. It is indeed significant, as D. Blamires has pointed out,[13] that Wolfram's vital definition of *minne*, 'reht minne ist wâriu triuwe' (532,10) occurs, not as one might have expected in the midst of the Parzival-action, but in a discourse by Wolfram during the first episode with Orgeluse. That he prized *triuwe* very highly is demonstrated in his depiction of other women, but not less does he value it in Orgeluse, where its manifestation is different.

Although Orgeluse loves Gawan, it is surely without the intensity with which he loves her. Her greatest love is for Cidegast. For him she has lived in the desire for revenge, and for him she mourns at the last. Of Cidegast himself little is known, save that he was loved by her and killed by the envious Gramoflanz. Her life lived in the hope of revenge and the tenacity and harshness which belie her great beauty are testimony in themselves to the power of her love for Cidegast. Added to this is her own praise of him:

> Mîn clâre süeze beâs âmîs,
> sô durchliuhtic was sîn prîs
> mit rehter werdekeite ger,
> ez wære dirre oder der,
> die muoter ie gebâren
> bî sîner zîte jâren,
> die muosn im jehen werdekeit
> die ander prîs nie überstreit.
> er was ein quecprunne der tugent,
> mit alsô berhafter jugent
> bewart vor valscher pfliehte.   (613,1-11)

She expresses, simply yet with profound sincerity, the love which existed between them when she says:

> ich was sîn herze, er was mîn lîp.   (613,27)

The strength of the love which she bore him was matched by her grief at his death:

> des muoz mir jâmer tasten
> Inz herze, dâ diu freude lac
> do ich Cidegastes minne pflac.   (615,30-616,2)

Yet it is characteristic of Orgeluse that her grief takes expression in active hatred of the man who killed Cidegast and in a relentless desire for revenge. The contrast with other bereaved women in *Parzival* is a striking one: Herzeloyde and Sigune withdraw into isolation and lonely grief, while Belakane is remembered in the image of the lonely turtle-dove. The difference in the reaction of Orgeluse is an emphatic one and altogether typical of the activity which distinguishes her from almost all the other women characters, in whom a passive acceptance of life is an essential aspect of true and mature womanhood. That Orgeluse does not conform in this respect to Wolfram's ideal picture is interesting for his whole conception of her nature. To some extent, of course, he was guided by his source, although, with Chrétien's version in its unfinished state, the figure of l'Orgueilleuse was never developed, and Wolfram was free to extend it, as indeed he did, far beyond the original which was his inspiration. Possibly, however, he wished to distinguish the goal of Gawan's chivalry, Orgeluse, from that of Parzival's, Condwiramurs. The two knights are very different, the bold and gallant Gawan a much less complex figure than Parzival, whose story is one of failure and despair before he comes to success. Consequently, whereas Condwiramurs is a woman of great spiritual depth, serene and composed, Orgeluse is one of activity and ceaseless exertion.[14] This is far from admitting, however, that she is the 'thoroughly worldly beauty' whom B. Q. Morgan finds. Such a figure as a major female character would be quite unacceptable to Wolfram, who gave even to Antikonie a certain nobility at the last.

In giving Orgeluse a wealth of sensitivity and deep-rooted passion while at the same time not detracting from her essential power of action, Wolfram created a figure who is indeed 'infinitely subtle' and who is also unique among his women characters. He has created a woman who transcends the rôle which he has given to her as the partner of Gawan, and, because she transcends it, M. F. Richey can justly say: "She stands alone, and we realize the disproportion between her solitary strength and the purely spectacular rôles of her fellow-actors."[15] She is a woman, who, although she is akin to Gawan in courage and resolution, comes close in some respects to

Parzival himself. Like him, she lives in single-minded devotion to one aim, to avenge the death of Cidegast. The expression of the affinity between Parzival and Orgeluse comes with their meeting, which is mentioned only later and so given a remoteness which could not have been present in a meeting actually witnessed. She tells Gawan:

> mînen lîp gesach nie man,
> ine möhte wol sîn diens hân;
> wan einer, der truoc wâpen rôt.　　(618,19-21)

It is learned how Parzival, as intent on his single quest as she on hers, refused the love of the beautiful Orgeluse:

> ich bôt im lant unt mînen lîp:
> er sprach, er hete ein schœner wîp,
> unt diu im lieber wære.
> diu rede was mir swære:
> ich vrâgete wer diu möhte sîn.
> 'von Pelrapeir diu künegîn,
> sus ist genant diu lieht gemâl:
> sô heize ich selbe Parzivâl.
> ichn wil iwer minne niht:
> der grâl mir anders kumbers giht.'　　(619,3-12)

Because it is remote from the present occasion, the encounter takes on a strange significance, for it was inevitable that Parzival should reject Orgeluse's offer, and yet it seems also inevitable that the two should have met during the course of their lonely and persistent quests. Related as it is so much later, it has lost much of the emotion which must have attended it at the time, and it now possesses a symbolic value, the coming-together of two great forces which then went their separate and relentless ways. Orgeluse saw in Parzival, the greatest of all knights, the only one to whom she could ever offer her love, and the one who could have accomplished her task for her; and Parzival rejected her, intent on his quest for the Graal and loyal as ever to his wife. Though the danger is potentially present, Parzival is not to become the true successor in suffering to Anfortas: he is not to fall a prey to the charms of Orgeluse. Yet the meeting remains a significant one, for it brings Orgeluse closer to the most important issue of the work, and it also brings her into closer relation with Condwiramurs.

The comparison which Parzival thus makes of Orgeluse with his wife is reminiscent of the first view of Orgeluse, when Wolfram himself had said of her:

âne Condwîrn âmûrs
wart nie geborn sô schœner lîp.   (508,22-23)

No greater praise could he offer, for Condwiramurs is supreme in beauty as in all else and must remain so. The comparison points forward, a long way it is true, to the revelation of Orgeluse as a truly noble woman, whose behaviour is motivated by her great love for Cidegast. It has a further significance, however, although this becomes apparent only later. It was Orgeluse who brought about the suffering of Anfortas and the sorrow of the Graal Family. Only one of her great beauty was worthy of the love of the Graal King: only for love of her could the noble Anfortas transgress. It is for Condwiramurs, the only woman who surpasses her in beauty, to relieve the grief and suffering which Orgeluse has inflicted and to become consort to the new Graal King. The sorrow of the Graal has its source and its termination in womanly beauty.

Orgeluse, then, is deeply involved in the sorrow of the Graal Family and is thus central to the story of Parzival's quest. This is, of course, not known when Trevrizent tells Parzival of the transgression of Anfortas (478,17-479,2). Only when Orgeluse tells of how she accepted the love of Anfortas in the hope of avenging Cidegast does her story become linked with that of Parzival. Her account of the tragic outcome of that love, too, adds to the poignancy of her history, for now she must suffer not only the loss of a lover

210

but share also in the grief of the whole Graal Kingdom, on which she has brought such suffering:

> glîchen jâmer oder mêr,
> als Cidegast geben kunde,
> gab mir Anfortases wunde.   (616,24-26)

That she loved Anfortas is clear from her grief, though this is mingled with a sense of responsibility for the wide-spread suffering and sorrow: it is surely the combination of the two which leads her to say that her suffering was greater than her suffering on the death of Cidegast. Her love for Cidegast remains the greatest love of her life, but the last which Wolfram tells of Orgeluse is that she weeps with joy when she learns of the release of Anfortas, the man whom she had also loved (784,4-7).

As the cause of the downfall of Anfortas, Orgeluse is the physical manifestation of the pride which is stressed as the reason for his humiliation, and it is surely no accident that Wolfram links with this downfall through arrogance the woman whose name is Orgeluse. The significance of her name is two-fold, pointing both to the pride in Anfortas of which she is a symbol, and her own pride, evident in her treatment of all those who seek to serve her, and of Gawan in particular. Yet the basic meaning of her name is softened a little by its graceful form, just as her arrogance is softened by her beauty and mingled with regal dignity, rather than the arrogance of pure conceit of her French predecessor.

In the hints which are never fully developed, of a pact with Clinschor (617,7-618,5), Wolfram adds yet another facet to the already complex character of Orgeluse. He involves her with the magic which is a part of the story of Gawan, and supplies also a severe test of his love and valour. The pact with Clinschor does not, however, mean that Orgeluse is in any way herself in possession of magic powers. Though a complex and subtle figure, she is essentially a real person. Because she is very much a woman who understands the world, and who combats its problems with force and strategy, she is an apt partner for Gawan. In her he finds a perfect partner, the culmination of his relationship with Obilot, which was one of service with no hope of reward, and that with Antikonie, which was based on physical attraction, no demands being made on his service. In Orgeluse he recognizes a woman whom he can love and serve with hope of reward, and she too recognizes at last that he is worthy of her love: the mutual respect and understanding between them is contained in the moment when they look one another straight in the eyes:

> Gâwân der kurtoys
> und de herzoginne von Lôgroys
> vast an ein ander sâhen. (619,25-27)

This moment comes after Orgeluse's account of her meeting with Parzival, when she has told how he refused her love, and Gawan, for his part, has praised Parzival very highly, telling her that, had she gained his love, this would have been the ultimate honour for her (619,21-24). Perfect understanding has been achieved between the two of them, then, the woman who is beautiful but less beautiful than Condwiramurs, and the man whose only victor will be Parzival. Yet, though Gawan remains in his own sphere, belonging essentially to the more worldly part of the work, Orgeluse transcends it and becomes involved also in the wider issue, which is the destiny of the Graal.[16]

NOTES

1. *Studies of Wolfram von Eschenbach*, p. 95.
2. Although one has to judge from the work in its unfinished state, it seems fair to assume that l'Orgueilleuse was never to gain greater prominence than that of the central female figure in the Gauvain episodes.
3. *Studies of Wolfram von Eschenbach*, p. 96.

4. In fairness to him, it must be remembered that he is treating *Parzival* only so far as it has a parallel in *Le Conte del Graal*. He takes no account, therefore, of the relationship of Orgeluse to Anfortas. Nevertheless, his view of her can hardly do justice to Wolfram's concept of her.

5. There is a quality in this description which recalls the first sight of Sigune.

6. cf. Lexer *Mittelhochdeutsches Wörterbuch*: *reizel*: 'reizmittel, lockspeise, bes. die im vogelkloben angebrachte.'

7. ed. cit. 6684ff.

8. cf. 130,5; 187,3; 176,10. With the description of Antikonie's mouth as 'heiz, dick unde rot' (405,19), Wolfram implies also a sensuality which is not present in these other examples but is perhaps an additional factor in his description of Orgeluse.

9. B. Q. Morgan (p .196), speaking of l'Orgueilleuse, says: 'Nowhere is there a single pleasing trait of character, and Gauvain's devotion is quite inexplicable.'

10. In the French version, on the other hand, Gauvain is reluctant to cross the river (ed. cit. 8487ff.) and does so only after the woman has scorned his timidity. It is true that Gawan does match Orgeluse in strength of purpose at this point, although in general M. F. Richey is probably right when she says: 'She stands alone, and we realize the disproportion between her solitary strength and the purely spectacular roles of her fellow-actors . . . , and the brave and debonair Gawan, despite his prowess, is cast in too light a mould to sustain, in all seriousness, her task of vengeance.' *Studies of Wolfram von Eschenbach*, p. 97.

11. See 531,19ff; 591,12ff; 601,1ff.

12. cf. W. Mohr ('Parzival und Gawan' in *Wolfram von Eschenbach*, ed. H. Rupp. Wege der Forschung 57, pp. 287-318): 'Und schließlich Orgeluse—auch sie ein Mensch, der durch ein schlimmes Schicksal verhärtet wurde und sich in Prinzipien

des Menschenhasses verbiβ: Ihre Verkrampfung löst sich durch Gawans beharrlichen Minnedienst' (p. 305).

13. pp. 404-405.

14. In his very interesting discussion of the relationship between Gawan and Orgeluse (p. 400ff), D. Blamires draws attention to the parallel, yet quite distinct, relationships of Parzival and Gawan with Condwiramurs and Orgeluse: 'But as Gawan is differentiated from Parzival and represents Wolfram's view of courtliness, so also Orgeluse differs from Condwiramurs. We have already seen how Gawan is characterized as *kurtoys* and *höfsch*, epithets which never occur in connexion with Parzival. . . . The key-word for the relationship between Gawan and Orgeluse is *kurtoys*, and in their story Wolfram explores as thoroughly as he is able all aspects and implications of the idea of *courtly* love, exemplifying the various stages of the *minne*-relationship from the knight's initial devotion to consummation in the bond of marriage' (pp. 401-402).

15. *Studies of Wolfram von Eschenbach*, p. 97.

16. Because there is this sense that Gawan belongs to one sphere and Orgeluse to another, I would not wholly accept the statement by D. Blamires (p. 403) that they are 'finally united in a fully mutual relationship.' The assessment by M. F. Richey (quoted in note 10 above) seems a more apt one.

PART V

The Minor Women Characters

WOLFRAM'S SKILL in characterization extends also to the minor characters, so that even those who make a fleeting appearance achieve a degree of individuality. They are memorable in their own right, yet they are also important for the contribution they make to the complete picture of womanhood which Wolfram creates in his three narrative works. A close study of such women shows them to be completely in accordance with the general pattern in his work. Many of the minor women characters—some of whom appear only briefly or perhaps not at all in person—echo and anticipate the more prominent ones, and the result is a perfectly consistent whole, in which each plays a part, whether great or small, yet without sacrificing her essential individuality. Some of them—Clauditte, Ekuba, Schoette, for example—appear in the work for only a few lines and yet are vivid and memorable. There are, however, many women who must rank among the minor characters but still receive from Wolfram rather lengthier treatment than might be expected. It is as though, with the vivid interest in single characters which is evident from his treatment of the more important figures, Wolfram became engrossed in them as he created them, so that they grew beyond the rôle which they were to fulfil.

Such a character is Bene, the young daughter of the ferryman Plippalinot. Though her rôle appears to be a very simple one, she increases in complexity as the narrative continues. However, to see in Bene anything more than a minor character would be to overestimate her. She is not significant to the work as a whole, but confined to the Gawan-action. She attends to Gawan's comfort in her father's house, and she acts as intermediary in the love between Itonje and Gramoflanz. Yet, like many of the characters concerned with Gawan's adventures, she echoes, on a different level, characters in the main part of the work.[1] From the beginning, her willingness to serve Gawan supplies a link. As Cunneware helped Parzival (332, 22-23), Bene helps Gawan with his armour (549,15; 560,17-18), and the picture of Bene cutting his meat for him, though possibly in itself a conventional gesture, is reminiscent of Belakane's eagerness to serve Gahmuret at table. Above all, perhaps, it is Liaze who comes most readily to mind, for she, too, sat at table with her father's guest and prepared food for him (176,16-21). In other respects, however, Liaze and Bene are not alike, and the relationships are different. Liaze and Parzival were well-matched, and the marriage which did not come about between them was nevertheless fulfilled in the marriage of Parzival and Condwiramurs. Bene is the daughter of a ferryman and can hardly aspire to the love of a knight. Like Obilot, she grieves as Gawan rides away (562,8; 562,15-16), but she grieves, not, like Obilot, because she has lost him, but, as Cunneware for Parzival, because she fears for what may befall him. When Bene next meets Gawan, she kisses his stirrup and his foot (621,16), and this gesture Martin interprets rightly as being 'Zeichen der tiefsten Untertänigkeit.'[2] Once more, the relationship is seen as one of devoted service, rather than of love, and one is reminded of Cunneware, who could never be Parzival's wife, yet remained his devoted friend. On two occasions, Bene lends her cloak to Gawan (552,20-22; 622,1-4), and one remembers Repanse de Schoye. Yet the gesture, though it echoes that of the Graal Bearer, is without symbolic depth and simply exemplifies Bene's desire to serve Gawan: again, one is reminded of the essential difference in levels of the two parts of the work.

Strangely, Bene reappears in the work, one of the few women to have two distinct rôles, for next time it is as intermediary in the love of Itonje and Gramoflanz that she acts. Here, too, she shows herself ready to help and intensely loyal. On numerous occasions she is seen to perform small services:[3] she is constantly willing to aid her mistress Itonje, hence Gramoflanz also, and her master Gawan. She is brought into conflict, however, when it transpires that Gramoflanz is preparing to fight against the brother of Itonje. Like the major heroines, Bene, too, experiences deep distress, resulting from her love and loyalty:

> dô Bêne daz gehôrte
> mit wærlîchem worte,
> daz ir hêrre ir frouwen bruoder was,
> der dâ solde strîten ûfme gras,
> dô zugen jâmers ruoder
> in ir herzen wol ein fuoder
> der herzenlîchen riuwe:
> wan sie pflac herzen triuwe.   (694,9-16)

Though her *triuwe* is never tried to the extent of that of Herzeloyde, Sigune, Condwiramurs or Gyburc, Bene nevertheless possesses it to the full. In accordance, however, with this lighter side of the work which is the Gawan-action, a solution is found in the reconciliation through King Arthur of the two opponents. In this, too, Bene is the intermediary, for it is she who goes to Arthur (714,10-16). She who has striven throughout to bring Itonje and Gramoflanz together is instrumental in the reconciliation which allows the marriage to take place. The last that is heard of Bene is that she rejoices at the happiness of her mistress and Gramoflanz:

> Bên was frô, dô daz geschach.   (729,30)

Her rôle is a modest one, entirely selfless, and unobtrusively she vanishes when her task is fulfilled.

An equally vivid character, though, like Bene, one who must rank as a minor heroine, is Arnive. She too belongs to the Gawan-action and is of no significance to the main theme of the work. Her appearances are brief, yet she is remembered for her essential individuality. Wolfram speaks of her as 'Arnîve diu wîse' (574,5), 'diu alte küniginne wîs (578,4), and she constitutes one of the most delightful pictures of mature womanhood. Of her Wolfram says that youth never came to old age with such womanly honour (656, 4-5), and from this one may conclude that he sees Arnive as the prototype of the noble old woman. Yet she is far from being a mere type, a description which is applicable in fact to none of Wolfram's heroines. As the wife of Utepandragun and the mother of King Arthur, Arnive occupies a position of some importance, but she is remembered, not really for her queenly power, but rather as an old woman with the wisdom of experience. It is this wisdom which characterizes her and is revealed in her actions. As Gawan lies sorely wounded after his fight with the lion, Arnive comes to his aid (574,27ff). While the other women are lamenting, she comes forward with practical help (578,4ff). She quickly takes charge of the situation, arranging for a bed and a fire for the wounded knight, and for the removal of his armour. It is then she herself who tends his wounds, smoothing on them a strange ointment and bandaging them; and it is she who gives him a herb which brings him the sleep he needs. Like no other woman in *Parzival*, Arnive is active and practical. Later it is she who, realizing the distress of Itonje, summons her son Arthur to her and, with Bene, helps to bring about a reconciliation. Arnive renders practical aid, based on experience and prompted by a shrewd assessment of the situation.

To this basic picture of Arnive, of the wise queen, the understanding mother and the old woman with strange skills, Wolfram has added some further details, which make of Arnive a lively, realistic figure. It would appear that much of her knowledge has been acquired as a result of her relentless desire to be informed of events. This is not exactly mere inquisitiveness, for it is coupled with a feeling that, if she knows what is going on, she may be able to help matters. When she learns of the message which Gawan is sending to Ginover, she waylays the squire who is bearing it, and she grows angry when he will not divulge his secret (627,1-4). Not content with one refusal, she tries to trick Orgeluse into telling her Gawan's identity (627,12-18). Again, but again in vain, she tries to obtain the information from the squire when he returns (652,26-653,14). This would seem strange behaviour, perhaps, but since Wolfram clearly admires her shrewdness and wisdom, one must assume that her curiosity and persistence are justified by the intention which prompts them. Obviously, since Arnive goes to such lengths to try to discover Gawan's secret, her power is by no means limitless. She is not omniscient: even the magic pillar now in her possession was stolen from Sekundille (592,18-19). In fact her seemingly magic powers are confined to a knowledge of medicines, which, she says, derives from Cundrie (579,23-580,1): she is no sorceress, but a wise old woman, outstanding as one of the very few examples of old women in Wolfram's works, and memorable in her vivid, though relatively brief, rôle.

Willehalm, too, has the figure of a noble old woman, Irmschart, the mother of Willehalm. She is vividly drawn, too, although her appearance is, again, a relatively brief one. The rôle which Wolfram gives to her follows very closely that of her counterpart, Hermanjart, in the *Aliscans*,[4] but she is consistent still, both with the new tone of *Willehalm*, and with Wolfram's whole picture of womanhood.

The fact that she is a mother is important in Wolfram's view of her character and in his treatment of her rôle. The influence which is due to her motherhood is not, however, a passive influence, as it is with Belakane or Herzeloyde, and Irmschart's rôle is not a passive one. Willehalm is prompted to speak out in the first place by the conviction that the woman who gave him life will come to his aid (144,24-30), and he is not disappointed. Irmschart echoes Gyburc in her courageous appeal to her men. While they are lamenting the death of Vivianz, it is Irmschart who urges them to leave their grief and turn their attention to giving aid to Willehalm (152, 11-27). Like Arnive, she is active, despite her age,[5] and, like Arnive, she comes forward with practical aid, while others are giving way to lamentation. This does not mean that she is not grieved, but that she sees what must now take precedence. As in the *Aliscans*,[6] it is Irmschart who steps between Willehalm and his sister and so prevents her daughter from coming to real harm and her son from committing further violence in his rage (147,22-24). Here, too, Wolfram reminds his audience that she is their mother. Her desire to keep the peace between her son and daughter is stressed when she sends Alyze with Willehalm's message of forgiveness (160,1-16). With the wisdom of experience, she sees that this is not the time for petty quarrelling, that they must unite to help Willehalm. As Arnive joined with Bene to reconcile Gawan and Gramoflanz, so now does Irmschart join with Alyze, the young and the old united by a wisdom which seems to escape those who are between them.

It is the final gesture of the scene which links Irmschart most emphatically with Gyburc. She offers her treasure to Willehalm to finance his war, ready and glad to give her wealth to the cause she believes in, and she is the first to do so, setting an example to her reluctant son-in-law. She does more, too, for she expresses her willingness to fight herself in defence of Willehalm; her *triuwe* as a mother is strong and ready to be tested:

> '.... harnasch muoz an mînen lîp.
> ich pin sô starc wol ein wîp,
> daz ich pî dir wâpen trage.
> der ellenthafte, niht der zage,
> mac mich pî dir schouwen:
> ich wil mit swerten houwen.'   (161,5-10)

The prospect of the old woman in armour and wielding a sword in the face of attack supports the picture of Gyburc herself. *Willehalm*, indeed, is the place for a new image of woman, and Gyburc and Irmschart together show that the truly noble woman is capable, if need arises, of inspiring the men about her and of leading them into battle.

The only remaining woman in *Willehalm* is the somewhat puz-

zling queen of Ludwig. Though the reasons are different, one encounters here a similar problem as with Obie and Antikonie. Her
callous rejection of her own brother's plea for aid places her in a
most unfavourable light, so that the ill-treatment she receives at
Willehalm's hands is seen as her just desert, although one may regret the uncontrolled rage of Willehalm which allows it. Her subsequent change of attitude when she learns of the deaths of their
kinsmen and the loss at Alischanz does not really serve to erase her
former behaviour, even though her intervention helps to persuade
King Ludwig that Willehalm must be given aid. Though she laments now the loss of so many kinsmen (164,10-165,27), one remembers that previously it was she who recognized her brother as
he sat alone and dejected, yet urged her husband to bar the doors
against him (129,19-130,2). It would seem that her change of heart
has been prompted as much by fear of Willehalm and by the memory of his harsh treatment of her, as by a genuine sense of loss and
desire to help.

In this suspicion one is supported, surely, by Wolfram himself,
for his treatment of her suggests his own disapproval. She is the only
woman whom he does not call by name, and in view of his interest
in names, which led him on all other occasions to supply a name
where it was lacking in his source,[7] this surely implies at the least
a lack of interest, even a positive dislike of her.[8] There is a further
significant omission: Wolfram applies no adjective to Ludwig's
queen, and this again is quite exceptional. The omission suggests
also that Wolfram could not bring himself to utter a word of praise
or affection for this woman. The problem, then, is rather different
from that encountered in the case of Obie and Orgeluse, where he
showed that true love and virtue lay beneath the surface and was
ultimately to reveal itself. Even in the case of Antikonie he managed, though with some difficulty and perhaps even embarrassment,
to delineate a character who was not wholly unattractive. This he
cannot do in the case of Ludwig's queen, and he does not attempt to
justify her actions. Her presence is necessary, both in fidelity to the

223

source and for the sake of the plot at this point, but of all Wolfram's women characters she alone lacks a place in an otherwise consistent whole.

A fascinating figure, who never actually appears, but whose name occurs a number of times in both *Parzival* and *Willehalm*, is Sekundille. Though she is not developed to the same extent, she resembles Ampflise, and the resemblance is both in her rôle and in Wolfram's treatment of her. For Sekundille, too, remains in the background, a force in the life of Feirefiz, as Ampflise is in the life of Gahmuret. Like Ampflise, Sekundille is doomed to lose the man she loves dearly, but Sekundille, a less tragic figure than Ampflise, dies before he returns and so is spared the pain of the loss.

Like Ampflise, Sekundille is a queen, and there are a number of isolated references to her, all pointing to her wealth. Wolfram refers to the precious stones and the gold in her land (519,2-17) and to the rich silks which are made there (629,20-27). There are similar references in *Willehalm* to the exotic riches of Queen Sekundille (125,28-30; 248,26-249,1; 279,17-280,1). Such references are used indirectly, in comparisons often, for clearly the wealth of Sekundille is renowned. In *Parzival* such mentions of her occur long before she emerges as a character in the work. They help to build up a picture of the exotic and the mysterious. The strange history of the hideous Cundrie and her brother (519,2-520,1) adds a little more to the mystery which surrounds Sekundille. The explanation which Wolfram gives of the strange pair succeeds also in linking Sekundille with the Graal. Her exact relationship with Anfortas remains obscure, like so much of her story, but it explains how the subject of a heathen queen became the messenger of the Christian Graal.[9]

It is the battle between Parzival and Feirefiz which brings Sekundille to the fore. Here she appears as the inspiration of the heathen knight, and for a time it seems that her spirit will lead him to victory. In this combat between such equally matched opponents, the power of the women is also equal. Thus, for a time, Sekundille is placed with Condwiramurs, and greater praise can hardly be given. Her name and the name of her city echo throughout the battle, nor does the end of it, which is brought about by the magnanimity of Feirefiz, bring dishonour on her name. Sekundille is clearly a noble woman, who loves, and is loved by, the only knight who is a match for Parzival. There is only one thing which she lacks, and this is the one thing which can take Feirefiz from her; she has not known baptism, and the conversion to Christianity of Feirefiz means his separation from her. It may be argued that Repanse de Schoye has already caused this separation, for he falls in love with her on sight, and this new love takes the place of all love he has ever known, including that for Sekundille (811,8-16). For Wolfram, however, great love is the way to faith, and so one may well regard his falling in love with Repanse de Schoye as his actual conversion, of which his subsequent baptism is the formal sign. Like Tybalt, Sekundille is the innocent sacrifice to a higher ideal. She, no less than the husband of Arabel, is powerless in face of the power of the Christian faith. With his constant compassion for human suffering, Wolfram could not, however, allow Sekundille, who had been so deeply in love with Feirefiz, to endure the pain of seeing him the husband of another woman. He releases her, and the news comes of her death (822,19-20).[10]

The burden of the woman to endure pain as the consequence of love is shown again in the brief portrayal of Schoette, Gahmuret's mother. She is in perfect accord with the other women in *Parzival*, for throughout this work the heroines are seen to love and to grieve because of their love. Schoette is remembered for a single scene when her son takes his leave of her, and the leave-taking is made all the more poignant by Wolfram's remark that Gahmuret is never to see his mother again (12,16-17). As Herzeloyde is to do after her, the widowed Schoette grieves at first and pleads with him to stay (10,15-16). Realizing, like Herzeloyde, that she cannot rightly keep him with her, she releases him. Herzeloyde will give to Parzival some basic rules of conduct to take on his way: Schoette, too, wishes that gifts should accompany her son, and she gives him rich silks and velvet to take with him (11,14-19). Only once more is Schoette mentioned.[11] When Gahmuret is at Herzeloyde's court and has learnt of the death of his brother, he immediately enquires after his mother, only to learn that she died of a broken heart, having suffered the death of her husband and elder son, and the absence of Gahmuret himself (92,24-30). Once more, she is linked with Herzeloyde who also endured for a time the loss of her husband but finally died when her son left her. That Wolfram sees this as the way of noble womanhood is clear from his praise of Herzeloyde, and Schoette, too, though her rôle is such a slight one, is remembered for Wolfram's description of her as 'daz wîplîche wîp' (10,17).

The picture of Wolfram's women is not complete without reference to Schoysiane, the first Graal Bearer. Though she never appears, she nevertheless achieves a degree of fame, as the equally virtuous predecessor of Repanse de Schoye, and the mother of Sigune. Perhaps inevitably, in view of the sacred object with which she is entrusted, Schoysiane shares some of the mystery which enshrouds her sister. Like Repanse de Schoye, she too was supremely virtuous and supremely beautiful (*Titurel* 10,1-2; 14,2), but her memory is surrounded by the tragedy of her early death and the grief of her husband. Schoysiane is always spoken of in the past tense,[12] and even her name is surely suggestive of the joy which she lost so early, and which was lost to the world in her.[13] Schoysiane's beauty and virtue live on in her daughter (*Titurel* 33,1-4), yet she has bequeathed also to Sigune the power to love as intensely as she herself loved Kyot, and in Wolfram's view of life, such love must bring suffering and grief with it. As a daughter of the Graal, Schoysiane bequeaths also to Sigune the suffering which is part of the legacy of all members of the Graal Family. Her own share in this legacy took the form of an early and tragic death, and her daughter is to endure the death of her lover and years of grief, until Parzival lifts the burden from the whole of the family. Schoysiane, then, like Herzeloyde, lives on in her child, and, as the predecessor of Repanse de Schoye, she is intimately linked with the Graal and the theme of the whole work.

At the back of such women as Sekundille, Schoette and Schoysiane are others, to whom reference is made only in passing, but who nevertheless contribute to the picture which Wolfram gives of the tragedy of human life. Mahaute and Annore are two such women, victims of the life of chivalry which takes their menfolk from them (178,16-24 and *Titurel* 126,1-127,2; 346,15-19). Their stories echo, though with less emphasis, those of Belakane, Herzeloyde and Sigune. Similarly, the history of Clauditte and Olimpia, which is never told, must come close to that of Sekundille, who loses Feirefiz to a greater love (811,11-16). By allowing these shadowy figures to exist behind the more prominent ones, Wolfram gives depth and reality to the situations which he presents: the tragedies he shows are universal ones, with the women as their victims. Because their own fates echo those of the major heroines, these faintly drawn characters attain also a depth which could not otherwise be theirs.[14] They belong with equal right to the vast spectrum which Wolfram's works display.

Itonje is a heroine in whom is revealed clearly the essential difference between the Parzival-action and the Gawan-action. Like Obie, she loves and suffers for a time, but she too knows the happy fulfilment of her love, unlike many of the women involved in the Parzival-action. The picture which Wolfram gives of Itonje is one of a charming and very courtly young girl, deeply in love with King Gramoflanz. In some ways, it is a very conventional picture, and Itonje's demeanour is very much that of the perfectly bred lady of the court. Wolfram's characters rarely remain limited by convention, however, and Itonje, too, rises to some extent above the type of the love-lorn maiden.

Her situation, after all, is an unusual one, for her love for the mighty Gramoflanz, whom she has never seen, is secret, and she finds herself in a dilemma when she has to kiss Orgeluse and the two knights who ride constantly in pursuit of Gramoflanz. This she does because Gawan has asked it of her, but it represents to her a failure in loyalty towards her lover (634,17-24). The situation is further complicated when she enlists the aid of Gawan, unaware that he is her brother, and when later she is brought to the terrible realization that her brother and her lover are to face one another in combat (710,9-18). Her grief is profound, and for a time her dilemma seems insoluble. In accordance with this lighter side of the whole work, a solution is found, however, when King Arthur intervenes and effects a reconciliation. Thus, though the conclusion is a joyful one, Itonje has not escaped the grief which, for Wolfram, is the constant companion of love:

> stæter freude se niht vergaz:
> doch kôs man an ir ougen schîn,
> daz si diu minne lêrte pîn. (723,20-22)

The comparison, and the inevitable contrast, between Sigune and Itonje is suggested in the words of Arthur to Itonje:

> ôwê, liebiu niftel mîn,
> daz dîn jugent sô hôher minne schîn
> tuot! daz muoz dir werden sûr.
> als tet dîn swester Sûrdâmûr
> durch der Kriechen lampriure. (712,5-9)

In these words he echoes very closely the reaction of Herzeloyde when she first learns of Sigune's love for Schionatulander:

> Ich klage et daz du bist alze fruo sîn âmîe.
> du wilt den kumber erben, des Mahaude phlac bî dem talfîn
> Gurzgrîe.
> (*Titurel*, 127,1-2)

Circumstances are set, then, for a repetition of the tragedy of Sigune, but the tone of the action at this point does not allow it.

The complexity of the love of Itonje serves to distinguish her from the conventional noble lady wooed by a powerful knight.

Though her nature and her rôle rest in this convention, Wolfram's intense interest in individual characters ensures that Itonje, too, is a memorable figure. She is remembered for her youthful yet powerful love, her grief when she realizes her position, but perhaps above all for the power of her love over King Gramoflanz. He who has appeared as a harsh, unscrupulous man, mellows in the face of her sweetness and love. Wolfram says of him that his hostility melts away before her, like snow in the sun (728,13-17). Thus the one who has held so many in fear of their lives is conquered by the love of a young girl. Once more, then, beauty and sweetness in a woman are shown to possess the power to reconcile. The coming-together of Itonje and Gramoflanz closes the Gawan-action, and the contrast with the main tone of the work is expressed most emphatically by the very presence of Parzival and the need he feels to leave (733, 20-30). Parzival does not belong here, any more than Itonje can be placed with Sigune or Herzeloyde. Though she is a noble woman, possessing the intensity of love which could lead her, like them, to tragic greatness, this is not required of her. Instead she ranks with Wolfram's minor heroines, contributing in her own way to the greater pattern of womanhood.

For a few moments another woman comes forward, to offer Parzival words of praise and consolation, after Cundrie's attack has plunged him into grief and dishonour. This is Ekuba, the heathen queen of Janfuse. With Cunneware and Jeschute, she goes forward to comfort Parzival (327,21-25). Thus compassion, which is a principal virtue of the major heroines, reveals itself in the gesture of this woman whose rôle is such a slight one. Cunneware and Jeschute are bound to Parzival by the strong bonds of friendship and gratitude, but Ekuba is a stranger, a heathen, who yet sees Parzival's greatness and is moved by the disaster which has befallen him. She acclaims him for his good looks and his noble bearing, asserting that all Christian people are honoured in him (329,4-10). Though he rejects the possibility of consolation, Parzival is clearly grateful for her words, as he is later for the companionship of Cunneware as he departs. It is characteristic of Wolfram's generosity towards all human beings that he allows a heathen woman to offer this gesture to Parzival. Virtue knows no barriers, and this black woman is equally well able to bring comfort to Parzival as any other virtuous woman. What matters is that she possesses the power of pity and love which will at last bring him back to God.

Ekuba is important, too, for the news she brings of Feirefiz. She tells of his wealth and fame (328,5-30), and her assertion that he has never been defeated in combat anticipates the moment so long after, when Parzival will almost succumb to the might of his half-brother. In this single speech of Ekuba, the two great men are brought together, as they will one day be in combat. The son of Gahmuret and Belakane must remain in the minds of Wolfram's audience, though he is remote from the action, until he is brought back into it with such force and significance. In Ekuba is seen once more the intense interest of Wolfram in the individual character. Though the two functions she fulfils could have been fulfilled in another way or by someone else, he chose to create this new character who appears in the work, to dominate it for a few lines, and to disappear immediately afterwards.

Although she is a very slight character, Clauditte must also be mentioned among Wolfram's minor heroines. She is remembered as the little girl playing with Obilot, and she shares in the charm of her more significant friend. Together they form a delightful picture of childhood, from the time when they are discovered playing the game of rings (368,10-12) to Clauditte's simple offer to give Obilot one of her dolls for Gawan, if they are prettier than her own (372,16-21). Clauditte acts as messenger between Gawan and Obilot, taking him the sleeve from her dress (375,19-20), and she is as innocent yet sincere as her friend. The picture of their friendship, childish yet firm, is a very true one, and the observation of life which must have made it possible is perhaps most apparent when Wolfram allows Obilot to demand that her little friend too be taken on to a knight's horse (373,9). As so many of the minor characters echo more prominent ones, so does Clauditte echo Obilot, exemplifying with her the beginnings of the charm of womanhood.

Finally, one must look at the character of Ginover as Wolfram shows her. He is dependent here to a large extent on the traditional conception of Arthur's Queen. Like Arthur, she is at the centre of the courtly life, and, like him, too, she is a rather passive figure, the impulse and the goal of acts of chivalry but not herself coming forward as an active character. Because the life of the Round Table is constantly in the background of the work, Ginover too is constantly appearing throughout it. She is always present when Wolfram wishes to stress the courtly environment.[15] She is an essential part of this environment, and Wolfram's picture of her gives to his audience what they have come to expect of Arthur's Queen.[16] Convention, which Wolfram could hardly have changed even if he had wished to, demanded that Ginover should be a gracious lady, remote to some extent, yet ready to hear the pleas of the knights in her service. This is Wolfram's picture of her, too. She intercedes on behalf of Urians, and it is to her that Segramors turns when he desires Arthur's leave to engage in combat (286,15-16). She takes the love-lorn Itonje into her care (731,2-3), and she performs all these acts with the grace and dignity of one who is first and foremost a queen. Significantly, Wolfram hardly ever applies an adjective to Ginover. In speaking of other women characters he frequently adds a word in reference to their beauty and their virtue: Ginover is 'frou Gynovêr diu künegîn (698,18), 'frou Ginovêr' (143,22; 387,7), and often simply 'diu künegîn' (646,23; 647,28; 650,23). Once he makes the simple statement 'diu was kurtoys' (727,18), and he speaks of her once as 'diu kurteise' (651,5). These are, however, restrained, formal compliments, suggesting the extent to which Ginover, even in Wolfram's conception of her, is still the traditional type of queen, perfect in courtly breeding, but lacking in distinct individuality.

Basically, then, this is the figure of Ginover in *Parzival*, the con-

ventional queen of Arthurian romance and more nearly a stereo-
typed figure than any of Wolfram's women characters. Yet even to
her Wolfram gives a little of those qualities which are manifested
more fully in his own creations, where he was free from all convention. It is for her grief at the death of Ither that Wolfram himself remembers Ginover, when he is reminding his audience of the
noble women of whom he has spoken:

> welch was froun Ginovêren klage
> an Ithêres endetage! (337,13-14)

As though speaking on behalf of all women who lament at Ither's
death, Ginover delivered a speech of some eloquence over his body
(160,1-30). Though the power of the gallant Ither over women is
known to have been great, one may argue that this speech is nevertheless in some ways a conventional one, which can hardly have its
source in deep personal grief, since it was Ither who had challenged
her husband. More convincing, perhaps, is her sorrow at Gawan's
absence, and her delight when the squire brings news of him (645,
1-6). On this occasion, too, she expresses her regret at the events at
the Plimizoel, which took away from her, not only Gawan, but
Parzival, Jeschute, Ekuba and Cunneware too:

> grôz jâmer nâch der werden diet
> mich sît von stæten fröuden schiet. (646,21-22)

In general, however, it is still Ginover, the conventional Queen of
Arthur, whom Wolfram shows, though such brief moments when
she betrays more ordinary human sentiments suggest that he meant
to imply womanly virtue beneath her regality. The absence of individual characteristics in Ginover serves to draw attention, however, to the intensely individual nature of almost all the other minor
women characters. Ginover stands alone, as indeed does Arthur,
as a character who was too much a part of the background of the
work to be changed or re-created to any extent.

232

The variety of Wolfram's minor women characters is remarkable. Each one is as much an individual as are the major heroines, and each one is extraordinarily memorable in her own right. Wolfram's method of portrayal is varied, too. Some of the women, like Bene, Itonje and Arnive, are fairly dominant for a while and vital to the plot at that time. Others, like Irmschart, Schoette, Clauditte and Ekuba, achieve memorability in the briefest possible space of time, often in a single, vivid picture. A particular distinction belongs to two women, Sekundille and Schoysiane, for both are a strange kind of presence in *Parzival*, extraordinarily familiar, yet never for a moment appearing in person.

Sekundille and Schoysiane are particularly striking instances of another aspect of Wolfram's range of heroines, too. Each one echoes a more dominant heroine, for the fate of Sekundille is close to that of Belakane and Ampflise, and Schoysiane shares the distinction of Repanse de Schoye. Clauditte echoes Obilot, and Schoette, in the brief account of her parting from Gahmuret and her later death, foreshadows Herzeloyde, as the devoted and heart-broken mother. The skill of Wolfram in allowing his minor characters to echo and anticipate the more central ones in this way contributes an essential feature to the overall depiction of the heroines, whom he sees both as individuals and as parts of a perfectly integrated whole.

NOTES

1. See Marianne Wynn: 'Parzival and Gawan—hero and counterpart,' *Beiträge zur Geschichte der deutschen Sprache und Literatur*, (Tübingen), 72, 1950, pp. 1-39.
2. *Kommentar* 621, 16.
3. See, for example, 642,1ff; 642,29; 663,9ff.
4. See B. de Kok (pp. 92-95).
5. Wolfram refers on a number of occasions to her age: 143,1; 160,1; 160,22. He clearly wishes to draw attention to the discrepancy between her age and her action.

6. ed. cit. 2805ff.

7. For example, Herzeloyde, Cunneware, Condwiramurs, Jeschute, Repanse de Schoye, Cundrie, Obie, Obilot, Antikonie.

8. In the source, the queen was called Blancheflor (ed. cit. 2548; 2767). It may be argued that Wolfram, remembering both the 'amie' of Perceval and the mother of Tristan, did not wish to give one of his heroines the same name, but it is unlikely that such a consideration would have troubled him in the case of this woman.

9. See above p. 135.

10. It is significant to compare this brief statement with the narration by Feirefiz of the death of Belakane of love for the man she has lost. In his treatment of Sekundille, Wolfram finds no place for sentiment which might have blurred the essential issue.

11. The mention of her in *Titurel* 126,4 is not significant to the study of her character.

12. Except in *Titurel* 10,1.

13. Wolfram clearly desires to link Schoysiane and Repanse de Schoye in their names too, for each contains the word *schoye* with the remainder of the name indicating the fate of this joy.

14. In a different way, Wolfram uses the scene of the woman with the knight dying in her lap whom Gawan encounters (505, 1-16) to support the scene of Parzival's first meeting with Sigune. There is the difference in intensity which characterizes the difference between the Parzival-action and the Gawan-action, but the parallel is nonetheless clear.

15. For example 143,21-24; 698,17-21; 731,1-3.

16. In 143,21-24 Wolfram draws attention to the precedent which Hartmann von Aue had clearly established in his portrayal of Arthur, his Queen and his Court.

Conclusion

TOGETHER the heroines of Wolfram's three narrative works fulfil his promise at the beginning of *Parzival*, to tell of the nature of womanly woman. The picture which emerges is an idealized one, as was to be expected from this early statement of his intention. Though not all the women attain the height of perfection of the greatest heroines, they nevertheless all contribute towards the final picture. The heroines may be seen to form a broad spectrum, in which each character stands in her own right, adding her particular shade to the whole, carefully gradated formation. That this is the case emerges from the close study of the women as individuals, for it becomes apparent that they share the same qualities, which are emphasized to a different extent in different heroines. The virtues which Wolfram sees as the essentials of womanhood are most strikingly present in Herzeloyde, Sigune, Condwiramurs and Gyburc, but they are present also in the young heroines, who have still to attain the mature virtue of the central women characters, as well as in those women whose rôles are not so extensive, in Belakane, Repanse de Schoye, Jeschute, Liaze, Cunneware and Cundrie. These women, like those who may genuinely be called 'minor heroines,' echo the more prominent ones.

Similarities become apparent during the close study of the women characters; it is not only that the virtues recur, but also that the situations of the women echo one another. This feature of Wolfram's heroines is a highly complex one, however, for while, for example, Herzeloyde recalls Schoette, she is linked also, in her love for Gahmuret, with Belakane, and Belakane herself bears a resemblance to Sekundille and Condwiramurs, and is clearly also the forerunner of Gyburc. As a wise old woman, Irmschart is linked with Arnive, as a devoted mother with Schoette, but her militant loyalty unites her also with Gyburc. Such resemblances, of which there are very many, add to the complexity of Wolfram's portrayal of his heroines and make of the whole range a fascinatingly intricate whole, in which the component elements are linked on all sides, without for a moment sacrificing their particular individuality. However close the resemblances may be at times, the situation changes slightly from case to case, so that none of the women is an exact repetition of another. Thus one may justly speak of a 'spectrum' in reference to Wolfram's heroines, for the women partake of the same qualities, which have as many manifestations as there are women.

From a close examination of the heroines as individuals and from the observation of the relationships among them, there emerges also a very clear picture of Wolfram's ideal of womanhood. This ideal, of course, is demonstrated above all in the four central heroines, but it is confirmed again and again by the other women. Of the many women characters whom Wolfram portrays, only two do not conform to this ideal, and both of them owe their presence in Wolfram's work to his loyalty to his source. Although Antikonie and Ludwig's Queen do present a problem, in that they disturb an otherwise consistent picture of virtue, Wolfram's treatment of them—his not entirely successful attempt to redeem Antikonie and his evident dislike of Ludwig's Queen—suggests his own feeling that these are not the women he wishes to present, and that they betray their sex by their behaviour. In a negative way, they draw attention to the extraordinary consistency in the remainder of the heroines.

The ideal of womanhood consists for Wolfram in three virtues which he prizes above all others. These are the virtues of *triuwe*, *kiusche* and *diemüete*. In *triuwe* Wolfram sees the basis of all perfect relationships, and the supreme feminine virtue. It includes the loving devotion of a woman to her husband, to her lover, to her son, but it finds its highest expression in the love of a human being for God. This *triuwe* is shown to the full in the four central heroines, but it is also an essential attribute of all the women, even, ultimately, of Antikonie. Above all, it is Sigune who is remembered as the embodiment of *triuwe*, in her single-minded devotion to her dead lover. Yet, in its various manifestations, *triuwe* is revealed very emphatically in the other heroines: in Herzeloyde, who by her *triuwe* to her dead husband through her son will be saved from the pains of hell, in Condwiramurs, whose *triuwe* is tested in the years of separation from Parzival, in Gyburc, whose *triuwe* to her husband and to God is given active expression in her defence of Orange. In the ways which lie open to them, all the other heroines, too, reveal and confirm their *triuwe*.

By *kiusche* Wolfram understands more than simply chastity, for it is the loyalty of a woman to her womanhood, her purity in all ways, and the total absence of falsity. This requirement is clearly fulfilled by the major heroines, but it is in Belakane, Jeschute and Repanse de Schoye that Wolfram stresses the virtue most firmly. In Jeschute, *kiusche* shines through her rags and mocks at the accusations of her husband. In Belakane and Repanse de Schoye, it is seen in its full significance, for it has a distinctly spiritual value, a substitute for baptism in the case of Belakane, and in Repanse de Schoye the virtue which allows her to bear the Christian Graal.

The virtue of *diemüete* is most evident in Herzeloyde and Gyburc, and in both of them humility reveals itself in the readiness to accept poverty. Their humility is the poverty of spirit which places no importance on worldly status and material wealth, and it is shared by Sigune and Repanse de Schoye, who withdraw from the world in their devotion. Another aspect of humility is revealed in the readiness to serve, which one recalls in Cunneware, in Belakane, in Bene, and in the unquestioning acceptance by Jeschute of the harsh treatment of her husband. Humility radiates from the Pil-

grim's daughters, from Alyze and from Obilot, yet never is its manifestation quite the same: always there is the genius of Wolfram to
vary it and present a new facet of the same virtue.

These, then, are the qualities of the ideal woman, and they are
in contrast to the virtues which Wolfram prizes in his noble knights.
In the men he looks for loyalty in love, it is true, but this is to be
expressed in noble combat, in the constant pursuit of fame and adventure. His knights must show themselves brave in battle and
merciful in victory, but this demands activity. It is the women who
possess the abstract power of love, whereas the men reveal their
love in action and physical effort. The love of Gahmuret for both
Belakane and Herzeloyde is indisputable, yet he seeks to display
it in deeds of valour and the pursuit of fame, while they remain behind, in unquestioning acceptance of the absence which they must
endure as part of their love. Herzeloyde is left to gaze after her son,
for whom the parting does not represent a denial of love, any more
than it did for his father, when he refused to remain with Schoette.
Most clearly does Wolfram point to the contrast, however, when he
says of Condwiramurs that she has all she could desire, for Parzival, no less in love with her, is not content in the way that she is
content, but desires to go in search of adventure, a desire which
gives most potent expression to his love for her. Both Gahmuret and
Parzival ride away, leaving their wives to bear their sons, and the
picture of motherhood of all three women is a restful one, epito-
mizing the passivity which balances the active restlessness of the
men.

The nature of woman, as Wolfram sees it, is passivity, but this
is not a negative quality at all, but a positive and immeasurably
powerful one. The power of woman rests in her essential being,
and she exercises her greatest influence not by what she *does*, but by
what she *is*. The power which the women exert is often the power
of their very presence, and this is most evident in the heroines of
Parzival, above all in Sigune, Herzeloyde, Condwiramurs, in Liaze,
Belakane and Repanse de Schoye. It is the case, too, with the young

heroines, the Pilgrim's daughters, Obilot and Alyze. Only Gyburc, in circumstances which she alone among Wolfram's heroines must face, transcends this passivity and reveals the same virtues by active means.

By the very impact of their perfect natures, then, Sigune, Herzeloyde and Condwiramurs are able to direct Parzival and in a strange way, both by direct contact and by his heritage from them, to govern his nature and so ultimately to lead him to the supreme spiritual goal. Nor is it only the central heroines who act upon him in this way, but many of the others, too, Cunneware, Jeschute, Liaze, Cundrie, Repanse de Schoye, the Pilgrim's daughters, influence him, when for a time their paths cross his and their perfection becomes apparent to him. Obilot and Alyze, too, exert an influence on Gawan and Willehalm, by their very presence as examples of virtuous womanhood. Ampflise and Orgeluse, on a less spiritual level, exert a power over Gahmuret and Gawan, by the force of their personalities. Though Gyburc's achievement lies in her active defence of Orange and her positive plea for mercy, it has its source in the courage and faith which allow her to act in a situation where activity is demanded: her power nevertheless rests in the perfection of her own nature.

As individuals the heroines of *Parzival* are seen to possess the power of love and faith, the power to heal and to reconcile, but together they clearly demonstrate the power of womanhood as an abstract concept. The spirituality of this power is apparent from the fact that so many of the women contribute in some way towards Parzival's achievement of the highest goal of Christian knighthood, which is coupled with his return to faith in God. Those women who do not come into contact with him, like Obilot, Belakane and Ampflise, are endowed nonetheless with powers as noble women which would have allowed them to contribute also, had they had the opportunity to do so.

Because womanhood as an abstract force is given a place of such significance in *Parzival*, the fitness of Gyburc to fulfil her rôle in

Willehalm becomes apparent. The message of the earlier work echoes in this single heroine, to whom is given the burden of expressing alone the theme of *Willehalm*, that the way to God lies through love. When perfect womanhood in *Parzival* has led the hero to his return to faith, it is apt that the heroine of *Willehalm*, with virtues equal to those of her predecessors, should stand alone and defend the faith which has come to her through love.

Such, then, is the great rôle of woman in Wolfram's works, and his notion of the ideal is manifested in the impressive array of women characters. While each of these women achieves memorability in her own right, and so contributes to the essential variety and the exciting texture of Wolfram's narrative, each still nevertheless bears out his notion of the ideal and helps to give it most potent expression. That this ideal is a vital force in Wolfram's work can hardly be disputed, for the evidence is plain, expressed in many ways and on many levels. Yet to the twentieth century the very notion of ideal womanhood may seem distasteful, savouring perhaps too much of a sentimentality which does not appeal to modern taste. To ignore its significance in the work of Wolfram von Eschenbach is, however, to reject a central factor in his view of life. His concept of the rôle of woman anticipates the closing words of Goethe's *Faust*: womanhood, in its perfect form, has the power to guide man, and an interpretation of Wolfram's works which fails to take into account this basic belief must fail in its understanding of Wolfram.

Select Bibliography

1. *Reference and general background works*

BENECKE, G. *Mittelhochdeutsches Wörterbuch*, ausgearbeitet von W. Müller and F. Zarncke, (reprint) Hildesheim, 1963

BLOCH, M. *La Société féodale*, Paris, 1939

BUMKE, J. *Die Wolfram von Eschenbach Forschung seit 1945. Bericht und Bibliographie*, Munich, 1970

CHANDLER, F. W. 'A Catalogue of names of persons in the German Court Epics,' M.A. thesis, London, 1936

CROSS, F. (editor) *The Oxford Dictionary of the Christian Church*, Oxford, 1957

HOFER, S. *Chrétien de Troyes, Leben und Werk*, Graz-Cologne, 1954

KER, W. P. *Epic and Romance*, London, 1896

LEXER, M. *Mittelhochdeutsches Wörterbuch*, Leipzig, 1872-1878

LOOMIS, R. S. *Arthurian Literature in the Middle Ages*, Oxford, 1959

MALE, E. *The Gothic Image* (Originally: *Religious Art in France: XIIIth Century*), translated by D. Nussey, 1913, (reprint) London, 1961

RICHEY, M. F. *Essays on Mediæval German Poetry*, Oxford, 1969

SALZER, A. *Die Sinnbilder und Beiworte Mariens in der deutschen Literatur und lateinischen Hymnenpoesie des Mittelalters*, Darmstadt, 1967

SCHULTZ, A. *Das höfische Leben zur Zeit der Minnesänger*, (2 vols.), Leipzig, 1889

SCHWIETERING, J. *Die deutsche Dichtung des Mittelalters*, Darmstadt, 1957

TAYLOR, H. O. *The Mediæval Mind* (2 vols.), 4th ed., Harvard, 1959

WECHSSLER, E. *Das Kulturproblem des Minnesangs*, Halle, 1909

2. *Editions*

WOLFRAM VON ESCHENBACH, ed. K. Lachmann, 6th complete edition, by E. Hartl, Berlin, 1927, (reprint) Berlin, 1960

CHRÉTIEN DE TROYES: *Le Roman de Perceval ou Le Conte du Graal*, ed. W. Roach, Geneva and Paris, 1959

Aliscans, Kritischer Text von E. Wienbeck, W. Hartnacke, P. Rasch, Halle, 1903

HARTMANN VON AUE: *Erec*, ed. A. Leitzmann, Tübingen, 1963

PRIESTER WERNHER: *Maria*, ed. C. Wesle, Halle, 1927

3. *Select Literature on Wolfram von Eschenbach*

ACKERMANN, P. 'Who is Kundrie—what is she?,' *The Literary Review*, Fairleigh Dickinson University, Teaneck, New Jersey, Vol. 2, no. 3, 1959, pp. 458-468

BAUER, G. 'Parzival und die Minne,' *Euphorion*, 57, 1963, pp. 67-96

BAYERSCHMIDT, C. F. 'Wolfram's Christian Faith,' *Germanic Review*, 29, 1954, pp. 214-223

BLAMIRES, D. M. *Characterization and Individuality in Wolfram's 'Parzival*,' Cambridge, 1966

BOESTFLEISCH, K. *Studien zum Minnegedanken bei Wolfram von Eschenbach*, Königsberg, 1930

BUMKE, J. *Wolfram's 'Willehalm*,' Heidelberg, 1959

EHRISMANN, G. 'Wolframprobleme,' *Germanisch-Romanische Monatsschrift*, 1, 1910, pp. 657-674

EHRISMANN, G. 'Über Wolframs Ethik,' *Zeitschrift für deutsches Altertum*, 49, 1908, pp. 405-465

ERTZDORFF, X. VON 'Fräulein Obilot: Zum siebten Buch von Wolframs *Parzival*,' *Wirkendes Wort*, 12, 1962, pp. 129-140

FOURQUET, J. *Wolfram d'Eschenbach et le Conte del Graal*, Paris, 1938

GIBBS, MARION E. 'The Rôle of Woman in Wolfram's *Parzival*,' *German Life and Letters*, 21, 1968, pp. 296-308

———. 'Wrong Paths in *Parzival*,' *Modern Language Review*, 63, 1968, pp. 872-876

GIESE, INGEBORG 'Sigune. Untersuchungen zur Minneauffassung Wolframs von Eschenbach,' Dissertation, Rostock, 1952

GÜNTERT, H. *Kundry*, Heidelberg, 1928

GROOS, A. B. " 'Sigune auf der Linde' and the Turtledove in *Parzival*," *Journal of English and Germanic Philology*, 67, 1968, pp. 631-646

HEISE, URSULA 'Frauengestalten im *Parzival* Wolframs von Eschenbach,' *Deutschunterricht*, 9,2, 1957, pp. 37-62

JOHNSON, L. P. 'Characterization in Wolfram's *Parzival*,' *Modern Language Review* 64, 1969, pp. 68-83

JOHNSON, S. M. 'Herzeloyde and the Grail,' *Neophilologus*, 52, 1968, pp. 148-156

KEFERSTEIN, G. *Parzivals ethischer Weg*, Weimar, 1937

KINZEL, K. 'Die Frauen in Wolframs *Parzival*,' *Zeitschrift für deutsche Philologie*, 21, 1889, pp. 48-73

———. 'Beiträge zur Erklärung und Beurteilung des *Parzival*,' *Zeitschrift für deutsches Altertum*, 30, 1886, pp. 353-365

KOLB, H. 'Die Blutstropfen-Episode bei Chrétien und Wolfram,' *Beiträge zur Geschichte der deutschen Sprache und Literatur* (Tübingen), 79, 1957, pp. 363-379

KOPPITZ, H.-J. *Wolframs Religiosität*, Bonn, 1958

LABUSCH, DIETLINDE 'Studien zu Wolframs Sigune,' Dissertation, Frankfurt am Main, 1959

MARTIN, E. *Parzival und Titurel: Zweiter Teil, Kommentar*, Halle, 1903

MEISSBURGER, G. 'Gyburg,' *Zeitschrift für deutsche Philologie*, 83, 1, 1964, pp. 64-99

MERGELL, B. *Wolfram von Eschenbach und seine französischen Quellen, I—'Willehalm,' II—'Parzival,'* Münster, 1936-1942

———. *Der Gral in Wolframs 'Parzival,'* Halle, 1952

MOCKENHAUPT, B. *Die Frömmigkeit im Parzival Wolframs von Eschenbach*, Bonn, 1942

MOHR, W. 'Obie und Meljanz. Zum 7. Buch von Wolframs *Parzival,'* in *Gestaltprobleme der Dichtung. Günther Müller zu seinem 60. Geburtstag am 15. Dezember 1955*, Bonn, 1957

———. 'Parzival und Gawan' in *Wolfram von Eschenbach*, ed. H. Rupp, *Wege der Forschung*, 57, Darmstadt, 1966, pp. 287-318

MORGAN, B. Q. 'Some Women in *Parzival,' Journal of English and Germanic Philology*, 12, 1913, pp. 175-198

PANZER, F. *Gahmuret. Quellenstudien zu Wolframs 'Parzival,'* Heidelberg, 1940

POAG, J. F. 'Wolfram von Eschenbach's Antikonie,' *Germanic Review*, XLI, 2, 1966

PSCHMADT, C. 'Jeschute,' *Zeitschrift für deutsches Altertum*, 55, 1917, pp. 63-75

RAHN, B. *Wolframs Sigunendichtungen: eine Interpretation der Titurelfragmente*, Zürich, 1958

RAMONDT, M. 'Zur Jugendgeschichte des Parzival,' *Neophilologus*, 9, 1924, 15-22

RANKE, F. 'Zur Symbolik des Grals bei Wolfram von Eschenbach,' *Trivium*, 4, 1946, pp. 20-30

RICHEY, M. F. *Gahmuret Anschevin*, Oxford, 1923

———. *Studies of Wolfram von Eschenbach*, London, 1957

———. *Schionatulander and Sigune*, London, 1927, (reprint) 1960

———. 'The *Titurel* of Wolfram von Eschenbach: Structure and Character,' *Modern Language Review*, 56, 1961, pp. 180-193

———. 'The Independence of Wolfram von Eschenbach in Relation to Chrétien de Troyes as shown in *Parzival* Books III-IV,' *Modern Language Review*, 47, 1952, pp. 350-361

SACKER, H. *An Introduction to Wolfram's 'Parzival,'* Cambridge, 1963

SATTLER, A. *Die religiösen Anschauungen Wolframs von Eschenbach*, Graz, 1895

SCHRÖDER, W. 'Süeziu Gyburg,' *Euphorion*, 54, 1960, pp. 39-69

————. 'Armuot,' *Deutsche Vierteljahrsschrift*, 34, 1960, pp. 501-526

SCHRÖDER, W. J. *Der Ritter zwischen Welt und Gott*, Weimar, 1952

————. *Die Soltane Erzählung in Wolframs 'Parzival,'* Heidelberg, 1963

SCHUMACHER, MARLIS *Die Auffassung der Ehe in den Dichtungen Wolframs von Eschenbach*, Heidelberg, 1967

SCHWIETERING, J. 'Sigune auf der Linde,' *Zeitschrift für deutsches Altertum*, 57, 1920, pp. 140-143

SINGER, S. *Wolframs Stil und der Stoff des 'Parzival,' Sitzungsberichte der Kaiserlichen Akademie der Wissenschaften zu Wien, Philosophischhistorische Klasse* 180. Bd. 4, Abhandlung, Vienna 1917

————. *Wolfram und der Gral. Neue 'Parzival'-Studien*, Bern, 1939

STAPEL, W. 'Wolfram von Eschenbachs *Parzival,' Wolfram Jahrbuch*, 1955, pp. 9-27

WALSHE, M. O'C. 'Notes on *Parzival* Book V,' *London Mediæval Studies*, Vol. 1, Part 3, 1939

WAPNEWSKI, P. *Wolframs 'Parzival': Studien zur Religiosität und Form*, Heidelberg, 1955

WEBER, G. *Der Gottesbegriff des 'Parzival,'* Frankfurt, 1935

————. *Parzival, Ringen und Vollendung*, Oberursel, 1948

WESLE, C. 'Zu Wolframs *Parzival,' Beiträge zur Geschichte der deutschen Sprache und Literatur*, (Halle) 72, 1950, pp. 1-39

WILLSON, H. B. 'Einheit in der Vielheit in Wolframs *Willehalm*,' *Zeitschrift für deutsche Philologie*, 80, 1961, pp. 40-62

―――. 'The symbolism of Belakâne and Feirefîz in Wolfram's *Parzival*,' *German Life and Letters*, 13, 1959/60, pp. 94-105

WOLFF, L. 'Der *Willehalm* Wolframs von Eschenbach,' *Deutsche Vierteljahrsschrift*, 12, 1934, pp. 504-539

―――. 'Wolframs Schionatulander and Sigune' in *Studien zur deutschen Philologie des Mittelalters. F. Panzer zum 80. Geburtstag*, Heidelberg, 1950

WYNN, MARIANNE 'Parzival and Gawan—Hero and Counterpart,' *Beiträge zur Geschichte der deutschen Sprache und Literatur*, (Tübingen) 84, 1962, pp. 142-172

4. *Other works used*

CHARRIER, C. *Héloise dans l'histoire et dans la légende*, Paris, 1933

EHRISMANN, G. 'Märchen im höfischen Epos,' *Beiträge zur Geschichte der deutschen Sprache und Literatur*, 30, 1905, pp. 14-54

GRIMM, J. AND W. *Kinder- und Hausmärchen*, Große Ausgabe, Berlin, 1890

de KOK, B. *Guibourc et quelques autres figures de femmes dans les plus anciennes chansons de geste*, Paris, 1926

MAURER, F. *Leid. Studien zur Bedeutungs-und Problem-geschichte, besonders in den großen Epen der staufischen Zeit*, Bern and Munich, 1951

MUSTARD, H. M. and PASSAGE, C. E. *Parzival*, translated into English, New York, 1961

RICHEY, M. F. *Herzeloyde in Paradise*, Oxford, 1958

VICAIRE, M.-H. *Histoire de Saint Dominique*, Paris, 1957

WERNER, E. 'Zur Frauenfrage und zum Frauenkult im Mittelalter: Robert von Arbrissel und Fontevrault,' *Forschungen und Fortschritte*, 29, 9, 1955, pp. 269-276